Porsche

THE

Carrera dynasty

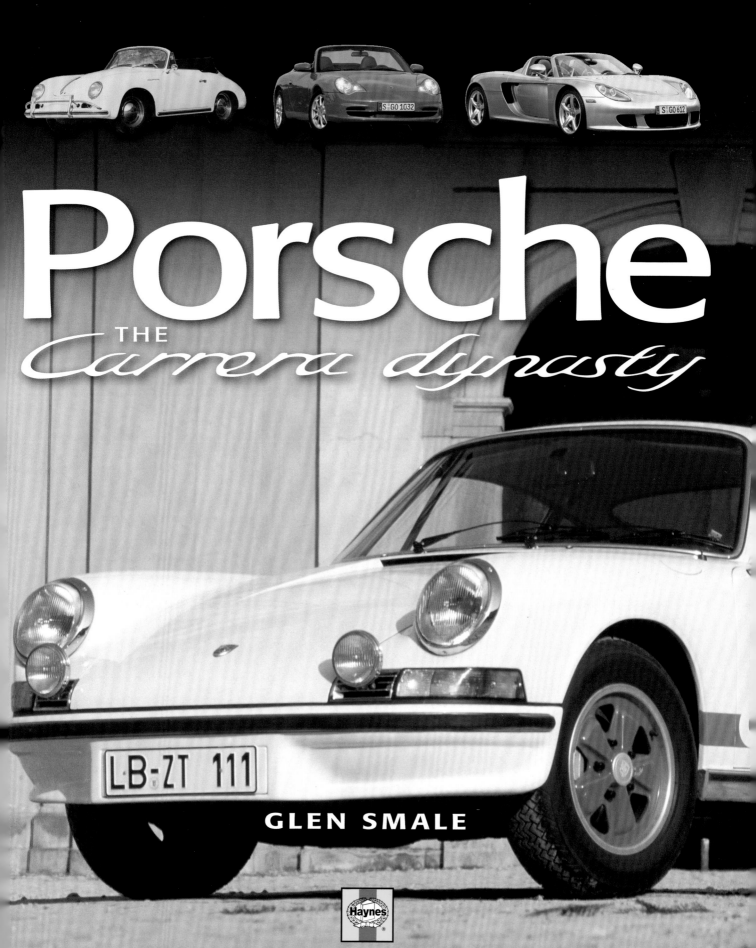

Porsche
THE
Carrera dynasty

GLEN SMALE

Haynes Publishing

British Library Cataloguing-in-Publication Data:
A catalogue record for this book is available
from the British Library

ISBN 1 84425 209 4

Library of Congress catalog card no. 2005935262

Published by Haynes Publishing,
Sparkford, Yeovil, Somerset BA22 7JJ, UK
Tel: 01963 442030 Fax: 01963 440001
Int. tel: +44 1963 442030 Int. fax: +44 1963 440001
E-mail: sales@haynes.co.uk
Website: www.haynes.co.uk

Haynes North America, Inc.,
861 Lawrence Drive, Newbury Park,
California 91320, USA

Designed by Helen McTeer
(helenmcteer@tiscali.co.uk)
Printed and bound in Great Britain by
J. H. Haynes & Co. Ltd, Sparkford

Contents

Dedication

Three very important people have played a major role in this book, from as early as the idea stage. To my dear wife, Elke, without whose help in translating and transcribing endless hours of German interviews, reading countless pages and showing absolute faith in my work this book would not have been possible – a huge thank you. To my two wonderful children, Margaux and Robert, who had to put up with my moods and constant requests to 'turn the music down', thank you too, for your patience.

Acknowledgements

No book on the subject of Porsche can be the work of just one person, as there are just too many facets to the history of this fascinating marque, not to enlist the assistance of others. For this reason, I would like to thank those tireless folk at the Porsche Historisches Archiv in Stuttgart, for their unwavering help in researching this book, both on my visits to their offices as well as back at my computer.

These include Archiv manager, Klaus Parr (recently retired) and his successor Dieter Landenberger, Jens Torner, Dieter Gross and Yvonne Knotek. In Porsche's head office, I would like to thank Michael Baumann, Michael Hölscher, Klaus Bischof and Nicole Nagel. Many hours were spent interviewing Porsche personnel both past and present, and these include Rolf Sprenger, Thomas Hartmann, Jürgen Barth, Herbert Linger, Dr Heinz Rabe, Anatole Lapine and Georg Ledert.

Through the Porsche Club of Great Britain, Peter Cook in the Club Archives was a big source of help, as was Robin Walker, Eoin Sloan and Andrew Horsell. I would also like to thank the Press Office staff of Porsche Cars Great Britain, in particular, Nick Perry who assisted with material as well as press cars for testing. I would also like to thank racing driver and journalist Tony Dron for his time in answering many of my questions.

Many hours were spent in the entertaining company of the late Ian Fraser-Jones and his charming wife, Jeannette, in Johannesburg. Jeannette kindly made available Ian's entire library of cuttings and albums and I thank her for her time and permission to use this material and the family photographs in that section. Assisting with the identification of South African photos were Bunny Wentzel and long-time motorcycle and racing ace, Paddy Driver.

From further afield, Marco Marinello has kindly provided photographs and given up valuable time to search through his personal archives. I am also grateful to Pete Stout of *Excellence* magazine and Scott George of the Collier Museum who supplied important details of the 550 Spyder. Kaye and Wilfried Mueller (Germany) and Paul Lawrence (UK) also provided valuable background to the Porsche Carrera Cup history.

I would also like to thank the many others who in various ways provided time by just listening to my enthusiastic ramblings on the subject – they may not have known it at the time, but they acted as important sounding boards for me. Two names I would like to mention in this respect are James Worthington and Greg Pickers – I really appreciated their time.

Without the contributions of those mentioned above, this work could not have been completed.

Glen Smale
Buckinghamshire
December, 2005

Introduction

Why is it that some automotive names conjure up images and memories so vivid and so colourful that, at the sound of the name, it is almost like being there when that car was launched, or when it crossed the winning line for the first time, against all the odds? What's in a name, anyway?

More than just identifying the car concerned, a name can link a vehicle with a certain moment in history when the achievement gained was so significant as to attract the attention of not only the competitors and spectators but also the wider motoring world. La Carrera Panamericana – a little known, dusty and dangerous race through some of the most inhospitable territory imaginable – was a trial that separated the tough drivers from the rest, and it tested the endurance of machinery to the absolute limit. There, a protruding rock or the treacherous terrain was as likely to put paid to your race as much as the encountered wildlife. Buzzards, donkeys, sheer vertical drops and impossibly narrow village streets crammed with enthusiastic onlookers all played a role in the high mortality rate of cars and drivers alike.

These were the conditions into which both men and cars were thrown in 1950, to fight it out to the line, and where only the fittest survived. It was often shrewd driving and a conservative approach that got the competitors to the finish line. Why, one might ask, does anybody even consider participating in such a risky and potentially hazardous rally? The answer lies in the inherent competitive nature of a racing driver. The greater the challenge, the greater the reward for winning, not in financial terms, because in the early 1950s that was not important, but for the sheer honour of success and achievement.

It was this environment into which the little Porsche 550 was thrust back in 1953, when the future of a small and relatively new German auto manufacturer was staked on the successful completion of a gruelling challenge in a far-off land. A year later and against all odds, this vehicle, with its revolutionary four-cam motor, excelled itself and surpassed the expectations of many critics and supporters alike. However, this adventure had a broader goal, to attract the attentions of a large and lucrative American market.

Success for the Porsche 550, lifted the manufacturer into the spotlight and in the process they had beaten far superior machinery with much larger engines, support crew and budgets. This conquest meant that Porsche had earned the attention of both the competitors and the sports car market, the effects of which would be felt for many decades to come. So significant was this achievement, that the company decided to build a production model celebrating the name of this event, and thereby capturing the hard-won memory for future generations.

The Carrera name needs little introduction today, but that is due largely to the untiring efforts of the company in its pursuit of engineering excellence, which it has built up over the decades. The Carrera model has come to be associated with this early Mexican success and, through time, it is a name that Porsche has reserved for its highest performing cars, the pinnacle of the genre, and as such the name Carrera has been applied to various models during this time. It is this theme that forms the basis of the study contained in these pages.

However, the Carrera badge, despite such an illustrious and triumphant birth rite, was dropped from the model range in the mid-1960s, only to be reintroduced again in 1972. This respected nameplate has come a long way over the years, in a turbulent automotive world, surviving several downturns in the market, yet wherever the name is mentioned it never fails to capture the imagination. The Carrera badge has evolved over the past five decades into a marketing name which today represents the whole 911 model line-up, not a move that was welcomed by all Porsche enthusiasts at the time.

Until 2003, that is – when the world was introduced to the company's latest creation, the Carrera GT. Putting this remarkable car into context, the Carrera GT represents a modern version of an early street-legal 550 with a hint of 356 Carrera Speedster. Through this state-of-the-art supercar, Porsche once again captured the spirit of the Carrera and it is to the credit of those early engineers, that the reputation and bloodline of the Carrera has continued to flourish.

The Carrera heritage was so significant in its early days that the Carrera four-cam engine was used both for road-going cars as well as race cars. In fact, seldom has there been a more flexible platform on which to build such a staggering variety of cars, from normal sports cars to mighty race cars, four-wheel-drive and also rally cars.

Some followers may not have approved of the application of the Carrera badge to the whole 911 model range in 1983, feeling that it diluted the legend somewhat. Others have said it was necessary to restore Porsche's fortunes during the troubled 1980s. One thing is for certain, it has ensured that the Carrera badge has survived for 50 years in an uncertain and unpredictable automobile industry – the strength of the legend

has spanned two different centuries and that name still commands the same respect today as it did in 1955.

Just as a royal family carries the name of its forefathers through history, so too can the name of Carrera be traced back through the years to its roots. This book is intended to show that family lineage, the heritage and the royal bloodline of a name that was born in Mexico half a century ago; the most revered name in the Porsche sports car history – Carrera.

BELOW Porsche Carrera GTS. (Author)

TIMELINE

1931	**1939**	**1944**	**1947**	**1948/49**	**1950/51**	**1952/53**
Porsche GmbH set up.	Berlin to Rome race (60K10).	Porsche development team moves to Gmünd, Austria.	Work begins on Project 356.	First 356 registered with Austrian authorities.	First 356 leaves plant in Stuttgart, Germany.	Work begins on 4-cam motor (Project 547).
Rabe and Komenda				356 No. 1 wins class	March 1951,	

CHAPTER ONE

In the beginning. . .

'If one does not fail at times, then one has not challenged himself.'

Porsche Cars North America Inc.

By virtue of their individual characters, motoring pioneers and visionaries are born into their role. Very seldom, if ever, do iconic motoring personalities grow into this position through passage of time, and neither can education alone qualify one for this role. Famous industry names such as Ferrari, Bugatti, Chrysler, Citroën, Ford, Renault, Lyons, Royce, Benz, Daimler, Porsche, and many more, did eventually cut their own path in the motor industry, but some of these personalities worked for other motor manufacturers first, before branching out on their own. Most of these people, and others like them, started work in a mechanically related field, but soon found that their strength and passion lay in creating and manufacturing motor vehicles of their own design, for an ever-growing market. Ferdinand Porsche worked for Lohner, Austro-Daimler, Daimler-Benz, Steyr, Auto Union and others before setting up his company, but sadly he never worked for the auto manufacturer that carried his name, as he died in the same year in which it was established. However, a common thread runs through all of these names, and that is, they all eventually went solo, establishing their own large, multinational motor manufacturing concerns.

It has been said that the cream always rises to the top of the milk. The story of how the company, Dr Ing. h. c. F. Porsche AG came into existence is well documented, as is the rise to prominence of the brilliant engineer and motoring visionary, Dr Ferdinand Porsche.

Possessed with a motoring vision, Porsche had the gift of being able to motivate his engineers to produce a motor vehicle just as he envisaged it in his own mind. Being able to look ahead and to predict the requirements of a vehicle that would outperform the established names in the field, shows not only courage, but demonstrates an understanding of the dynamics that a sports car must possess, in order for it to be both unique and superior in the market. Ferdinand Porsche was not an inventor, but he had the ability to identify a suitable engineering solution to any challenge confronting him, by applying some existing technology in a unique way, and in many cases, improving on that technology in the process.

Never satisfied with 'good enough', motoring pioneers such as those mentioned above, have traditionally forged their own path. Whether their products were renowned for speed, quality, endurance or simplicity, they have today all become synonymous with their own specific hallmark. While pre-Second World War sports cars mostly relied on large-capacity engines and power to achieve their goals of winning races, it was Ferdinand Porsche who sailed against the wind of current practice, so to speak, believing that higher vehicle speeds could be achieved by smaller engined cars with sleek and streamlined bodywork. While Porsche's critics were privately amused at the prospect of a 1,100cc sports car actually being able to achieve anything of note, it was Ferdinand's son, Ferry Porsche, who set about showing the motoring world that this formula could work.

OPPOSITE Ferdinand Porsche in his design office at 24, Kronenstrasse, Stuttgart in 1937.

Looking back through the annals of history of the motoring industry, the founders of most of the large motor manufacturing organisations have all possessed an ability to attract the best skills in the industry to their company. Ferdinand Porsche was no exception, and despite having built up a rather unpredictable and demanding reputation in the workplace, he nevertheless attracted the attentions of fellow automotive engineer, Karl Rabe, when he established his own design consultancy in Stuttgart on 25 April, 1931. Fortunately for Porsche, Rabe, who had worked together with Porsche previously, had an understanding of the way in which his boss worked and this enabled him to interpret Porsche's ideas, turning them into reality.

Another highly skilled engineer and designer, Erwin Komenda, was persuaded by Porsche to join the fledgling design consultancy as the manager of its bodywork construction department in November 1931, leaving behind a highly paid job at Daimler-Benz. Amongst Komenda's most notable achievements up to that point, the KdF-Wagen (or Volkswagen Beetle as it was later called) and the beautifully styled bodywork for the first

Auto Union racing car, must rank as some of his most significant work. Erwin Komenda stayed with the Porsche company from 1931 to 1966 and was chief of the Porsche body designing department, eventually being responsible for the 356, 550 and 911 models, which all achieved iconic status.

Almost all motor manufacturing organisations have developed out of a strong central belief in the ability of its founders and key personalities, as well as the quality of its products. It is this same principle that cemented the relationship between Ferdinand Porsche and Hans Ledwinka, despite their glaringly different characters. Both men possessed an enviable amount of creative potential and the desire to see their creations in the 'metal' as finished products. Porsche's style was more forceful, while Ledwinka adopted a more creative approach to problem solving, but it is this dovetailing of styles that ensured a lasting and productive relationship. Common to both men, however, was their single-minded attitude in seeing a project through to its end, sometimes overcoming seemingly insurmountable obstacles in the process.

With financial assistance from Adolf Rosenberger, whom Ferdinand Porsche had worked with at Mercedes Benz, Porsche continued to assemble his team. One of the most important members to join the company was none other than his 21-year-old son, Ferry.

In order to escape the constant Allied bombing of Stuttgart towards the end of 1944, Porsche's development team was evacuated to Gmünd in Carinthia, Austria, while Porsche and his family moved to Zell am See, situated in the picturesque Austrian Alps, in the province of Salzburg.

With Ferdinand still in prison in France, the seed planted earlier in Ferry's mind by his father – that is, the idea of producing a sports car bearing their family name – began to grow and take shape. Dominated by poverty and isolation in the small Austrian village, life for the engineers in Gmünd was far from glamorous. However, in 1947, despite enduring the many sacrifices and difficulties of working in an old converted sawmill, Ferry Porsche and Prof Eberan van Eberhorst started work on Project 356.

ABOVE Erwin Komenda (1938).

Why build a sports car?

'He just simply wanted to build a sports car', explains Klaus Bischof, manager of the Porsche Museum in Stuttgart-Zuffenhausen.

The urge to build a sports car bearing his own name, had been with Ferdinand Porsche since his early days as an engineer, even while working for other manufacturers. Following a request by Count Sascha Kolowrat to build a 1.0-litre lightweight racer, Porsche produced a vehicle which showed some promise. Later, during a brief spell with the Daimler company in Austria, he again built a small blown 2.0-litre straight-eight race car. With experience gained during his years with other motoring companies and by producing a bewildering variety of other mechanical and hydraulic products, Ferdinand Porsche realised that he would have to go solo if he was to avoid further frustration in his career. In 1931, he opened his own consultancy in Zuffenhausen, Stuttgart, under the name – Dr Ing. h. c. F. Porsche GmbH – Konstruktion und Beratung für Motoren und Fahrzeuge – which was essentially a development office concerned with engine and vehicle design. From its small beginnings, thanks to the varied projects undertaken by the organisation, the firm rose to around one hundred employees by the start of the Second World War.

This desire to build an eponymous sports car bearing his own name continued to gnaw away in Ferdinand Porsche's mind. Following the development and apparent potential of the KdF-Wagen, the prospects of building a KdF-based sports car using Volkswagen components seemed too good not to explore, but this was not to be, at least in 1937. Undeterred, father and son Porsche continued to dream about one day designing and building their own sports car which would hopefully be made possible through the funding they were to receive for the design of the KdF-Wagen and other projects.

Although the idea of having a prototype racing car funded by the state-run VW organisation had been dashed, pride in the sport of motoring was something that ran deep in Germany. Always on the lookout for a juicy Nazi propaganda opportunity, Major Hühnlein, head of motorsport

in the Third Reich, sought to create a sporting event which could be used to maximise the launch of the new KdF-Wagen in Germany, the nation's new 'people's car'.

A race from Berlin to Rome over 800 miles of autobahn, and run over the national roads of three different countries, would bring unprecedented exposure to the new KdF-Wagen, winning valuable popularity from the German people in the process if, of course, the cars performed well. To this end, Porsche was commissioned to build three prototypes that not only utilised KdF mechanicals but which also looked similar to the KdF-Wagen, so that they would be easily recognisable to the public as a production derivative. This project, given the designation 60K10, enabled Porsche to borrow from the design work already carried out on an earlier internal project, the Typ 114 design, and thereby recoup some of the cost of this work already carried out by the firm. The '60' signified

ABOVE Front and rear views of the 1937/38 Typ 114 'Sportwagen' scale model that never went into production, but which served as a basic design for the Typ 64.

OPPOSITE In Gmünd (Carinthia), Austria, Porsche KG took over the premises of a sawmill in the summer of 1944, in order that work could continue without the risk of Allied air attacks. Porsche remained there until moving back to Stuttgart in 1950.

its link with the Model 60, or KdF-Wagen, while the 'K' referred to its special body (Karosserie) manufactured by Reutter, and '10' was the body style within the KdF family of models.

Although the Typ 114 never made it off the drawing board, this vehicle would have undoubtedly set the racing world on fire with its advanced 1,493cc V10 engine configuration and lightweight, streamlined coupé body. Also known as the F-Wagen (for its designers, Ferry and Ferdinand), this vehicle had a mid-engined rear-wheel-drive layout running through a five-speed gearbox, a very innovative concept for the 1930s. Similarities between the 114 and the 60K10 were however evident, illustrating the lessons already learned in the design of the former.

The Komenda-designed Model 60K10 project ultimately formed the basis of the bodywork for the Porsche 356, the first sports car to display the classic Porsche lines. This project would unquestionably prove to be the starting point for the realisation of Porsche's dreams, to build his own sports car in the future.

It has to be said that the Komenda-designed 60K10 KdF-based streamlined racer was the forerunner of all Porsche-badged vehicles. Started in the fall of 1938, the three prototypes, sporting an aerodynamic sports coupé with a streamlined roof and an aluminium body, were completed by the summer of 1939. The design used the front of the existing KdF-Wagen body while the rear incorporated the familiar ventilation slats below the rear windscreen. Larger valves, twin carbs and

BELOW The Typ 64 outside the Porsche Villa, Feuerbacherweg 48, Stuttgart – this home is still in the Porsche family today. The first ever VW Beetle was assembled behind the garage doors in the background.

THE 60K10 DETAILS AND SPECIFICATIONS

Body/Model	Coupé/60K10
Number produced	Three
Engine	VW flat 4-cylinder
Displacement	1,131cc
Maximum output	45hp
Transmission	4-speed manual
Brakes	Drums
Maximum speed	90mph (150km/h)

a higher compression ratio boosted power to 45bhp, sufficient to give the car a top speed of 91mph (150km/h). Prior to the Second World War, Porsche's experience with the development of the KdF-Wagen had shown him that the VW engine was well suited to running for prolonged periods at sustained high speeds, especially on the smooth new autobahns of Germany, and hence it would be ideal for powering the 60K10 in the up-coming Berlin–Rome race.

But, unfortunately, these cars were never raced in anger. With the storm clouds of war looming menacingly over Europe, the ambitious race was called off and these radical cars were put to private use. One of them, driven by Bodo Lafferentz, a KdF official, was subsequently damaged in an accident and not seen again. Of the remaining two cars, one was used by Jakob Werlin of Porsche while the other was used by Ferdinand himself throughout the war. After that, the car was sold to Austrian motorcycle ace, Otto Matte, who won the Alpine Rally with it in 1950.

However, the significance of these three vehicles cannot be overemphasised and the lessons learned in their construction were clearly carried over into the early 356 design work.

Porsche's philosophy was to go light

Despite participating in races against his father's better judgement, knowledge gained by Ferry Porsche in his younger days as a racing and test driver with Wanderer and Auto Union, was to stand him in good stead in the future. This applied in particular, to the understanding of good sports car dynamics, road holding and handling. Although the war intervened, and Ferdinand Porsche (who was awarded the title of Honorary Professor in 1940) was imprisoned in the chaotic aftermath at the end of hostilities, his plans to create a sports car bearing the family name came to fruition due to his son Ferry who later breathed life into a dream which had been shared by both father and son.

BELOW Typ 64 (or 60K10) outside Werk 1, Stuttgart on 6 September, 1939.

ABOVE The Typ 64 undergoing road tests around Stuttgart during the early years of the Second World War.

Up until the 1950s, it was accepted that a driver could enter almost any motor vehicle in motorsport events, including family saloon-type cars, such as Saab, Rootes Group cars, Ford Zephyr, Renault 4CV and others. Although this is perhaps a light-hearted way of explaining the situation, it is to all intents and purposes, correct. This situation is certainly one of the contributing factors that pushed manufacturers to create smaller and higher performing cars that were better suited to competition, in an effort to attract the attention of the more serious drivers.

Performance cars available to privateer drivers on the market at the time (late 1940s) were limited mostly to expensive Italian makes (Ferrari, Maserati and Alfa Romeo), some British makes (Aston Martin, Jaguar and others) and Mercedes Benz. The common denominator amongst these cars, and for that matter almost all of the other sports cars on the market, was that they were of large capacity (most were above 3.0-litre), front-engined and somewhat heavy. Porsche saw this as a limiting factor in the performance equation, as nobody at that point had seriously dabbled with a smaller mid- or rear-engined layout.

Ferdinand Porsche stuck rigidly to the principle that speed was not merely a factor of big engines and brute power. In fact, at a time when most other motor manufacturers found that increased performance was a product of larger capacity engines with complex technical innovations, he instead sought to reduce weight in the car thereby generating more speed. Higher speeds were also a factor of streamlining and simplicity of shape, and by looking at the advanced VW Typ 60K10 one can see this principle in action.

To appreciate why Porsche cars were so successful both on the road and in competition, it is necessary to understand their philosophy and why Ferdinand even considered a mid- or rear-engined layout, when nobody else had really gone along that route. Ferdinand Porsche had been responsible for developing some of the most noteworthy performance machinery of that time, including the mighty Mercedes S, SS, and SSK-series of vehicles, but it was the Auto Union and the Cisitalia (Typ 360) that had left him with the ideas which he considered worthy of developing.

In an interview with the author, Jürgen Barth, multiple race winner and Porsche engineer and driver, explained: 'If you have a light car, you don't need so much power and you don't need so much fuel, because, at the time it was also an important point in the Porsche racing philosophy, that we needed to build cars that were not using so much fuel.' He continued, 'but the main thing was the fuel consumption combined with good aerodynamics in a light car. That is an easy principle.'

'It was the genius of the designer, saying: "I want more weight on the rear axle for doing everything like, going up the hill in rain, in snowy conditions, in bad conditions with mud and whatever else",' is how Jürgen Barth explained the extraordinary foresight and brilliance of the engineer, Dr Ferdinand Porsche.

Klaus Bischof, manager of the Porsche Museum in Stuttgart, confirms this: 'Enjoyment means fast driving with good handling – a light car. That is why he used an aluminium body to achieve good handling with speed.'

In placing the engine behind the rear axle, 'There was a big advantage in braking', Herbert Linge explained, 'because the weight came forward onto the front axle, and there was a big advantage in acceleration. There was also a big advantage in the rallies if you could "throw" the car. If you know how to play the violin, you could work it very nicely', he added laughingly, implying that with a sensitive touch a skilled driver could make the car 'dance' or perform just the way he wanted it to.

With this knowledge, Porsche undoubtedly saw the potential for further mechanical development of the VW power plant, utilising the rear-engined layout already proven in more than 1.8 million miles of testing. The successful development of the KdF-Wagen, or Beetle as it became affectionately known, showed Porsche that the VW mechanicals could be adapted to suit their requirements. With performance dynamics and vehicle size in mind, this concept provided them with a workable platform on which to develop their model according to a strict weight and cost budget.

By opting for an air-cooled engine, Porsche was able to place the engine anywhere within the body, as the power unit was not reliant on a water-cooled radiator. An air-cooled engine was also a lighter unit and by placing the engine at the rear of the car Porsche was able to do away with the need for a prop shaft, which transferred drive from the engine to a final drive unit as in a conventional front-engined, rear-drive layout. A front-engined vehicle at that time was by nature a fairly large beast, relying on cubic capacity to outgun any opposition. The larger the engine, the faster you could go, but the heavier the whole package became. By simply reversing that process and wrapping the resultant design in an all-enveloping and sleek body style, the weight reduction and improved resistance to wind was so advantageous as to increase performance substantially.

Rolf Sprenger explains: 'If you have a closer look to the real Porsche No. 1, it was a mid-engined one, and sports cars and race cars had that system [at the time].' Acknowledged as the preferred layout for optimal road holding and performance,

BELOW The 1948 Porsche 356/2 Gmünd Coupé sitting pretty in the Austrian countryside. Note the split windscreen and extremely narrow tyres.

Ferry Porsche and his colleagues constructed their first car in this way.

This engine layout and body style combination helped achieve Porsche's goals in terms of weight, as his early prototype weighed only 1,674lb (759kg) and thereby offered unrivalled speed, acceleration and fuel economy. Returning a fuel consumption of only 24mpg (11.79 litres/100km), this altogether acceptable package could not have been achieved with any other engine and body configuration.

Early 356 development

Officially, the Porsche 356 project began life on 11 June 1947. Based on earlier ideas generated by his father, Ferry Porsche, together with his engineers in Gmünd in 1947, set about giving form to the first Porsche-badged vehicle. Designing and developing a new car was a far from easy task in the early post-war years. Stuck away in the mountains of Austria, supplies and equipment for vehicle production were hardly available from the corner store, and so engineers and fitters from the fledgling company had to travel by truck to

Germany to obtain this material. Much of what was needed was sourced from Volkswagen, but the engineers had to scrounge whatever they could for free from other engineering firms as well, as finances were also not in plentiful supply. Being limited in so many ways, it is hardly surprising, that the early 356s borrowed so heavily from the Volkswagen technology.

As we have seen, Ferry Porsche was positively influenced by the advantages of the rear-engined layout as a result of the work already done by his father on the KdF-Wagen. Rolf Sprenger remembers: 'Since he knew the basics of the Volkswagen, he probably thought "I can develop it, and I can convert it to a sports car".' Sprenger continues, 'and my former boss, Mr Klauser, told me that he, as well as the young Ferry, did some test driving with the Volkswagens in the 1930s.' Hans Klauser was a research engineer at Porsche before the war, after which he became the general manager responsible for after-sales tasks for Porsche KG.

As a result of design and mechanical information already available from other projects, provisional bodywork structures and frames for the proposed sports car were completed by the 17 July

BELOW Porsche 356 No. 1 pictured in Gmünd in 1948. Standing next to the car are, from right to left: Ferdinand Porsche, his son Ferry and body designer Erwin Komenda.

OPPOSITE The famous 356 No. 1 Roadster – the car that started it all.

1947. Erwin Komenda's bodywork for the first car, Porsche 356 No. 1 was stream-lined and sporty and this vehicle, an open-topped Roadster, was registered on 8 January 1948. Porsche's Gmünd-based group assembled a running prototype of the little Roadster and it was shown off to the gathered press at the Swiss Grand Prix in July 1948. Put conservatively, the press was more than just a little impressed by the newcomer.

The prototype, Porsche 356 No. 1, was fitted with a high-compression flat-four cylinder 35bhp 1,131cc Volkswagen power plant, reversed to give a mid-engined layout with the gearbox mounted behind. The first Komenda-designed 'Roadster' body was based on a tubular frame, with torsion bar suspension, cable-operated drum brakes and low-slung, light-weight aerodynamic bodywork. Although 356 No. 1 featured a mid-mounted engine, subsequent production versions differed dramatically in their chassis layout.

Just five weeks after 356 No. 1 was completed, the car scored an 1,100cc class win at the

PROTOTYPE 356 NO. 1 (K45-286) DETAILS AND SPECIFICATION

Body	Aluminium cabriolet body designed by Erwin Komenda, handcrafted by Friedrich Weber and mounted around a tubular steel framework with mid-engine layout.
Engine	VW 4-cylinder, air-cooled boxer engine of 1,131cc and 7.0:1 compression ratio
Fuel supply	Down-draught carburettor
Power output	35bhp @ 4,000rpm
Maximum speed	84–87mph (135–140km/h)
Transmission	4-speed gearbox mounted ahead of rear axle
Suspension	Taken from the VW
Dimensions	Length: 3.86m
	Wheelbase: 2.15m
Windshield	Two-piece unframed glass
Weight	585kg (1,287lb)

BELOW Production of the
Typ 356 Coupé in
1948/49, Gmünd.
Pictured left is Erwin
Komenda, and right is
Otto Husslein.

BELOW RIGHT Porsche
Typ 356/2 Gmünd
Coupé being worked
on outside the Gmünd
works in 1948. In the
background is 356 No. 1.

Innsbruck City race in the hands of Herbert Kaes,
Ferry's nephew, marking the beginning of an
astonishing history in motor racing. The Porsche
was homologated by the state government of
Kärnten in Austria on 8 June 1948, hence the 'K'
in the car's registration, 'K45-286'.

With public enthusiasm for the sports model
running higher than expected, Porsche realised
that turning his little sportster into a commercial
success would be difficult, because the hand-
hammered aluminium skin over the space frame
would be cost-prohibitive. So Porsche wasted no
time in drawing up a completely different chassis
that significantly altered the basic layout of the car.
These drawings for the production 356 were,
however, completed before the prototype was even
finished. The result was a spartan, ground-hugging
two-seat Roadster whose rounded lines established
a styling theme that would evolve over the lifetime
of the 356. The most advanced element in the
configuration of the first 356 was its simple,

compact and rounded shape which featured no
sharply defined edges.

Rather than a space frame, the new production car
had a monocoque chassis formed from sheet steel,
and the midships engine placement was abandoned
in favour of a rear-engine layout. For this model, the
second car, 356-002, he used a basic VW platform
chassis and running gear. The rear engine layout
also offered much greater luggage carrying capacity
as the space behind the front seats was freed up and
this area could also provide two small seats for
occasional rear passengers, albeit a bit cramped.

Herbert Linge explained how Ferry Porsche
initially saw his sports car with a mid-mounted
engine. 'This was not good for sales of a car for the
normal road because you have no luggage room in
the back, nothing in the front and with more
noise, and this was not good. So the engine had to
move back to get more room in the inside. Also in
the wind tunnel, with the engine in the front, the
front is higher', he said.

The initial design requirement for the car was that it should be fast, comfortable with 2+2 configuration and to be a fliessheck, or fastback shape. Both coupé and cabriolet were unique and different from anything that had preceded them in the sports car world. The engines were located in the 'wrong' place; they were air-cooled, there was no radiator grille and the fenders and headlamps blended into the body. Advanced and unconventional it most certainly was, as there wasn't a car like it anywhere.

During the winter of 1948/49, production in Gmünd was slow and irregular. The first production models were each unique in detail and built by hand. Fifty of these hand-crafted aluminium-bodied coupés were completed in Gmünd, but Porsche never planned large-scale production of the 356 at the mountain-locked Austrian manufacturing facility. When plans were made to move the production operations to Stuttgart in 1948, it marked the beginning of

a close working relationship with the nearby Reutter coachworks which was to become the main supplier of Porsche bodies for nearly two decades, before being annexed into the Porsche organisation. With the later move back to Stuttgart, the 356 underwent another transformation, this time from an aluminium body, to steel.

Porsche proceeded to hire a section of the Reutter workshops because the American army still occupied the original part of the factory using Werk 1 as a vehicle repair shop, so Porsche production couldn't continue there. The Reutter's company, which had been building a range of large cars, found itself with spare capacity due to the low demand for big cars at that time, so Porsche simply transferred their manufacturing operation across the road to their building.

The Typ 356 made its motor show debut at Geneva in the spring of 1949. The 1,086cc engine retained the same 73.5mm x 64mm over square bore and stroke of the VW, but instead, was fitted

RIGHT Ferdinand Porsche with son Ferry (1950), in front of a Porsche 356 Gmünd Coupé in the courtyard of the Porsche Villa.

BELOW An early 356 Gmünd Coupé undergoing testing – note the string taped to the body to assist with streamlining.

with a pair of downdraught Solex 26VFJ carburettors.

In 1950, with the beginning of Porsche 356 production at the Stuttgart works, the first pale grey-painted Porsche 356 left the Reutter plant. Initially, it was believed that only 500 Porsche 356 sports cars could be produced per year at a rate of about 40 cars per month. To the relief of Porsche and his engineers, the public's reaction to the production model was favourable. Even though equipment levels were basic, to say the least – the 356 had no fuel gauge or tachometer – the little sports car obviously had what was necessary to handle well and run strongly, with an 80mph (129kmh) top speed.

Even though the Porsche platform would remain based on VW components for a few more years, the process of constant and incremental improvement that had begun in Gmünd, continued. Reutter's exemplary workmanship was evident in the quality of components and in overall fit-and-finish. Porsche styling, while not everyone's cup of tea, drew strong support from a growing army of avid admirers, its sleek design achieving an amazingly low drag coefficient of 0.296 – still remarkable today, and an unknown fact until the 1980s when an early car was tested in the wind tunnel.

Pre-A 356 (1950–55)

In 1951, Porsche's range of engines was expanded to include 1.3-litre (1,286cc) and 1.5-litre (1,488cc) displacements, although the 1,500cc engine did not become generally available to the public until the early spring of 1952. Output had increased from the original 1,100cc model's nominal 40bhp to 44bhp and 60bhp respectively. In 1950/51, seven lightweight Gmünd coupés were built for competition purposes and were renamed 356 SL (see Chapter 2).

More performance – why?

Following the early class success of the first of the 356 (Gmünd-manufactured prototype 356 No. 1) at the 1948 Innsbruck City race in the hands of Herbert Kaes, it was patently clear to the factory engineers that their newly born sports car had great competition potential.

It is easy to get emotionally carried away with performance goals of a new vehicle and to forget about the economics of building a production car, but the Porsche engineers were able to see how both goals could be reached, each benefiting the other. The first experimental 356s used the VW flat-four with 1,131cc capacity, whereas the early production 356s had a reduced capacity of 1,086cc in order to fall within the 1,100cc sports racing class. In the early cars, power in the 356 was up from the VW's 25bhp to 40bhp thanks to the twin Solex 26VFJ carburettors.

Before the factory itself started building race cars, Porsche was working with several private racing drivers, Walter Glöckler and Heinrich Sauter probably being the best known. Having recognised the Porsche for what it was, Glöckler, together with his workshop manager, none other than the talented engineer Hermann Ramelow, and with the help of Porsche engineers, set about building his own body and chassis to accommodate the Porsche engine and gearbox.

Walter Glöckler, son of a wealthy German motor dealer, had built up a successful racing reputation and when the family organisation acquired a VW dealership, it included the rights to sell Porsche cars. This gave Glöckler access to not only the potent

The death of Professor Ferdinand Porsche

While 1951 was a good year for business, the world bid farewell to Ferdinand Porsche who died on 30 January that year. This was indeed a tragedy as he was not able to witness his sports car dream achieve its ultimate prominence. Dr Ing. h. c. Ferdinand Porsche was acknowledged as a leading automotive engineer for five decades, before his son Ferry launched the car that bore his name. Fortunately for automobile enthusiasts the world over, Ferry proved himself to be an able custodian of the reputation created before him, as he injected the much-needed managerial and marketing expertise, sufficient to carry the organisation into the future.

The last photograph known to have been taken of Ferdinand Porsche before his death, as he enters his company's premises in Stuttgart-Zuffenhausen in 1950.

Porsche sports cars, but it also enabled him to build a valuable relationship with the engineering and factory staff in Stuttgart-Zuffenhausen.

The first of these Glöckler cars was completed in 1950 and featured a 48bhp 1,086cc engine which was turned around and mounted ahead of the rear axle with the gearbox behind, just like the prototype 356. In order to extract the most out of the Porsche engine, Glöckler built a simple ladder-type frame with the 356 No. 1 style suspension and this was clothed in an attractive streamlined custom, lightweight body constructed by Weidenhausen, a small body shop in Frankfurt. The whole package weighed in at a mere 980lb (445kg). It was in this car, with its light aluminium body, that Glöckler notched up a sensational victory in the 1950 German 1,100cc sports car class championship, albeit with his car wearing a VW nose badge.

In August 1951, the second Glöckler Spyder, now rebadged as a Porsche, had a roller bearing 85bhp 1,488cc factory engine as used in the successful 356 competition coupés (this was still the basic VW power plant but in enlarged and tuned form).

It won its class in an important hill-climb event, setting a new class record in the process, but on the faster circuits, Glöckler attached a small, streamlined coupé top which further improved the aerodynamics of the car. This vehicle was then sold to Max Hoffman, the Porsche general representative in America, where it continued to be successfully campaigned for some time. A third Glöckler Porsche, more closely resembling a 356 up front, was produced the following year, 1952, using a conventional 356 floorpan, rear engine and trailing arms for easier handling, while two more mid-engined Glöckler Porsches were built for other customers.

There followed many more successes across Europe for each of the Glöckler Porsches in the hands of several different drivers. More importantly though, these results did much to boost the confidence of the small but dedicated band of engineers at the Porsche works.

The importance of the Glöckler Porsches is very significant, both from a design perspective as well as from a mechanical one. Glöckler worked very closely with Porsche engineers, and advances made through co-operation with talented privateer racers such as these, proved to be invaluable to the company. Furthermore, by offering factory assistance in this manner, Porsche was able to experiment on the race track without the burden of running a full factory race department, which, for a fledgling motor manufacturing company, was the most prudent way of doing things. In addition, ambitious racing drivers, who had recognised the performance potential of the small German cars, were able to provide Porsche with valuable feedback gained on the track, experience that the company put to good use.

The Glöckler–Porsche relationship thrived as a result of a shared understanding of racing and a mutual desire to succeed. The quality of the Porsche mechanicals was matched by the exquisitely crafted chassis and bodywork of these cars. In this way, the Porsche engineers and management were convinced by the professionalism and the many successes of this privateer racer, which in turn fuelled the desire for further cooperation between the two parties.

Despite the positive progress described above, Porsche and his engineers were only too aware that they, as a motor manufacturer, were still not building real racing cars. Up to that point, they had been merely dabbling with the sport. The 356 was in reality a touring car with sporting potential, but, more importantly, Ferry Porsche realised that along with success on the track would come a great many more vehicle sales. Herein lay the secret to the company's growth.

However, Porsche could not rely on privateers alone to provide them with competition success as this would prove unreliable in the long run, and more crucially, such activities were not under their full and direct control. In addition, mere success on the race track in itself would not be sufficient to carry the name of the company in the future, it would also require a coordinated

BELOW A very early photograph showing the prototype Porsche 356 No. 1 followed by a Typ 64 during the 1948 Innsbruck city race.

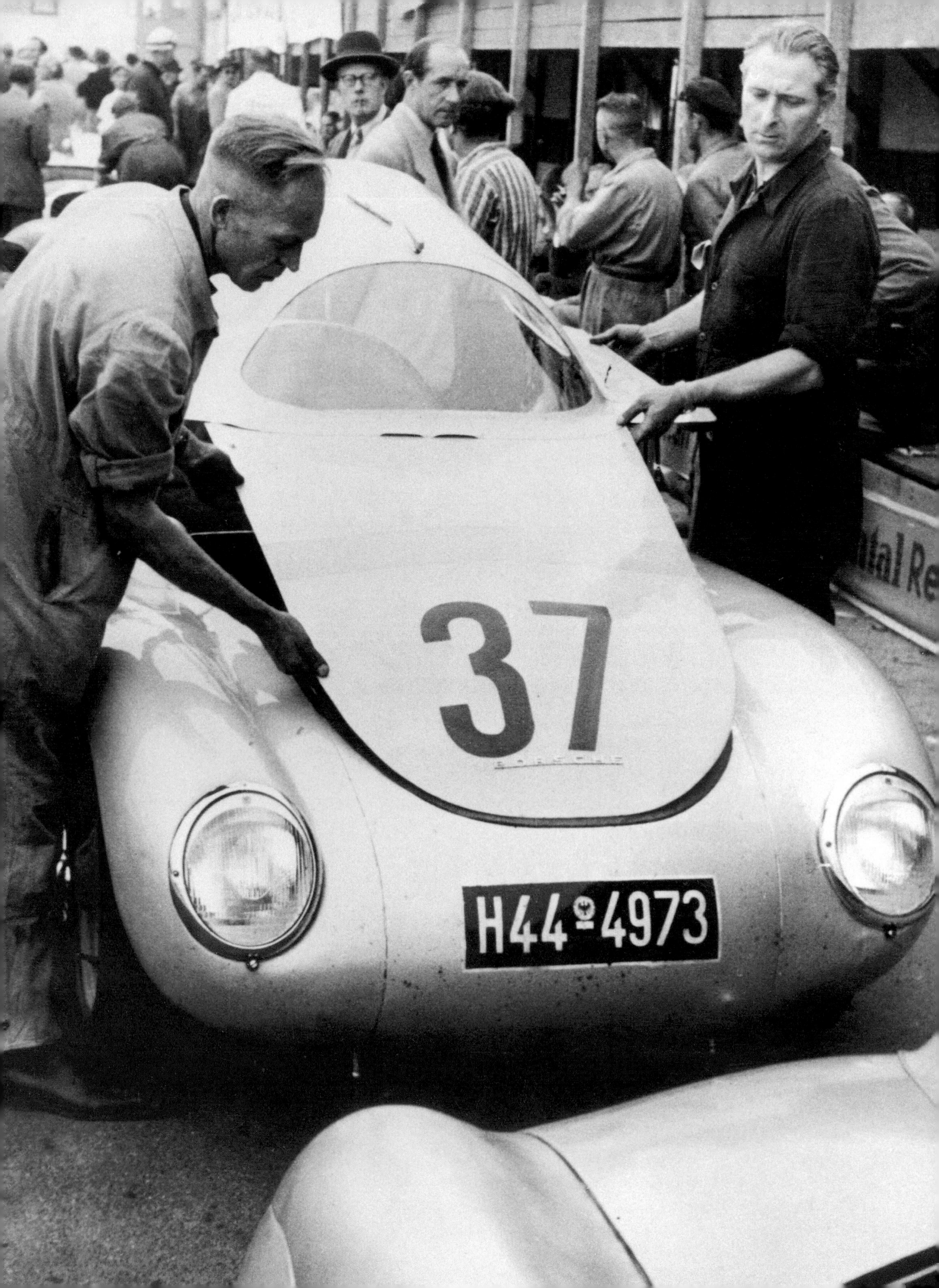
37
H44-4973

effort to maximise the publicity generated by its competition activities and to build a reputation based on these achievements. The arrival of Huschke von Hanstein in 1952 can be cited as one of the most important milestones in the development of the company's early motorsport fortunes. Being of aristocratic background, von Hanstein was well connected in social circles internationally, an attribute that would count strongly in his, and Porsche's, favour.

As Racing Director, not only did von Hanstein coordinate the factory's racing programme but he also actively searched for suitable events in new territories, thereby ensuring success over a wider area geographically. In this role, von Hanstein doubled up as the company's public relations

director, and as such was ideally placed to exploit opportunities guaranteeing greater publicity of race victories. A born publicist, von Hanstein, through his naturally persuasive manner, was always able to secure the best spot in the best publications and thereby maximising the impact of any sporting achievements.

With the combined factors of recent racing successes, a buoyant engineering department, and with a hungry motorsport manager in von Hanstein, plans could then be laid that would enable the company to develop its own racing cars and engines. This was becoming increasingly important for the company due to the growing competition being felt by Porsche internationally in the 1,100cc and 1,500cc racing classes.

OPPOSITE A 1951 Glöckler Porsche being fitted with the one-man streamlined top, but this restricted the driver's view.

BELOW Baron Huschke von Hanstein at his happiest: behind the wheel of a racing car, in 1955.

TIMELINE:

1952	**1953**	**1954**	**1955**	**1956**
Work begins on 4-cam engine (Project 547).	October, the 550 is unveiled at the Paris Salon.	First 550 production model available to sell. Hermann comes third in a 550 in the Carrera Panamericana.	October, Carrera becomes an official model name.	Maglioli victory in the Targa Florio in 550.

CHAPTER TWO

Competition driven

'If the race begins at 3, you must be ready at 3.
They will not wait.'

Porsche Cars North America Inc.

In a world in which performance cars and motorsport was dominated by larger, more powerful and more resourceful motor manufacturers, Porsche was, to all intents and purposes, relatively unknown as a sports car manufacturer on the international stage. However, the secret of their success lay most probably in their ability to adapt and respond to the needs of their customers and changes in the motorsport world, in a much shorter time frame than many of their competitors could. Coupled to this strength was the undeniable fact that the Porsche company was staffed by some of the most talented, focussed and motivated engineers and designers in the business.

In addition to this relatively strong position held by the company, Porsche was certainly in the top echelons of the game when it came to understanding performance cars, both from a mechanical and a design perspective. If there was a weakness, or a chink in the armour which offered any real threat to their progress, it was perhaps the size of the financial resources at their disposal, or rather lack of.

However, where there is a will, there is a way, and the resourcefulness and commitment of the Porsche engineers was certainly one of the company's strengths. Income earned from their consultancy for providing engineering solutions to other manufacturers and royalties from the sale of VW Beetles, ensured that the much-needed funds for the development of their other projects, kept flowing in.

Early 356 victories

June 1949 saw the first running of the famous 24-Hour endurance race at Le Mans following the cessation of hostilities. Attending the 1950 Paris Motor Show, the Porsches, father and son, were approached by Charles Faroux, one of the initiators behind the post-war Le Mans revival, to submit an entry for the race. Ferdinand Porsche, even in his poor state of health, saw the benefit that success in this event could bring the firm internationally, and this opinion was shared by Auguste Veuillet, Porsche's importer in France. Unfortunately, Ferdinand Porsche died before that could happen, and in the circumstances, Ferry Porsche understandably took his time in considering the proposal.

Porsche still had several of the aluminium-bodied Gmünd coupés languishing in the factory. These had not been sold since the introduction of the newer, steel-bodied production 356 which was built in Zuffenhausen, following the move there in 1950. These cars were not only much lighter due to their aluminium bodywork, but they had slightly narrower cabins resulting in a reduced frontal area and were thus better suited aerodynamically. During 1950/51, seven of the Gmünd 356s were revived by the factory for racing purposes. Undergoing a total identity transformation, they were given new chassis numbers and renamed the 356SL, which stood for Super Leicht.

For Porsche, running a team at Le Mans was no simple matter. It wasn't so much a question of

OPPOSITE Ferry Porsche with Karl Rabe in 1957. When the Dr Ing. h. c. F. Porsche GmbH company was formed in Stuttgart, Karl Rabe joined the fledgling organisation as chief designer and remained there until his retirement in 1965.

having the right car with the right engine set-up, and neither was the issue a shortage of top-rate drivers. For Porsche, participation in the Le Mans 24-Hour endurance race would represent the fledgling company's first entry into big time racing with an official factory team, and this for a company that had only produced its first car three years earlier. Ferry's decision also took into account the eventual publicity to be gained from such a venture should they be successful and heaven forbid, how to deal with a total disaster should it all go horribly wrong. Favourable publicity for the company depended solely on a good result as there was no money for any additional promotional or public relations campaigns.

The standard 1,086cc, 40bhp engine and standard 356 bodywork allowed the car to reach a top speed of 88mph (142kmh), which was adequate for swift travel on public roads, but by fitting wheel covers to improve airflow and by boosting the engine to 46bhp, the race version was capable of reaching over 100mph. Increased performance was also achieved from this motor when a special Fuhrmann-designed cam was fitted.

Initially, for the 1951 Le Mans race, Porsche planned a two-car team, but during pre-race testing one of the cars was totally written off, while the second was seriously damaged. Many teams would have walked away from the event right there, but Porsche considered the exercise to be worthwhile and a third car was duly prepared. Porsche was now down to just one car, that driven by Auguste Veuillet, the French Porsche agent, and Edmond Mouche. The Veuillet/Mouche car performed almost faultlessly, and the little Gmünd coupé came home in 20th place overall and first in the 1,100cc class. The 1951 results were repeated the following year, when three of these 356SLs ran in the 1952 Le Mans race. Thus started a tradition for the then still small Stuttgart manufacturer.

Four of the 356SLs were built to run the Liège–Rome–Liège Rally and then Montlhéry, France for record setting. At the end of September 1951 the Porsche factory used two Gmünd cars to break eleven world records. Running at the Montlhéry circuit, the Porsche 356 Coupés broke several speed records for both the 1,100cc and 1,500cc engine sizes, capturing the world record

BELOW Car No. 49 – the Porsche Typ 356 SL of Veuillet/Müller waits for the start of the 1953 Le Mans 24-Hour race.

RIGHT The 1952 Liège–Rome–Liège Rally – Helmut Polensky with Walter Schlüter in the Porsche Typ 356 Gmünd Coupé.

average speed over 72 hours at 94.7mph (151.9kmh). In the Liège–Rome–Liège Rally in August 1952, Helmut Polensky and Walter Schlüter led Gilberte Thirion in her Porsche to a remarkable first place overall. These cars were later sold off to private individuals.

In 1952, Max Hoffman imported three of these cars to America where he sold one of them to John von Neumann. Von Neumann campaigned car 356-063 in California, but due to mixed success as a result of braking problems, he chopped the roof off making the vehicle much lighter, a move which is thought to have sparked the idea for the eventual 356 Speedster.

Other European victories followed, including a class win in Monza in 1952, at the Sestriere Rally in 1953, the Belgrade Grand Prix, and the Alpine Rally

BELOW AND RIGHT For the 1953 Le Mans race, the 550 Spyders raced with the aerodynamic, detachable roof, although these were disliked by the drivers as they were very claustrophobic, stuffy and the engine noise resonated inside the thin metal canopy. (Car No. 44 was prototype 550-001).

Why the need for a factory racer?

'Engineering driven' – is the term typically used by Porsche when describing its philosophy of why they build sports cars the way they do. For 50 years this has been a fundamental factor in the company's drive for excellence.

Following the encouraging results on the circuits of Europe with what was essentially a tweaked VW pushrod power plant, several of the more ambitious racing drivers tried to extract even greater performance out of the little Porsche 356. Though the 356 had become a sales success in Porsche terms, the engineers realised that the model had a number of shortcomings when it came to international racing. The example of Glöckler, and others, showed that some of the

more determined racers were willing to modify their Porsche Roadsters to suit their own needs. These enthusiastic endeavours were not missed by the factory as the more serious drivers were lacking in power, and Porsche knew this.

The factory 356 Coupés had been campaigned long and hard across Europe, first with aluminium and then steel bodies. Although they had fared admirably, the steel body, while excellent for a production car, was just too heavy and its monocoque structure too flexible for optimum race car handling. In addition, competition from other manufacturers was beginning to make itself felt. OSCA proved a very real threat in the 1,100cc and 1,500cc class at Le Mans, while Borgward and EMW were also proving strong competitors.

In reality, by the summer of 1952, the 356 had

reached its development threshold as a serious contender in international motorsport and some far-reaching decisions had to be made about building a thoroughbred race car. Being a competition-orientated and technically innovative manufacturer right from the start, it was inevitable that Porsche would sooner or later sever the chains linking it to its VW ancestry.

Following the Le Mans event in the summer of 1952, Ferry Porsche approved two new design projects to be initiated under the management of Karl Rabe. One of the projects concerned a new higher performing engine, Project 547, which would fall to engineer Ernst Fuhrmann, while the other required the development of a purpose-built race car, the Type 550, to be designed by Erwin Komenda.

and, with that year's Le Mans 24-Hour race as their goal, the amount of time available was limited. As finance was another commodity in short supply, the Zuffenhausen team stuck to the same simple ladder frame used in the Glöckler car.

The first 550s were powered by the factory-prepared, highly tuned, 1,500cc pushrod engine (based on the VW power plant) mounted ahead of the rear axle to give an almost perfect 50/50 weight distribution with the driver aboard. The car's model designation, '550', was not derived from the weight of the car (550kg/1,210lb) as shown in the specification sheet, but rather in keeping with the design office number 550 for the project. Porsche designer, Erwin Komenda, was responsible for the bodywork which clearly shows, once again, that the inspiration for the sleek lines had come from the Glöckler cars.

The two cars ready for the 1953 Le Mans event were 550-001 and 550-002, with car 001 being driven by Helm Glöckler (cousin to Walter) and Hans Herrmann, while car 002 was given to the driver-journalist pairing of Richard von Frankenberg and Paul Frère. The company could not have wished for a better finish for the 550 on its debut, with von Frankenberg and Frère finishing just ahead of the Glöckler/Herrmann car, thereby taking the two top spots in their class and setting a new 1,500cc class record in the process.

Following its success at Le Mans earlier that year, Porsche publicly unveiled the mid-engined, two-seat prototype 550/1500RS production racer at the Paris Salon in October 1953 at a price of DM24,600, but it wasn't until late 1954 that the Porsche factory actually had a production 550 Spyder to sell to its customers.

The name 'Spyder' had been adopted for this model as it was thought that the original full title of 550/1500RS Spyder would be too much for most people to use regularly. Although the motor was based on the VW power plant, the unit was by now very much a Porsche engine, having been subjected to constant improvement by the Zuffenhausen engineers.

After more racing and with several victories under its belt, Porsche brought cars 550-001 and 002 back home to Zuffenhausen for a thorough overhaul, before being sold to a Guatemalan garage

ABOVE Porsche Typ 550 (car No. 45) of Richard von Frankenberg/Paul Frère during the 1953 Le Mans race.

OPPOSITE Here, the Porsche 550/1500RS is shown at the Paris Salon, October 1953 (top left).

What was the Typ 550?

The Typ 550's starting point was undoubtedly the early custom-built 356-based racer created by Volkswagen dealer Walter Glöckler of Frankfurt. As a result of the lessons learnt in the development of the Glöckler cars, the timeline for building the new 550 race car would not be that long as these were to be closely modelled on these cars. The task of building this new car fell to Porsche engineer, Wilhelm Hild, but work only started in early 1953

owner and racer, Jaroslav Juhan. The Czechoslovakian-born Juhan intended for these two cars to be driven in the fourth Carrera Panamericana, a tortuous 3,000km race through the 'outback' of Mexico, scheduled for 19 November 1953. One of these original 550s scored a class win in that event in the hands of José Herrarte, while the following year, it finished fifth in class driven by Chavez.

By the time the prototype 550-001 ran in its first race in 1953, the drawings of the production version of Porsche's purebred racer had already been completed, although final designs would not be signed off until the following year. Those first two cars had served as a vitally important test bed for the company's thrust into the sport as a mainstream competitor. Also, with these two 550s, Porsche had successfully bridged the time gap between their modified but by now outclassed 356 Coupés and the introduction of the second project approved by Ferry Porsche back in 1952, the development of a higher performance motor – Project 547.

PORSCHE 550 TIMELINE AND TECHNICAL SPECIFICATIONS

Year	Car type	Engine capacity	Engine type	Power output	Maximum speed
1951	Glöckler -Porsche	1.1-litre	Tuned VW 4-cylinder pushrod motor	93bhp @ 5,500rpm	200km/h (125mph)
1952	Glöckler -Porsche	1.5-litre	Tuned VW 4-cylinder pushrod motor		
1953	Typ 550 launched at Paris Salon, Oct. 1953, but production only started in 1954	1,488cc	Typ 528 4-cyl pushrod motor	98bhp	200km/h (125mph)
1955	Typ 550 with flat welded tube frame	1,498cc	Typ 547 4-cam motor	110bhp @ 7,800rpm	220km/h (137mph)
1956	Typ 550A with lattice tube frame	1,498cc	Typ 547 4-cam motor	135–148bhp @ 7,200rpm	240km/h (150mph)

This table shows some of the milestone developments of the VW and Porsche engine types and the capacity used in the 550, and the introduction of the Project 547 four-cam motor.

Project 547 – the four-cam motor

The brief given to Dr Ernst Fuhrmann, a brilliant engineer who at the time was only 33 years of age, was to build a higher performing, air-cooled 1.5-litre boxer engine capable of producing 100bhp from the outset. The new engine was to follow the general format of the existing 1,500cc pushrod motor, and should therefore not exceed the physical dimensions of this unit, but it should also allow much greater development potential in the future, in fact right up to 2.0 litres. Fuhrmann decided early on that the motor would have two camshafts per bank which were shaft driven rather than chain or belt driven.

Herbert Linge picks up the story: 'Fuhrmann was really trying to build an engine which could also be used on the road, which was very difficult in the beginning; it was just so expensive for a road car.'

Initially, this motor would only be for competition purposes, which meant that it was destined for the 550 racing car. It must be pointed out that although the 550 model cars were being developed at the same time as work was being done on the 547-engines, the first two prototype 550s, were never intended to receive the four-cam motor. Although the engine drawings were finished by late 1952, the first unit was only ready for dynamometer testing by Easter the following year.

The complex, light alloy 1,498cc engine had four camshafts and produced 110bhp at 7,800rpm. It had twin ignition which meant two plugs per cylinder, two camshaft driven distributors and two coils.

The motor was fitted with a Hirth four roller-bearing crankshaft and was dry sumped with a

large oil pump and a separate oil tank. So complex was the motor, that Porsche mechanics had to be specially trained before working on it, as an engine rebuild could take up to a week. The simple task of replacing the spark plugs required the use of a special double-articulated plug wrench, which often proved too much trouble for owners.

Jürgen Barth recalls the complexity of the engine at the time: 'I know the motor is complex, because when I was an apprentice I had to learn on this engine and it takes a lot of experience before you can get it right.' He marvelled at what a brilliant engineer Ernst Fuhrmann was: 'Because air-cooled engines have a way of expanding because of the aluminium, and so you have to have a system with overhead camshafts which can cope with this expansion, and the only way of doing so was with shifting seals in the rods. So it was a unique feature at the time.'

Engine testing was frequently carried out in cars by the mechanics who worked on the engines. 'At the time, we took all the cars, whatever was available, even the mechanics. We had Weutherich [later, James Dean's mechanic] at the time, he was the mechanic building these engines and even he tested the cars. Sometimes he crashed them, quite often he crashed them', Barth added laughingly.

The Spyder started it all – or was it the 356?

In an attempt to unravel the process which led to Porsche producing a higher performance road car, one must trace the initiative back to the company's early competition days. Just as the Glöckler-Porsches led to the 550 Spyder and ultimately the Fuhrmann four-cam motor, so too did the Porsche 356 lead to the 356 A Carrera in response to the need for greater performance by Porsche's customers.

The first four-cam engines were road tested in the Porsche 550, but Fuhrmann felt that they would also be suitable for installation in the production 356. In 1954, a 100bhp version was put in Dr Porsche's personal 356 Coupé, which was known affectionately around the factory as 'Coupé Ferdinand'. This was one of the first vehicles, chassis number 5056, built in Stuttgart-Zuffenhausen. It derived its name from its first use

PREVIOUS PAGE Porsche 550 Spyder, body number 550-001, now fully restored and residing in the Collier Motor Museum, America. (*Collier Museum*)

as a present for Professor Ferdinand Porsche's 75th birthday on 3 September 1950.

However, following the Professor's death, 'Coupé Ferdinand' was promoted to a full experimental vehicle within the test department and was used for a total of eight years in a wide variety of tests relating to the engine, chassis, gearbox, electrics, bodyshell and tyres. On 9 October 1958 the car finished its active service during which it had changed colour six times, been driven for more than 415,000km (257,000 miles). Today, this car can be found in the Porsche Museum.

'Coupé Ferdinand, fitted with the Fuhrmann engine, was a big hit with the factory staff and, as a result of this successful development, a Gmünd coupé was entered in the 1954 Liège–Rome–Liège marathon race. It performed remarkably well over the four-day event in the hands of Helmut Polensky and Herbert Linge and, as a result, Ferry Porsche decided that a small production run of these 356s with the four-cam engine was justified.

Even though the car's engine performance had been increased dramatically, it nevertheless proved itself to be very reliable even in long-distance events. The substantial percentage increase in horsepower led to a similar increase in performance and, although complex, the Fuhrman engine, as it became known in the factory, also proved its reliability in the long-distance races. Antole Lapine explains: 'Because, in none of the Spyders was the four-cam referred to as anything but the "Fuhrmann" engine and with respect for the brilliance of its designer, any reference to this engine as such, was much to the chagrin of Ferry Porsche.' Lapine laughingly adds that both men were not very tall individuals and feisty – they 'couldn't stand each other'.

It had been the company's experience that customers always looked for more power from their cars. As Rolf Sprenger recalls: 'And then they put it [a more powerful engine] in the production car, as we did in the later years, whenever we had some experience from the races we developed our production engines.' It is estimated that in the early days, up to 20 per cent of Porsche customers hungered for more power, and in order to prevent those who wanted to spend more money from slipping away to buy a Ferrari or Maserati, a stronger engine was needed in the Porsche production car range.

BELOW Hans Herrmann at the wheel of the class-winning 550 Spyder in the 1954 Mille Miglia. Herrmann and Linge finished sixth overall.

Were the European victories not enough?

'Ferry Porsche liked lightweight, easily manoeuvrable sports cars of consistently functional design; this was the foundation for the 550 Spyder's career' – an extract from the Porsche Museum catalogue.

The essence of a true athlete is power, weight and timing – these aspects must obviously be present in the correct proportions in order for that athlete to succeed. In the same way, the extract from the Porsche Museum catalogue above represents these same attributes which must be present in a sports or racing car in order for that car to be successful in competition. The 550 Spyder was the true athlete of its time.

The racing success of the Porsche 550/1500RS Spyder has been a major, if not the major, contributing factor to Porsche's initial racing and commercial success. From these beginnings, most of the company's later growth and development

can be traced, both on and off the track. Success with the 550 in Europe at the Le Mans 24-Hour event between 1953 and 1955 confirmed both the durability and the capabilities of the small race car. Still running with the pushrod engines, the first two 550s, cars 550-001 and 550-002, were ready for the 1953 Le Mans 24-Hour race. 'Out of the box' they were placed first and second in their class.

The story of the 1954 Mille Miglia in which Hans Herrmann and Herbert Linge finished a creditable sixth place overall, is well documented, but the tenacity of the drivers is matched by the plucky endurance of the machinery. The year was crowned with the famous third-place finish in the Carrera Panamericana, the one event in the company's motorsport history on which this whole story is based.

The following year, things only got better, with a fourth place finish overall in the Le Mans event, a win in the 1.5-litre class and a first and second place finish in the 1.1-litre class. The Porsche was also awarded the Index of Performance for the car

RIGHT The Typ 547 four-cam engine designed by Ernst Fuhrmann, as fitted to the 1955 Porsche 550/1500 RS (Rennsport) Spyder.

with the best combined speed and economy for the entire race field. Later that year, in September 1955, the 356A Carrera was introduced to the public at the IAA in Frankfurt as a full production model for the road (see Chapter 3).

If the 1954 Carrera Panamericana had been the most important Porsche 'triumph' to date, the 1956 Targa Florio must surely rank as the most significant and memorable. Umberto Maglioli single-handedly drove his 550 A to overall victory in sweltering heat to win by a massive margin of 15 minutes. The 550 had by now become the 550 A thanks to a lighter and stiffer lattice tube frame which made this model one of the best handling Porsche race cars to date.

The Solitude circuit not far from Stuttgart, had long been considered Porsche's home track. In 1956, they had the chance to show the home crowd what the 550 A was capable of and in the hands of Hans Herrmann, Graf von Trips and Richard von Frankenberg, the Spyder achieved remarkable 1–2–4 place finishes. The Fuhrmann-engined Porsche had indeed matured into a formidable machine.

For the faster circuits, hard tops were fitted for better streamlining. During the years of 550 production, from 1953 to 1957, a total of 137 race cars of the 550-series and all its derivatives, were built. Where it was not uncommon to find only one or two cars produced by other manufacturers within one model in a single racing season, this was a notable tally for any race car manufacturer. The 550-series had been so successful that they formed the basis of future models such as the formidable RS59, RS60 and RS61 Typ 718 race cars.

With such an enviable record of victories and other top finishes, one must ask why Porsche, at a time when resources were not plentiful, felt it necessary to look to the far flung corners of the globe for further conquests. Races in Europe were the most competitive in the world and certainly very plentiful – was this not enough for the fledgling company?

BELOW A studio photo of the famous Porsche Typ 356 Coupé Ferdinand (1950).

TIMELINE:

1952

Gmünd Coupé wins Liège Rally with pushrod engine.

1.5-litre 'Super' engine introduced at 1,488cc.

1953

Easter, 547 engine runs tested on dynamometer.

550-02 wins 1,500cc (pushrod) class in Panamericana.

1954

August, 547-engined Gmünd Coupé wins Liège Rally.

Herrmann third overall in Pan-americana with 547-engined 550-004.

1955

September – Carrera 356 intro at Frankfurt Motor Show.

October – Paris Salon – Fuhrmann Carrera wrecked.

1956

Carrera 356 listed as production car for first time.

1957

Carrera split into GS and GT models.

1958

Carrera 1,600cc engine introduced.

CHAPTER THREE

Going west

Thoroughbred – (thu'-ru-bred') – being of aristocratic birth and showing the characteristics of that birth.

Odhams *Dictionary of the English Language*, London, 1946

The definition of the word thoroughbred is most relevant at this point, as it captures the qualities of a privileged lineage, a special and rather distinctive heritage. Above is an appropriate explanation for the word, from the same period as the Carrera's birth.

La Carrera Panamericana – The origin of the Carrera legend

In studying the origins of Porsche's Carrera badge, it is important to understand the circumstances in which this model name came about, and to grasp some of the ambience surrounding the world of motorsport in the 1950s. Things were not quite so complex back then and legends were sometimes born out of simple traditions and, on occasions, even unintentionally.

At the end of the 1940s, the combined countries of the Americas agreed to resume the building of the highway connecting the countries of the western hemisphere, effectively uniting the two Americas by way of a north–south road. Known as the Pan-American Road, it covered a staggering 16,000 miles (25,700km), stretching from Alaska to Chile.

In celebration of the completion of the Mexican section of the road, known as the Inter American Highway, and in order to attract public attention to the project, the Mexican government proposed the creation of an international border-to-border

road race, an idea that was immediately accepted. It was planned that top rate drivers would be invited to participate, a concept that was self-fulfilling as the event was being billed as a tough challenge. If one well known driver signed up, the others couldn't afford not to be there.

The Spanish word 'carrera' means competition or race, and so the name given to this great Mexican event was simply La Carrera Panamericana, which in English translated to the Pan American Road Race. The event was first held on 5 May 1950 (later, events were held in November), and was officially classified as a rally, although in reality, it took the form of a no-holds-barred race across some of the harshest and most dangerous terrain in motorsport at that time. Stretching from Tuxtla Gutiérrez in the south near the Guatemalan border, to Ciudad Juarez near El Paso on the American border, drivers had to tough it out over the 2,000-mile course with little in the way of maps, or even support crew for some. By way of a comparison, the Carrera Panamericana was twice the length of the Mille Miglia, over much more rugged terrain and far from any of the major manufacturers' support structures. Rules were sketchy at best, and so the race became an all-out contest to get from the start line to the finish line as fast as possible, with the mere matter of 2,000 gruelling miles (3,200km) separating these two points.

The Carrera Panamericana was only run for five years (1950–54) because of the high risk attached

OPPOSITE Carrera Panamericana – the 550 Spyder of José Herrarte finished first in the 1,600cc Sports Car Class.

to the event, for both drivers and spectators. The Mexican road race, designed to help advertise the Pan-American Highway and develop tourist interest in Mexico, had had its fair share of fatalities over the years, with two deaths in each of the first two races and another in the third year. Then in the 1953 race alone four drivers lost their lives. However, to spice things up somewhat, local spectators would take pleasure in 'bullfighting' the cars as they sped through the towns, trying to touch them at 120mph. Rutted and cobbled roads, high mountain passes with sheer drops threatened cars and drivers alike, so if the spectators, wild animals or the roads didn't get you then vehicle reliability most likely would.

In a report in *Autosport* (March, 1953), the Mercedes-Benz race director, Alfred Neubauer, described the event as: 'A combination of the Tripoli Grand Prix, the Italian Mille Miglia, the German Nürburgring and the 24-hour race at Le-Mans', and that was probably a conservative view.

Race conditions varied from a hot and humid tropical start, rising up from sea level to 10,000 feet with temperatures ranging from over 90°F to almost freezing, all within 72 hours. It is hardly surprising that it earned the title of the 'Toughest Race'.

These extreme conditions placed teams and drivers under constant pressure right from the start. Engines that performed satisfactorily at sea level sounded really sick at 10,000ft (3,000m), requiring teams to tune and retune their engines, as well as resetting carburettors and plug gaps on a regular basis. (Drivers also had to change to a colder range spark plug at high altitudes in the highlands.) Stretching almost the entire length of the country, the Mexican race was tough on both the drivers and their equipment as road surfaces consisted of a mixture of highly abrasive volcanic ash, with rock-strewn run-off areas and deep road-side gorges. A set of tyres was not expected to last much beyond 600 miles (960km).

BELOW Hans Herrmann en route to a memorable third place finish in the 1954 Carrera Panamericana race in his Porsche Typ 550 Spyder. The crowds lining the route often proved more of a danger than an encouragement.

The first race, in 1950, followed a route southwards from the US border to the southern town of El Ocotal, while the next four events saw drivers heading northwards. At first the Americans dominated with their Oldsmobiles, Cadillacs and Lincolns, but then the big Italian and German machinery took over in subsequent years with drivers such as Phil Hill, Karl Kling, Fangio, Taruffi and Maglioli, as well as a Texas chicken farmer by the name of Carroll Shelby.

In an interview, Herbert Linge told the author that the roads were 'very tricky'. There was little road safety to speak of, with sharp corners, steep hills, animals on the roads and the road surface was covered with dust from the surrounding countryside.

Linge remembers the stretch leading from Mexico City up to the border (with the USA): 'There were many long straights, sometimes up to 80 km (50 miles), just straight, the only thing in between were these vados, they could ruin your car if you hit them at full speed.' Vados was the Mexican word for a drainage ditch or gutter which ran across the road to channel the rainwater away after a heavy downpour, and although they were all supposed to be marked with road signs, these had frequently been removed by locals and it was very difficult to see a vados when covered with dust. In fact, Lancia driver, Felice Bonetto was killed in the 1953 event after his car hit a vados.

Why did Porsche go to Mexico?

It is not unreasonable to expect that few people in Europe had even heard of the Carrera Panamericana. Although this race may not have been as widely publicised as the Mille Miglia, Targa Florio or Le Mans, many famous racing drivers drove in the Mexican race.

Herbert Linge explains: 'All of the European drivers from Lancia and some of the Ferrari drivers had already driven in Mexico because there were no races in Europe, so they all had time in November to go to Mexico. The whole Lancia team was always there, you could see Fangio, Maglioli, Phil Hill; the whole Formula 1 drivers field all drove in Mexico. So the race was not well known in Europe, but for the teams and race drivers, it was well known and everyone was trying to drive there.'

Not many motor manufacturers would even consider participating in international motorsport after having been in existence for just a few years. Although Porsche did not field an official team in Mexico until 1953, many Porsche customers entered this event early on as privateers, and some came away with very impressive results. This perseverance by the privateers had several results, first, that it proved beyond any doubt that even the overweight 356 was still a worthy competitor in the face of stiff opposition, and secondly, it ensured factory engineers sat up and took notice of these results.

Did Porsche have a strategy that justified their trip to Central America? In the 1950s it was far simpler as many of the top international racing drivers of the era were wealthy in their individual right, often counts or barons, and so a quick phone call to a fellow noble would open the door. With Baron Huschke von Hanstein's contacts in the elite sporting circles of the FIA and further afield in those aristocratic cliques, racing events could be arranged in far-off destinations without too much difficulty. With the Carrera Panamericana being run at the end of the racing season – 'You always go

ABOVE Fürst Metternich speeds through the desolate Mexican countryside in his Porsche 356 Cabriolet in the 1952 Carrera Panamericana.

ABOVE The 356 Cabriolet of Fürst Metternich pictured in front of the Mercedes garage in Mexico City during the 1952 Carrera Panamericana. Seated in the rear is Herbert Linge (chief mechanic), while up front is Constantin Graf Berckheim (with cap) who drove a 356 Coupé, and Alfons Fürst zu Hohenlohe, a local German resident who entered both 356s in the event.

there in winter. It is warmer than in Germany, and sometimes the food is better', chuckled Jürgen Barth.

Over the five-year period during which the Carrera Panamericana was run, it attracted over two million spectators, more than any other motorsport event in the world up to that date. In order to break into the American market, the Carrera Panamericana event provided the perfect opportunity for the German manufacturer to make its entrance and to demonstrate the strength and reliability of their cars in the arena in which American cars competed, and in an event that was being followed by the American population. The Carrera Panamericana offered Porsche an ideal opportunity to demonstrate the ruggedness and reliability of its cars to a willing and enthusiastic audience, a market that had the resources to buy their products.

Herbert Linge recalls: 'When Fürst Metternich and Constantin Graf Berckheim entered private cars in 1952, they asked the Porsche factory if it

was possible to have any help there because nobody knew the car. I was with Max Hoffman in the States, so I was ordered to Mexico to manage these two cars. I was entered as the co-driver for Bergheim so I could take care of the two cars in the race. I was co-driver, mechanic, racing director and everything for these two cars. We got no sleep there.'

What they needed was a team of professional drivers and a vehicle with factory support that could exploit the full potential of their cars, and which would lift the name of Porsche into the spotlight, right on the doorstep of the lucrative American market. However, running a full factory race team required human and financial resources, of which Porsche had neither in abundant supply in the early 1950s. With the arrival of Baron Huschke von Hanstein as race manager in 1952, the prospects looked brighter, and he was able to use his extensive network of contacts in the international racing scene, to elbow his way into the burgeoning sport.

With Porsche's activities in the States, the company had to do something to increase its profile, while still not costing them too much money. The Carrera Panamericana seemed like a good idea as this event was closely followed by the American public and a good result there would highlight the strong mechanical abilities of the little 356. 'And as you know in the early Fifties, Johnny von Neumann, Max Hoffman and all the people started with the 356s and 550s in competition to show what a good car Porsche is and what good engines they produce and how durable the cars are', explained Rolf Sprenger.

US Porsche importer, Max Hoffman, had been energetically canvassing the Stuttgart management to take notice of the American market since 1950. At first, Ferry Porsche didn't think that the Americans would take much notice of the small cars from Germany, but Hoffman, as we shall see later, knew the market there better than most and he encouraged his Porsche customers to race their cars at the weekends. With small successes in the hands of privateers, the young 356 soon gained an enthusiastic following and the market indeed began to pay attention.

The Carrera Panamericana – US publicity?

One might wonder what justification there was in travelling halfway around the world, to a little-known country in Central America – little known that is, to the public in Europe – to take part in a race that very few outside of Mexico and America had even heard of. Certainly, for the first four years (1950–53), there was no pre-race publicity in Europe, and so one might question what the value would be of such an extravagant trip for the small Stuttgart manufacturer, but it was in the exposure gained in the American market which counted. With many key drivers from the United States taking part, and many others who raced in stock car events and the hot rod movement, they enjoyed strong support from their followers back home and the Carrera Panamericana enjoyed good publicity there.

According to Herbert Linge, 'In America, the race was well liked because all the stock car drivers from Indianapolis drove there in their Mercurys and Lincolns and the exposure helped them a lot

with sales.' With active support from Hoffman, the New York-based Porsche importer, he ensured that Porsche's achievements also received positive publicity in the United States.

In order to help finance the factory team in Mexico, Huschke von Hanstein struck a sponsorship deal with a California-based Porsche aero engine agent, Fletcher's Aviation and German electronics giant, Telefunken. One of the conditions imposed by Fletcher was that Porsche participated in an event at Turner's Air Force base en route to Mexico. This suited von Hanstein as it would also give Porsche some valuable exposure in America, and undoubtedly the name would still be fresh in the minds of the American public when reports filtered back from the upcoming Carrera Panamericana. The ever-alert von Hanstein never missed a trick when it came to publicity for the Porsche name, but despite a disappointing showing in both America and Mexico that year, the small cars from Germany attracted a lot of attention.

For the 1954 Carrera Panamericana, there was slightly more publicity in the local Stuttgart papers ahead of the race, based on the encouraging results of Porsche's previous year's participation, but

BELOW Fürst Metternich (right) stands alongside his 356 1500 Cabriolet during a stop in the 1952 Carrera Panamericana. Constantin Graf Berckheim, driver of the 356 Coupé is on the left. Note the engine capacity '1500 ccm' on the front lid.

BELOW Le Mans, June 1953 – the 550 Spyder (550-001) No. 44 of Herrmann/Glöckler leads the von Frankenberg/Frère (550-002) No. 45 car. Von Frankenberg/Frère finished 15th overall with Herrmann/Glöckler in 16th.

TOP RIGHT One of the first times the Porsche Typ 550 Spyder ran with the new Typ 547 four-cam motor (1953).

BELOW RIGHT José Herrarte stands next to his 550 Spyder (550-002) after the fourth running of the Carrera Panamericana in 1953. Herrarte finished first in the 1,600cc Sports Car class and 32nd place overall.

nothing too elaborate. Any press exposure tended to be after the event rather than before, as coverage depended on the degree of success achieved by the German manufacturer. The race had not yet earned anything like the level of interest enjoyed by the big European events such as the Targa Florio, Le Mans or the Mille Miglia.

Porsche racing successes 1952–54

As we saw in the previous chapter, Porsche realised after the 1952 Le Mans race, that they needed to construct their own purpose-built racer. The 550 race car was debuted at the 1953 Le Mans event but the famed four-cam engine would only be bench tested for the first time in Easter of that year, and so could hardly be expected to be ready to run at Le Mans just a few months later. Although they were still running on the VW-based pushrod engines at Le Mans that year, the company's assault on the French 24-hour endurance race produced some very encouraging results. Frère and von Frankenberg in 550-002 came home 15th overall and first in class with Helmut Glöckler and Hans Herrmann 16th overall in 550-001, and second in class.

The first Typ 547 four-cam motor was dyno tested during the Easter week of 1953 but would only be fitted into a car in August of that year, when Hans Herrmann drove it in practice at the Nürburgring. As this event was intended to be the swansong race for the soon-to-be-replaced 001 and 002 cars, Herrmann practised with the new 550-003 car equipped with the 547 engine. However, he preferred the older car 002 in that event, and 003 was parked instead and closely guarded, as Ferry Porsche and von Hanstein did not want any prying eyes to see what motor they had under the bodywork.

The first official competitive event in which the 547-powered 550-003 car was driven in anger was the Freiberg Hill-climb, in which Hans Stuck Snr drove it to third place. The power curve of the four-cam motor was such that peak power was only available at high revs within a very narrow power band, and the short and narrow hill-climb course prevented 550-003 from achieving a better place.

Mexico

Later that year, in September, car 550-004 was joined by its sister, 550-005, as they were prepared

for the trans-Atlantic trip, and the opportunity of representing Porsche for the first official factory team effort on American soil.

Once again, Herbert Linge was in attendance as race mechanic, this time accompanied by factory mechanic Werner Enz. Powered by the trusty pushrod engines, as the Fuhrmann four-cam motors were still considered to be under development at the time, these two cars performed disappointingly, although the crowds were suitably impressed with the performance of these newcomers. Unfortunately, the Mexican outing that followed their American debut proved equally disappointing with 550-004 piloted by Karl Kling, dropping out with engine failure while Hans Herrmann crashed in the remaining car, 550-005, with a broken steering column. Guatemalan, José Herrarte in 550-002, came home in 15th overall place, while Argentinean Fernando Segura's brand-new, totally stock 356 Super came in 16th, just behind Herrarte.

It should be noted here that both Herrarte (002) and Juhan (001 – although he did not finish) were also in cars powered by the old pushrod engines, and after Herrmann and Kling had both bowed out of the race, von Hanstein, in true fashion, set the Porsche mechanics to work supporting the two older cars. This move further illustrates the camaraderie amongst the Porsche personnel and non-factory drivers that existed at race meetings around the world.

Europe

Encouraged by the progress, if not the success, of the Porsche 550 in the USA and Mexico in 1953, the Stuttgart engineers continued to improve the 547 engine for competition. The 1954 Mille Miglia marked the international debut in a long-distance race of the four-cam motor in the 550 Spyder, just a month before the Le Mans event. Hans Herrmann and Herbert Linge drove their Spyders to a commendable sixth place overall, after the now-famous dice with a train in which Herrmann just managed to get across the level crossing before the barrier came down. Herrmann and Linge had driven the route in practice, and between them they had agreed a signal for the race in the case of an emergency.

During the race itself, rounding the bend just before the railway crossing, Herrmann noticed the train approaching out of the corner of his eye and at that moment, with Linge looking down at his notes, Herrmann struck his co-driver on the helmet and they both ducked instinctively under the closing boom. Linge recounts the moment: 'We knew there was a railroad crossing coming, I had it in my book and so when he hit my head, I knew immediately what is going on.' This is a racing story that will be analysed and discussed for many years to come.

In June 1954, the company's assault on the French 24-hour endurance race at Le Mans, produced some very encouraging results. The Herrmann/Polensky car (550-011) was sacrificed as the pace setter as its sole aim was to get the opposition to chase it in the hope that they would break before the Porsche did. After 14 hours, it was the Porsche that retired with a holed piston, while the car of von Frankenberg and Helm Glöckler

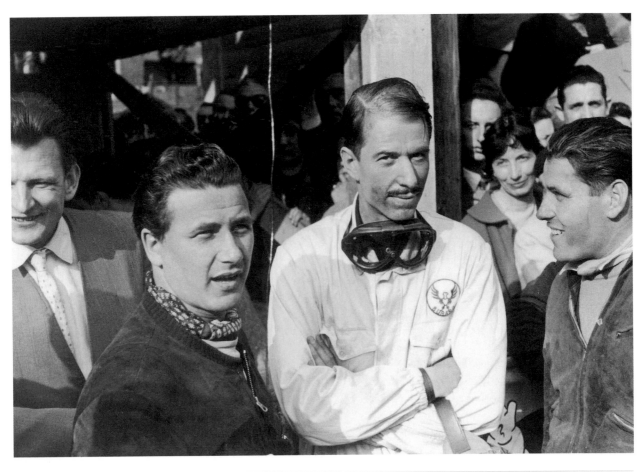

(550-010) had already gone out in the first hour leaving the cars of Jon Claes/Paul Stasse (550-012) and Gustave Olivier/Zora Arkus-Duntov (550-013) to carry the flag. The latter car of Olivier/Duntov (550-013) was fitted with the much smaller 1,089cc engine and finished a commendable 14th overall and first in the 1,100cc class. The Claes/Stasse car won the 1,500cc class and finished in 12th place with a holed piston, but only by attrition as the two cars ahead of it took themselves out of contention in a collision in the last hour, leaving the Porsche to limp home to victory in the class. Despite the circumstances in which victory was achieved, it proved that the Porsche power plant was once again extremely resilient.

For the Liège–Rome–Liège Rally of August 1954, Porsche called out of retirement one of its trusty aluminium-bodied Gmünd Coupés, and fitted it with a 547 four-cam Le Mans-type engine. Fuhrmann's plan was that if the engine could

survive the event, which included extremely demanding and gruelling sections in the Alps, it could survive pretty much anything that customers might subject it to – a plan which hinted at his earlier aspirations when developing the motor, back in 1952. Polensky and Linge were assigned to tackle this tough 3,000-mile (4,800km) rally, as it was Polensky who had won the event in a Gmünd Coupé in 1952, albeit with the proven pushrod engine. For the 1954 event however, the roof line of the Gmünd Coupé was lowered and a one-piece windscreen was fitted. In the interests of improved reliability, power was reduced to 105bhp, down 10bhp from the Le Mans set up, helping Polensky to bring the car home in first place.

Success in this event went down well with everyone at Porsche, but this was more so than with Ernst Fuhrmann, who had had personal plans to install this powerful four-cam motor in the 356 bodyshell from the outset. With interest in this quarter now aroused within the factory and

OPPOSITE TOP The 550 Spyder of Hans Herrmann is prepared in the Porsche garage during the 1953 Carrera Panamericana. He retired with a broken steering column.

OPPOSITE BOTTOM Participating in the 1954 Mille Miglia – from left to right: Günter Jendrick, Hans Herrmann, Fitch and Herbert Linge.

LEFT The famous painting of the incident where Herrmann/Linge just scraped under the closing railroad boom in the 1954 Mille Miglia. They went on to finish sixth overall, but this close encounter will live on for many years still.

ABOVE Victorious in the 'baby' 550 Spyder – Olivier/Duntov finished an impressive 14th overall in the 1,089cc-engined Spyder. Seated on the car's fender is Duntov's wife, Elfi (front left), while Huschke von Hanstein, with camera in hand is on the other fender, giving directions.

management, the 356/547 combination began to gather pace as a viable concept and Porsche subsequently decided to go ahead with the production version.

Mexico again

For the 1954 Carrera Panamericana, four 550s were entered. Lopez-Chavez was in Juhan's former car, 550-001, and Hans Herrmann drove Kling's 550-004 as the official factory entry sponsored by Fletcher Aviation and Telefunken. Fernando Segura was in 550-006 and Jaroslav Juhan was in 550-012. This was to be revenge time for Porsche as Hans Herrmann (550-004) won the 1,500cc class in jubilant fashion finishing third overall while Juhan (550-012) was second in class and fourth overall.

It is not well known that in the 1954 event, after

Mexico City, Segura complained that he was too tired and couldn't drive anymore. With the car well back in 52nd place, Linge took the wheel and for three days fought his way back up through the field to 16th, when Segura took the car across the finish line on the last day, still holding that position.

Jaroslav Juhan would later take 550-012 to other class victories in several South American endurance races, but by that stage the American motoring-mad public had already taken notice of Porsche's achievements and the German manufacturer was firmly in the spotlight.

Although the Carrera Panamericana was not the scene of Porsche's greatest racing accomplishment, with eleven wins in the Targa Florio and five wins in the Nürburgring 1,000km event, the Mexican race must nevertheless rank as one of the toughest. Climatic and race conditions apart, for the small manufacturer from Stuttgart this represented a monumental achievement as they were undoubtedly the lightweights in the field. With little by way of infrastructure outside of Europe, they had to be almost totally self sufficient. Any results thus achieved had to be down to driver talent and the reliability of the machine. Porsche decided that Herrmann's success in the Carrera Panamericana (behind the Ferrari 375s of Maglioli and Phil Hill) was well worth publicising and, added to its class victories at Le Mans, the company's endurance racing credentials were affirmed.

According to Klaus Bischof of the Porsche Museum, the race technicians in Mexico referred to the four-cam motor in the 550 as the 'Carrera' motor because that is the race in which the car was participating at that time. It was customary for the technicians to refer to engines in this way as it helped them to identify certain technical differences, just as they may simply refer to an engine as the 'Le Mans' or the 'Targa Florio' engine which may have been used in those events. The Carrera reference was to the engine only, not the car. The difference here was that the name stuck and the legendary engine was later to power the production 356 which gave birth to the Porsche Carrera legend.

ABOVE Hans Herrmann brings his Porsche 550 Spyder across the line in third place overall in the final Carrera Panamericana (1954). This must rank as one of Porsche's most important 'victories'.

PORSCHE 550 SPYDERS THAT COMPETED IN THE CARRERA PANAMERICANA IN 1953 AND 1954 DETAILS AND SPECIFICATION

DETAILS	550-001 AND 550-002	550-003 AND 550-004
Motor	4-cylinder boxer motor, air-cooled, two double carburettors	4-cylinder boxer motor, air-cooled, double ignition, four camshafts, dual Solex 40 PII carburettors
Engine	Typ 528	Typ 547
Displacement	1,488cc	1,498cc
Bore and stroke	80mm x 74mm	85mm x 66mm
Compression ratio	9.0:1	9.0:1
Power output	79bhp	110bhp at 7,000rpm
Gearbox	4-speed manual	4-speed manual
Chassis	Tubular frame	Flat tubular frame
Bodywork	Aluminium	Aluminium
Length, width, height	3,600mm x 1,540mm x 1,180mm	3,600mm x 1,540mm x 1,050mm
Net weight	550kg (1,213lb)	550kg (1,213lb)
Maximum speed	200km/h (125mph)	220km/h (138mph)

Porsche's international sales

Fortunately, Ferry Porsche, who for some time had been in charge of virtually every company function from engineering and production to marketing and forward planning, now took an even greater interest in expanding international sales in the early 1950s. He prioritised the establishment of a competition department and the expansion of additional external markets, the United States in particular. It could be said that these two areas became the focus of Ferry Porsche's activities for the rest of the decade. With sales in Europe and Britain anything but meteoric, Ferry realised that the American market held the key to the company's growth.

It is fair to say that the American car-buying public were going to be hard-pressed to part with their money for a small, foreign, up-turned bathtub of a motor car that had its engine at the wrong end. Furthermore, it was air cooled, it didn't make a lot of noise and it cost a whole lot more

than anything the 'Big Three' manufacturers in America could offer. Faced with this situation, Ferry Porsche was going to have his work cut out trying to sell the Porsche 356 to a nation as vast as America, where traditionally the company had not spent any real money on marketing or promoting its products. Advertising budgets were almost non-existent and there certainly wasn't even a marketing department to speak of.

As far as a marketing strategy was concerned, there wasn't one. There was no money to pay for extra staff to do this function, and there certainly was no money to employ the services of an external agency to carry out this task. Racing gave the company all the exposure it wanted, and in the right places, where motorsport enthusiasts would see the results, such as motor magazines or the sporting pages in the press.

Always looking for a public relations opportunity, Jürgen Barth recalls a story of how effectively von Hanstein used the media to get attention in the newspapers. Huschke von

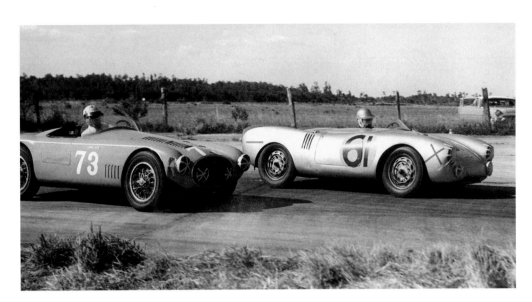

LEFT Sebring 1955 – (No. 61) Bob Davis in a 550 Spyder mixing it with some American muscle.

Hanstein, upon returning home from Cuba in 1958 following the recent kidnapping of Juan Manuel Fangio by the then young radical, Fidel Castro, arrived at the Stuttgart airport to a sea of journalists and photographers. Von Hanstein appeared in the doorway of the aeroplane at the top of the steps, wearing a helmet and holding a revolver in his hand, and announced to the assembled throng of media: 'This is the new equipment for race directors.' Very few people could pull off a stunt of such audacity as this so successfully, but von Hanstein was a master of media opportunism. With that type of publicity, the company did not need to spend money on expensive public relations campaigns, as von Hanstein was frequently on the front pages of the newspapers around the world.

The importance of von Hanstein's role as head of motorsport and public relations at Porsche cannot be overestimated during those formative years. During the early years of the growth of the sport, motor racing and public relations tended to be synonymous. At Porsche, especially, the functions of public relations, advertising, racing and engineering, all tended to blend in, and von Hanstein had the skill and ability to understand the delicate but enormously important relationship between these commercial elements. If an opportunity presented itself to further the company's reputation or to promote an achievement then it could be assured that von Hanstein would maximise such an occasion.

Huschke would himself write race reports for the well-known German motoring journal, *Auto Motor und Sport*, and he had the added bonus of having someone like Richard von Frankenberg on the staff who not only raced, but was also an accomplished journalist, so the company had respected journalistic resources to draw on.

In the early 1950s, Porsche had a small export sales department run by Ed Peter, and they naturally searched the globe for new markets. Distribution agreements were often set up in foreign countries as a result of a driver in that country competing successfully with the Porsche cars on the track. Just such an agreement was established with the French importer, Auguste Veuillet, who, following a string of track successes, agreed to sell the German cars in France. These agreements were frequently also the result of family ties with wealthy industrialists in other countries.

Jürgen Barth, winner of 1977 Le Mans 24-Hour in a Porsche 936 (with multiple other top race finishes to his name) and currently head of Porsche Customer Motorsport in Zuffenhausen, explained: 'I think at the time they didn't talk about marketing. They talked about selling and I think the customers did the marketing by racing these cars in the Fifties, and to the point, where these cars were beating all the big Corvettes and everything else. And that was all the marketing they had, and didn't need to do anything else.'

ABOVE December 1951 – Ferry Porsche (left) and Max Hoffman on the terrace of Hoffman's apartment on Park Avenue, New York.

The American connection

'He [Ferry Porsche] never made any decision without having long discussions with Max Hoffman and Johnny von Neumann, the big dealers in the States. We always figured about 55–65 per cent [of production] was going to be for the States, because we knew we could never build a car just for Europe', Linge recalls.

Max Hoffman, an Austrian born entrepreneur, had raced and dealt in all manner of cars in Europe, prior to the Second World War. However, around the time that hostilities broke out in Europe, he made his way to America in an attempt to set up and continue dealing in exotic motor cars from the 'Old World'. Unfortunately, soon after his arrival in New York, America too was at war and the demand for expensive imported motor cars evaporated overnight, as did the supply of cars, which at that point were primarily sourced from the Continent and England.

After the war, he again turned to the motoring world, his first love, establishing himself in 1947 in a glamorous showroom in Park Avenue, New York, where all the well-to-do shoppers would pass by. Hoffman signed distribution agreements with many top Continental manufacturers and so his empire began to expand. In 1950, he took delivery of the first batch of 20 VW Beetles and later that year he bought three Porsche 356s from the Stuttgart manufacturer, having been shown some photographs of the car back in 1948.

Hoffman met Ferry Porsche at the Paris Motor Show for the first time in 1950. It was a meeting that would set Porsche on the road to unprecedented growth and which would result in a business relationship far beyond the dreams of both parties. In characteristic and conservative fashion, Ferry Porsche substantially underestimated the demand for his cars across the Atlantic, telling Hoffman that he didn't expect to sell more than five cars a year in the American market and capping his expected total annual sales at 500 units. Hoffman told Porsche in no uncertain terms that if he couldn't sell more than five cars a week, he wouldn't be interested in distributing them in America at all. Both men were very wrong.

With the Porsche cars gracing the shiny floor of his Park Avenue showroom, Hoffman was once again bitten by the racing bug. He encouraged his customers to race their cars at weekends and in 1951, he bought Glöckler's first racer which had performed so well in Europe. Hoffman campaigned this Glöckler racer at a meeting at Palm Beach Shores, Florida, on 8 December 1951 and, despite being a non-finisher in its first race, Hoffman went on to race it at many American circuits, accumulating numerous victories in the process.

The factory sent Herbert Linge over to New York in 1952 to act as a support technician for the Hoffman organisation. In an interview with the author, Linge explained how he would be sent from New York to Miami and Chicago and even to Los Angeles just to service or repair customer cars. Even getting the American people to just look at the car was a bit of a problem in the beginning because they really didn't know the name very well, and so Hoffman entered the 356 in small local races at airports and small circuits while Linge was assigned to look after the cars. It wasn't long before spectators commented on how refreshing it was to see a factory technician looking after these cars, which is more than the other manufacturers such as MG and Jaguar were doing.

This opened up the market for the Stuttgart manufacturer, and so the cars became more popular. Linge would conduct driving lessons for the new customers because, in his words: 'These

American people who were used to automatic transmission and big engines, didn't know why there was a clutch pedal in the car. So we held driving schools to show the people how to use the gearbox, and that helped us a lot.'

Linge continues: 'For me, I was all by myself, there was no customer service people so I had to do everything. I had to start from zero, there was nothing there, I just had my tool box with me, that was it.'

As Porsches were raced by both Hoffman and his customers alike, their popularity increased and reputation spread such that Porsche cars created a buzz at the circuits wherever they were raced. The American public loved the little German racer, just as Hoffman had hoped. Hoffman's persistence and enthusiasm for the little-known marque was unquestionably one of the major contributing factors in Porsche gaining such a strong foothold

in America. He was later responsible for creating a national dealer network, including the all-important West Coast, where his friend John von Neumann raced and had his dealership, in North Hollywood, California.

At a time when an average V8 American family saloon sold for around $2,000, Hoffman knew the answer to increased sales lay in a cheaper, open-top version of the Porsche. Thus, in 1951, the America Roadster was born, a more affordable sporting tourer that would appeal to the younger buyer.

This version was not successful however, as the body had lost its flowing lines and when Heuer, the makers of this model, went out of business after just a handful had been produced, the America Roadster was destined for the history books. Although this had been the car that Hoffman had wanted, the costly manufacturing process still resulted, disappointingly, in a price tag of $4,500.

BELOW A new Porsche Typ 356 Speedster pictured outside the Max Hoffman, Motor Car Co., New York in 1955.

Operating from his garage, Competition Motors in North Hollywood, von Neumann was just as close, if not closer, to the racing fraternity than Hoffman was. As the marque became more established, it once again hit the pricing obstacle in the market place. As a weekend racer, the Porsche 356 was very capable of putting in a good performance, but at $4,500, it cost more than a Jaguar XK120 ($3,500) and was only half the size – not a good thing in America. Reports differ as to whether Hoffman or von Neumann first came up with the concept of a stripped out version of the 356 for competition, with supporters from both camps shouting equally loudly for their man. While von Neumann had the ear of the engineers in Stuttgart, it was Hoffman who carried the weight where it counted most, and Ferry Porsche eventually gave the green light for the building of a lightweight model, the Speedster. This was another example, where, through knowledge of the local market, Hoffman was able to persuade the factory to build models that he believed would improve sales in the US. Hoffman was also instrumental in naming the car, as he told Ferry that Americans liked to have names for their cars, not numbers and types. A name like the Speedster, conjured up images of performance, speed and character, and this helped to sell cars by creating a suitable identity. Unwittingly, the doomed America Roadster had paved the way for the new Speedster.

Klaus Bischof explains: 'We had Max Hoffman in America, who was the one that always had ideas as to how to market and especially to give [a car] identity. Max Hoffman has always had this identity skill. He always wanted to create synonyms which were understood by the whole world. And the whole world understands Carrera, Speedster, Spyder; that was his idea.'

The Speedster, first introduced in 1954, offered the dealers a sportier, more spartan car, both as a price leader ($2,995) and as an SCCA sports car racing production class contender. Tucked away in southern Germany, the Stuttgart engineers and marketers could not have been expected to have spotted this gap in the American market.

The America Roadster and the Speedster were both instrumental in raising the popularity of Porsche in the USA. In particular, the Speedster brought real race car performance to a great many people, and this model would play a more important role in the future with the arrival of a much more powerful engine, which was then still under development.

The Porsche Speedster

West Coast America, and in particular Los Angeles, was undoubtedly where Porsche would appeal most to the youthful set. Johnny von Neumann called it boulevard racing, posing, seeing and being seen by all the young and impressionable Americans who loved the social scene. Cruising from traffic light to traffic light in a slow and deliberate manner, or leaving twin black rubber tracks on the tarmac in a cloud of smoke, would ensure you equal amounts of attention from pedestrians and passers by.

Von Neumann, who was Hoffman's Porsche agent on the West Coast, knew the local market

there better than most. There was nothing more 'in' at that time than to cruise the boulevards with the top down, elbow over the door, where the boys watched the girls and the girls watched the boys. On the West Coast, on hot, sun-filled days or warm balmy evenings, anytime was a good time to cruise the streets or just pose at the beachside diner. Come the weekend, the loud shirt, swimming costume and surf board would be dumped in place of a pair of racing overalls and a helmet as the young studs headed for the race track.

The Porsche was the perfect imported sports car in which to live out this carefree lifestyle beside the lazy ocean. Von Neumann knew that the influential youth would queue up to buy a Porsche if only it were cheaper and so he continued to bend Hoffman's ear with this idea. He told Hoffman that he could sell just such a basic Porsche soft-top by the truck load, if attractively priced for under $3,000, as this would undercut the other imported sports cars by a sufficient margin. The car didn't need wind-up windows, and the interior was to be as spartan as possible not only to keep the costs down, but also the weight, to allow the

OPPOSITE John von Neumann competing in a Porsche Typ 356 America Roadster in Reno USA (1953).

BELOW Standing outside Porsche's Werk 2 in Stuttgart-Zuffenhausen, these Reutter-bodied 356 Speedsters await delivery in 1957.

enthusiastic owners to race their cars at weekends.

This wasn't such a simple decision for the men back in Stuttgart, as the company philosophy to date had been to manufacture quality cars with quality interiors and finishings. For Porsche to build a car down to a fixed price was not what they were used to, and without wind-up windows, it was almost inconceivable. But that is what Hoffman and von Neumann wanted, and so the Speedster was born.

As racing was central to getting the Speedster into the American market, it really needed to be a stripped-out car with a lightweight folding hood, side screens and a removable windscreen. With the exception of the factory test car and a 356 SL race car, the Speedster (chassis 80001, September 1954) was the first 356 to receive the Typ 547 four-cam motor. This is the car that von Neumann really wanted.

The production 'Carrera'

The Porsche 356 A 1500 GS Carrera (1955–59)

For the more sporty minded, the 550 Spyder was not a sensible car to offer Porsche customers in a production form, and so began the legend which saw the Fuhrmann four-cam engine being fitted to the 356 model.

In September 1955, Porsche introduced the Typ 356 A at the IAA Frankfurt (Internationale Automobil-Ausstellung), replacing the 356 model. The 356 A (the 'A' models were named internally as Type 1, and thereafter known by enthusiasts as

---

JAMES DEAN'S PORSCHE 550 SPYDER
(James Dean – 8 February 1931 to 30 September 1955)

To the American youth in the mid-Fifties, the life of James Byron Dean must have seemed idyllic. A successful young actor, living life in the fast lane, parties and a sparkling future all mapped out for him in the movie industry. His carefree way of life was being modelled by many of his admirers, although this lifestyle went against the grain of the older generation.

Dean loved dangerous sports such as rodeo riding, bullfighting, motorcycle and later motor car racing. In 1955, he was smitten by the racing bug and he bought himself a Porsche 356 Speedster to compete with in local races. This went against the advice of close friends and colleagues in the film industry and his film contract for the shooting of *Giant* precluded him from all racing activities during the filming for fear of the producers losing their star actor to some racing accident.

With the filming behind him and after a four-month lay off from all racing, he was itching to get back on the track and while he was no professional behind the wheel, he had enough experience to keep him in the middle of the pack. Free of any contractual obligations, he struck a deal with John von Neumann to trade his Speedster against a spanking new 550 Spyder, also securing the services of von Neumann's mechanic, Rolf Weutherich. Dean had his racing number, 130, taped on the car and he had the customiser, George Barris, paint a nickname on the deck lid: The Little Bastard.

With little time to acclimatise himself with the new racer, Dean set off from Las Vegas on Friday, 30 September 1955, for the race circuit at Salinas, some way to the north. Just before 6 o'clock that evening, James Dean was dead, his mechanic was seriously injured and the world had lost a talented star. The driver of an oncoming car had failed to see the low, sleek Porsche in the setting sun and turned in front of the speeding racer. Dean's side of the car got the worst of it, as the lightweight Porsche careered headlong into the solid sedan. He never stood a chance.

Rebel Without a Cause was released a month after Dean was killed on the highway, en route to his first race in the new 550 Spyder. In many ways, the title of this film summed up the life of this young tearaway. A rebel in his own right, Dean always did things his own way, seldom taking the advice of those closest to him, and ultimately paid the price for it.

Although the publicity that surrounded the whole accident and its aftermath was clearly not the kind that Porsche was looking for, it nevertheless brought the manufacturer's name into the spotlight in America, in a big way. Had any suggestion of a mechanical malfunction been laid at the manufacturer's door, this would have had catastrophic consequences for them in the market, but an inquest after the accident returned an open verdict – no single factor to blame, just a tragic road accident. Countless theories have been tossed about ever since the incident that fateful night, but the remains of The Little Bastard have never been found to this day. Although some mechanical components from Dean's Porsche did find their way into other Spyders, the bulk of the car simply vanished.

It is hard to separate the Porsche 550 Spyder from the legend of actor James Dean. In much the same way that Dean cut his own path, so too did Porsche, from the beginning, doing things his way when he knew them to be right. Dean was instrumental in popularising the name of Porsche amongst the youth in the USA and through his enthusiasm for the marque, James Dean helped to lift the name of Porsche into the realm of stardom.

'T-1' cars) was a logical development of the Porsche philosophy, being more comfortable, luxurious and easier to drive than the original 356. However, the star of the show was undoubtedly the new 356 A Carrera, a model born out of the company's vast experience in motorsport, and a model which could trace its mechanical lineage directly from the 550.

According to our definition at the start of this chapter, the term 'thoroughbred' could justifiably be applied to the brilliant Porsche 356 Carrera. In recognition of the achievements of the four-cam engine in competition, and in particular the Carrera Panamericana, the 356 production car destined to receive this engine was dubbed the Carrera. On the back of such illustrious achievements, one can conclusively say that the Carrera engine earned its stripes having been developed through tough competition, and subsequently the 356 A Carrera road car entered the history books at birth. With such royal parentage, the 356 A 1500 GS Carrera Coupé, to give it its full title, was quickly recognised by professional drivers and amateurs alike as a formidable machine.

In the motoring world, the creation of a thoroughbred is only achieved through the combined effort of engineers, designers and motorsport experts. Strong competition in Europe had raised the level of performance with each passing event, and the tiny Porsche had impressed at every turn. By being constantly challenged, the lessons learned on the track were applied by the factory engineers to each successive model.

BELOW This contemporary press photograph shows the Porsche 356 A 1500 GS Carrera Coupé in daily use. What other sports car of this era was so flexible?

The name Carrera was henceforth applied to all of Porsche's highest performing road going models, right up until the model's demise in 1965.

So great was the excitement generated by the Carrera at the Frankfurt and Paris shows, that von Hanstein requested Fuhrmann to send his own Carrera to Paris for a demonstration to an interested customer, as no production cars were yet available. Fuhrmann declined and a rather frustrated von Hanstein contacted Ferry Porsche directly to see if he could 'assist' with his request. Porsche, in his usual quiet and diplomatic way, convinced Fuhrmann of the importance of the situation, and the car was duly dispatched to Paris. Fuhrmann's worst fears were realised when he received news that his car had been written off by the customer. Once again, Ferry Porsche was brought back into the picture and Fuhrmann was given the actual show car as a replacement, a gesture which saw Fuhrmann even better off than before. This car had leather upholstery together

with all the extra trimmings that go with a 'show' car which rather amused Fuhrmann as he now had the best 356 Carrera in the company, actually the only 356 Carrera in the company, even before the boss had one.

A small number of pre-A Porsche 356 Carrera Speedsters were made in 1955, but it is very difficult to define the exact specification of these first models. They were regular Speedsters equipped with the four-cam engine but all had different options, built to the individual buyers' needs. It is thought that the first two four-cam 356 A Speedsters were not even badged 'Carrera', but this only came about on the third car.

The 356 A Carrera, a classic among classics

Undoubtedly, it was the Carrera which stole the show at the 1955 Frankfurt Motor Show, but it was only in 1956 that the Carrera would be mentioned in the sales literature as a full production model. Externally, the features

BELOW Photographed in 1955, the new Porsche 356 A Carrera Coupé (1956 Model Year).

OPPOSITE This picturesque photograph of a Coupé (MY 1956) demonstrates the everyday usability of the Porsche 356 A Carrera.

differentiating this sporty version from the standard Porsche 356 A were the model name 'Carrera' in gold-coloured script, which appeared along the front fenders and on the engine lid, as well as the dual exhausts and an oil tank which sat neatly under the left rear fender behind the wheel. The other difference was the price. For a German customer, the 356 A 1500 GS Carrera Coupé cost DM18,500 as against the standard 1600 Coupé at DM12,700, a difference of almost DM6,000.

In the interests of reliability, the 356 A Carrera was fitted with a slightly detuned version of the four-cam engine. Designated the 547/1 but still packing a hefty 100bhp, this unit far outperformed the old pushrod motors' 75bhp. Lower crowned pistons resulted in a drop in the compression ratio which in turn contributed to the slight decrease in power. In a 1955 factory

document, the four-cam engine was offered only as an option for the Porsche 356 Speedster, but in reality, all 356 models would receive the engine at one time or another. The combination of Speedster and four-cam engine was the sizzle that sold the steak. From a performance perspective, being lighter than both the Coupé and Cabriolet, the Speedster proved the ideal car for the four-cam Carrera engine.

Even in this detuned state, many customers misunderstood and misused the 356 A Carrera in this road-going guise. Designed to work hard, the engine did not like slow town driving which unfortunately the Carrera would be subjected to more regularly than was good for it. Porsche owners were not accustomed to revving their cars to 6,000rpm and beyond during normal daily driving, and plugs would habitually foul up which

BELOW The Porsche 356 Carrera of Storez/Buchet at a stop during the 1956 Liège–Rome–Liège event. This Reutter-bodied coupé was a racing prototype and finished first in the 2,000cc GT class and second overall.

resulted in many four-cam motors eventually being replaced with standard pushrod units. Whereas the 1,500cc pushrod engine would usually run out of steam at around 5,000rpm, the Carrera unit was only just beginning to get into its stride at that stage, revving right up to 7,500rpm without showing any signs of stress, which in 1955 was quite a feat.

In typical conservative fashion once again, Ferry Porsche only intended for 100 356 A Carrera models to be built, primarily for competition use – just sufficient for the model to be homologated for entry into international GT class racing. Between the years 1954 and 1959, however, a little over 700 356 Carreras were made, of which 167 of these were Speedsters.

The sporty Porsche was well suited to the tight and twisty roads of the Targa Florio and 1956 saw the 40th running of this famous Sicilian road race, through the mountainous, ten lap, 72km course. Only eleven days before the start of the 1956 event, on 10 June, Porsche decided to enter Umberto Maglioli in a 550 A Spyder, now pushing out an impressive 130bhp from the Fuhrmann four-cam engine. When the dust had settled at the end of a very hot and sunny race day, Porsche had won by a massive 15 minutes from second-placed Piero Taruffi in a Maserati 300S. The next eight places behind the Porsche were filled by five Maseratis, a Ferrari and two Mercedes-Benz 300SLs. This victory represented Porsche's first important overall victory in international motorsport, a mere eight years after the first Porsche sports car had seen daylight in that tiny mountainous village in Austria.

The T-1 version remained in production until the advent of the 356 A T-2 which was announced in September 1957. During that year, Porsche decided to split the Carrera range to suit the tastes of two emerging groups of buyers. Sales had shown that after the honeymoon period of Carrera ownership was over, some customers would not drive their cars in the winter months due to the absence of a heater, as by then the car had earned the nickname of 'the most expensive icebox in the world'. The high-performance factor simply did not outweigh the lack of comfort, engine noise and harsh ride by a sufficient enough margin for the

vehicle to remain an attractive proposition in the eyes of some owners.

On the other hand, there were those for whom the Carrera was an all-out sports machine and it was there to be driven hard. The lack of a heater and any interior trim did not deter these performance hungry buyers, who actually preferred not to have all the extra clutter in their race car. The only solution to keep the Carrera flag flying successfully, was therefore to create a car for each market and so Porsche introduced the 356 A Carrera GS and the GT models to satisfy the demands of both groups.

The 356 A 1500 Carrera de Luxe was the luxurious version and featured improvements in comfort and utility. Only the de Luxe was offered in a Cabriolet version and to keep those buyers happy, a petrol heater was installed.

The 356 A 1500 GS Carrera GT was a stripped-out racing version devoid of trim or any niceties. Available in either coupé or Speedster form, the GT was fitted with lighter bumpers, a larger fuel tank, bigger brakes but no heating system as this had been thrown out in the interest of weight saving. The 356 Carrera Speedster GT was lighter and quicker, thanks also to Plexiglas quarter lights, door windows and rear window, and was used by professional racing drivers and amateurs on both sides of the Atlantic. In the USA, the cars were entered in many SCCA competitions right up until the early 1960s.

During 1957, trials on the new Fuhrmann Typ 692 four-cam engine were being completed. From 1958, the Carrera models used this new 1,600cc engine which superseded the 1,500cc unit, further improving performance. Displacing 1,588cc, the 1.6-litre version retained the 66mm stroke but was enlarged to 87.5mm bore and the crankshaft was fitted with conventional plain bearings in place of the noisier Hirth roller bearing crankshaft. With the same carburettors and compression of 9.5:1 (de Luxe) and 9.8:1 (GT), the 1.6-litre unit developed 105bhp (engine 692/2) at 6,500rpm in the de Luxe version and 115bhp (engine 692/3) in the GT model. The differences otherwise between the GS and the GT remained as before, but the Reutter GT versions received aluminium doors and deck lids; the engine cover louvred at the sides

for cool air ducted to the carburettor air intakes; seats were made of aluminium (not steel); aluminium wheels with steel centres; spacers were used to increase track width; aluminium hub caps (not usually used); and Koni shocks used at all four corners.

The 1959-model 356 A Carrera GS was the heaviest and also the most luxurious Porsche yet, also offering more sound insulation than before. These changes were done in the interests of making the car more 'streetable', as the American market liked to call it. Even with the increased engine capacity, performance was not much better and so the pressure was on to resolve this. Despite factory support for their dealers in the States, sales were not encouraging, and unfortunately for the Carrera, despite their best efforts to remedy the situation, a less-than-favourable reputation had spread due to the car's requirement to be driven hard.

The 356 A Carrera GTs were known for their racing exploits and some drivers capitalised on the performance of these cars. One of these drivers, Bruce Jennings, earned the title 'King Carrera' after an SCCA championship win in 1964. Jennings won more races in a Carrera than any driver in history, campaigning as many as four GT Speedsters against much more powerful racers.

An estimated 148 GT Speedster Carreras were made over a four-year period and as a result these are extremely rare, because so few people wanted them at the time due to their rather firm and sporty characteristics. The 1959 356 A 1600 GS Carrera GT Speedsters are the very last of the Speedsters to be manufactured and are highly sought after today.

Porsche's profit margin on the 356 Speedster was small and so the car was dropped in 1958, to be replaced by the Convertible D ('D' for the car's body builder, Drauz). The Convertible D, of which 1,330 were made, boasted a full-height windscreen, a proper hood and a less spartan interior, superseded the Speedster in August 1958. Unhappy Speedster customers soon objected to the dropping of their favourite model as the Convertible D with its more luxurious interior was no proper Speedster substitute. To avoid further upsetting this small band of Speedster fanatics, the factory introduced the Roadster in 1960. A Carrera version of the Convertible D was not made, but a total of 25 Carrera Speedsters fitted with the 1,600cc four-cam engine were built in 1958/59. The Roadster was a development of the Speedster and the Convertible D, and represented a middle-of-the-road model for those open-top enthusiasts.

The Carrera GS engine was discontinued after 1959, although the uprated GT version was still offered to special customers. When the 'B' was introduced in 1959, the Carrera was only offered as a GT.

FAR LEFT The highly desirable 356 A Carrera Speedster (1958) was good for 125mph (200km/h) – astonishingly fast for a 1,498cc four-cylinder car in its day.

BOTTOM FAR LEFT This stunning 356 A Carrera Cabriolet (1958) does not have the chrome trim along the waistline as does the Speedster model pictured above it.

BELOW A Porsche 356 A 1600 GS Carrera GT (1959 Model Year) still hard at work at Sebring as late as 1962.

TIMELINE:

1954
Herrmann finishes third overall in final Carrera Panamericana.

1956
10,000th 356 rolls off production line.

1958
First win on African soil for Porsche is a Carrera – SA 9-Hour.

1959
356 B introduced in September.

1960
20 Carrera Abarth GTL coupés made.

1963
356 C introduced.

CHAPTER FOUR

Racing around the world

'As a sports car company, we have always seen the racetrack as a laboratory.'

Porsche Cars North America Inc.

The track successes of the 550 Spyders in 1955 and 1956 diverted the factory's attention away from the racing potential of the 356 A Carrera. Still a little too overweight to dislodge the lightweight Speedsters, the 356 A Carrera was neither the full-blown racer sought by the speed boys and neither was it the luxurious grand tourer desired by the image-conscious fraternity. Aimed directly at the competitive driver, the 356 A Carrera GT offered an all-out no frills alternative to much more expensive machinery available on the market. Unfortunately however, this announcement was made too late in 1957, and the model was only ready in time for the 1958 racing season.

However, the 356 A Carrera was still to have its day. On 13 March 1957, an assembled group of drivers, mechanics, technical personnel and FIA officials watched as the Speedster Carrera left the pits at Monza on a record-breaking run. Without any official backing from the factory, as Ferry Porsche did not want to draw media attention to the event in the case of failure, von Hanstein and Richard von Frankenberg arranged the preparation of a private car. Sponsorship from Bosch, Veedol (oil) and Continental tyres had been the brainchild of von Frankenberg, while the car that was used belonged to Rolf Goetze. The Carrera's engine was replaced with a specially prepared engine of slightly enlarged capacity (1,529cc) and a higher compression ratio. The drivers were the car's owner, Goetze, and another well-known Porsche racing driver, Paul Ernst

Strähle who set out to break records in the Italians' own backyard, on the high-speed section of the famed Monza track.

The idea was to run for 24 hours, but during the course of events an oil pipe broke, putting paid to their plans. They did however break the 1,000-mile and 2,000km records as well as the 12-hour record, all at an average speed of 116mph (187kmh). Satisfied but not elated, the group had to settle for these results but they had once again proved that mechanically the car was still capable of surprising the critics.

Already a happy hunting ground for Porsche and arguably the toughest rally event in the Europe, the 5,000km Liège–Rome–Liège Rally was run over some of the most challenging roads that the organisers could find. Almost all the major Alpine passes were included in the route, while two thirds of the total distance was run on gravel roads. For the 1957 rally, a 356 A Carrera driven by Frenchman Claude Storez with navigator Robert Buchet, demolished the opposition by accumulating a mere 20 penalty points, while the second-placed car, a Mercedes 300SL, attracted well over 600 points.

Across the pond, Bruce Jennings and Ken Miles raked in many SCCA victories in the little Porsche, so much so, that the organisers had to reclassify the Carrera into a higher class where it competed with Corvettes and Cobras. Victories were forthcoming in England, Australia and later in South Africa. Another driver, Ludwig Blendl, who had raced Porsches for some years,

OPPOSITE The 1957 Porsche 356A 1500 GS Carrera GT Coupé of Paul Ernst Strähle undergoing aerodynamic testing.

purchased a Carrera Speedster in which he competed in hill-climbs and interestingly, also in the ice races at Zell am See, Austria, a short distance from the Porsche family's holiday home.

In March 1958, Huschke von Hanstein and Herbert Linge drove their Carrera GT to victory in the 1,600cc class at the 12-hour Sebring meeting. Amazingly, this same car was then prepared for the Targa Florio later that year, where Wilhelm Hild was to pilot it. On the way from the factory to the event in Sicily, Hild drove the car to Greece where he competed in a hill-climb, then over the next three days, drove it over some of the most challenging roads in Europe en route to Sicily. Baron Pucci and von Hanstein put this car through its paces on the gruelling Targa course, winning their class in the process and finishing sixth overall. Such was the strength, durability and flexibility of the Carrera engine, that Hild was able to drive the car back to the factory following this Sicilian success.

The Liège–Rome–Liège Rally was to bring more success for Porsche, when in 1959, Paul Ernst Strähle took his Carrera to victory once again.

The 356 Carrera had shown the world that a company with limited financial resources, relative at least to the automotive giants around the globe, through consistent development and experimentation, could achieve unimaginable results. Having started out in motor car production just over ten years before, Porsche was now competing against the most sophisticated and expensive machinery that money could buy. And it had all started in a little wooden shed in a remote Austrian mountain village.

Racing in South Africa

The inaugural South African 9-Hour Endurance Race was held at the Grand Central circuit, Johannesburg on 15 November 1958. The first race of any kind is always a memorable one, if not

BELOW In the 1959 Liège–Rome–Liège event, Paul Ernst Strähle and Robert Buchet finished first overall and first in the GT class, a convincing victory for the 356 A Carrera.

just for the novelty of the event, then certainly for the anticipation leading up to the race and the chatter about who is expected to do well, the new drivers and especially the new cars. The media whipped the South African public into a frenzy ahead of the country's first 9-hour and the whole episode was filled with uncertainty, which all added to the drama of this first race meeting.

The South African motor racing scene was an especially active one. Not only was there always fierce rivalry amongst the local boys at the best of times, but a certain undercurrent of pride ran through this rather assorted group of combatants. There was the regular enthusiast-turned-racing driver who rather fancied his hand at the sport and then there was the more experienced driver, who although not a fully fledged professional racing driver, was nevertheless a talented individual who had racing sense, and who could be expected to turn in a very competitive drive in almost any type of vehicle.

A recent 24-hour motorcycle endurance race had just been successfully staged at the Grand Central circuit earlier that same year, and with the country's strong racing heritage, it was suggested that a 9-hour endurance race be held there for motor cars. With the likes of Clark, Hill, Moss, Bonnier, Surtees, McLaren and many others competing in South Africa during the European off-season, racing had become extremely popular in the country. Being exposed to sophisticated overseas machinery, the South African drivers, for whom such complex racing cars were simply far too expensive to buy, set about copying many of the advanced technical components found on these top machines. This is one of the prime reasons why local drivers, such as John Love, Ian Fraser-Jones, Doug Serrurier and others came to be even vaguely competitive with the overseas drivers.

Grand Central, north of Johannesburg, was in fact an old aerodrome circuit which had to undergo a transformation in every sense of the word in order to accommodate the race cars for the event. Ian Fraser-Jones, who had raced all over the sub-continent in the post-war years, was offered a drive in one of the newest Porsche 356 cars, imported by the owner of the local VW franchise, George Lindsay, who had also just acquired the

Porsche franchise. This lightweight 356 Speedster was then fitted with a Carrera engine by the mechanics at the Lindsay Motors workshop. The car was also fitted with a hardtop and additional louvres were cut into the engine lid to assist with cooling. Fraser-Jones, or 'Frones' as he was affectionately called in the press, enlisted the services of his friend and fellow competitor, Tony Fergusson, to drive this car in the first 9-hour with him.

Race day saw the track heaving with spectators, and as the start time of 2pm approached, the anticipation mounted. The drivers lined up for the Le Mans-style start with most of the attention focussed on the clear favourite, a 2.7-litre V12 Ferrari driven by D. Jennings and D. Philp (Scuderia Lupini racing stable), reputedly an ex-Mille Miglia car, and the one that everybody had come to see. The start was predictable enough as the Ferrari sped off into the distance, but one can only imagine the spectators' surprise when, after just three laps, Fergusson brought the Carrera Speedster past the pits in the lead. Unfortunately, the Ferrari continued to drop further back with overheating troubles, while the Porsche continued to slay the critics, even staying ahead on its index of performance.

ABOVE Ian Fraser-Jones at speed in the Carrera Speedster during the 1958 SA 9-hour race, which he and Tony Fergusson won.

BELOW The boys in the bar
– an interview session in
progress in the bar at the
Fraser-Jones home,
Chicane, in Johannesburg
during the International
Series of 1961/62. From
the left: Colin Chapman,
Huschke von Hanstein,
obscured, Trevor Taylor
(yawning after a long
night), unknown, Ian
Fraser-Jones and Ken
Anderson, a local reporter
conducting the interview.

According to Fraser-Jones, about a third of the
way into the race the brakes began to fade. During
one pit stop, Fergusson informed Fraser-Jones that
they had virtually no brakes at all, which brought
about a drastic change in their driving tactics. As a
result, they had to change down through the gears
for each corner much earlier, placing severe strain
on the Carrera engine, and there were fears that
the motor would not hold up under the additional
strain. Combined with the last remaining grip
that could be salvaged from the brakes, they
managed to keep the Carrera on the track. In fact,
once they had settled into this driving pattern,
their speed through the corners was actually faster
than before. As a result of not having the stopping
power that they had earlier, their higher speeds
through the corners made up for the speed they
lost in having to change down earlier when
approaching the corners and their lap times
hardly suffered at all. Once they had mastered
this new technique no additional pressure was
felt from the second-placed car.

The extra pressure placed on the engine did not
have any detrimental effect during the course of
the event and the tyres also held out with the
additional strain placed on them due to the higher
cornering speeds. This fresh confidence later
turned to concern for the gearbox, which was
also placed under strain far beyond its expected
performance, but it too held together right to the
end. At 11pm, the hooter sounded and fireworks
filled the sky as the Porsche team watched
with jubilation as the Carrera crossed the line
victorious. It was the first time that a Porsche
had raced on South African soil, and the laurels
had gone to a Carrera.

Huschke von Hanstein, never wishing to miss
an opportunity of promoting the company's
achievements, was quick to latch onto this victory
and in due course paid a visit to South Africa,
where he found the people extremely hospitable
and very keen on motor racing. In fact, in the
1950s and '60s, very few other sports boasted the
kind of hospitality which accompanied motor

racing events. In the outlying colonies, grand balls were frequently held in the most lavish of venues including palaces and diplomatic residences, where von Hanstein was at his aristocratic best.

The Fraser-Jones home in Johannesburg was set in the northern suburbs of this thriving metropolis, arguably the largest city on the African continent. In his home, aptly named 'Chicane', Fraser-Jones had the room alongside his sprawling garage and workshop converted into an entertainment and family room, where, due to the long hours spent in the workshop tuning and fixing race cars, he could at least be close to his family. It was during one of von Hanstein's trips to Johannesburg with the Porsche team for the single-seater races that Ian Fraser-Jones was to throw a party for close friends and race colleagues at his home, and at which the Stuttgart visitors were the guests of honour. Fraser-Jones at that time was campaigning an Abarth Carrera GTL in the Southern African racing series, a car which for some reason just did not come up to expectations. 'The Abarth engine was clearly a dud motor, because it would consistently oil up its plugs after only about two races,' he remembered telling von Hanstein some time before his visit.

Unbeknown to Fraser-Jones, the Baron and his team had a double agenda that evening, and while the party was in full swing, the Porsche mechanics slipped away from the festivities and set to work on the Carrera engine in the workshop, right next door to the party. They whipped the old engine out and installed a new motor straight from the factory, all while the music played and the cocktails flowed in the room next door.

With the job done, the signal was given and the Baron turned the conversation to matters motoring, and Fraser-Jones invited him into the workshop to take the discussion further. In the meantime, all signs of the engine swap had been tidied away and when the engine lid was lifted, Fraser-Jones could hardly believe what he saw! Ian remembered with fondness the privilege of racing and being associated with the Porsche team and drivers such as Taffy von Trips and Edgar Barth. 'My association with Porsche stands out as the highlight of my 20-year racing career,' he commented during an interview with the author.

It was gestures like this and others that made it special to belong to the wider 'Porsche family'.

This association was mutually felt, as in 1959 the factory offered 'Frones' one of the ten RS60 Spyders being manufactured for the following season. A local newspaper reported that with between 300 and 400 applications received by the factory for these new race cars, this was indeed a big compliment for the South African driver and was an indication of how highly they regarded his driving skill.

Development work

By the late 1950s, preliminary planning work for the new 356 replacement model had already been underway for some time, after Graf Albrecht Goertz, an independent automotive designer, had presented the Porsche management with a Plasticine model concept in 1957. This Goertz model represented the first stage in the planning process of a 356-replacement model. Two years later, in 1959, Butzi Porsche submitted an early T-7 concept idea of the 901 model, a four-seater version of the Typ 754 featuring a 2.0-litre four-cylinder Carrera engine. Komenda also submitted his version of the Typ 754, the T-9, but Ferry insisted that the new model was to be a 2+2 and not a four-seater.

F. A. Porsche then submitted the T-8 version of this concept in 1963, which was to become the final production version of the new 901/911 model, but while all this design and planning work was going on, the 356 still had many years of production life left.

Carrera – the 356 B and C

In the five years following the introduction of the Carrera into the 356 model line-up, a total of a little over 700 Carreras were produced, from 1955 until January 1960, most of which were race cars. If it wasn't for the customers' competition needs, the Carrera saga may well have ended in 1959 as during the period 1960/61, the Carrera was phased out and the only ones built were for the Privatfahrer, or non-works driver, and hard core street users.

The 356 B (1960–63)

Under Komenda's overall control, the 356 B emerged and was presented at the 1959 Frankfurt Motor Show. This model was introduced without a Carrera in the catalogue, its place being taken by the Super 90.

By 1958, Ferry Porsche and his team were working on ideas to update the 356 and the 'facelifted' 356 B T-5 was introduced in September 1959, for the 1960 Model Year. Throughout 356 B production which took place between 1959 and 1963, Porsche introduced some of the most significant developments, including a 12-volt electrical system which appeared for the first time in a Porsche production car. The T-5-bodied version was produced between September 1959 and August 1961, while its replacement, the T-6, was built between September 1961 and July 1963.

For a while, the potent 1,600cc competition Carrera GT engine continued and nominal output was boosted from 110bhp to 115bhp at 6,500rpm. The new Super 90 was introduced as a replacement for the 356 A Carrera, offering higher performance from its pushrod engine and improvements to the chassis did much to eliminate the car's tendency to oversteer. It remained one of the world's most reliable sports cars with Porsche's usual high standard of build quality. An even more potent 135bhp version of the four-cam engine was available in the Italian-bodied Abarth GTL racer, but more of that later in the chapter.

BELOW In true style, Porsche's PR guru, Huschke von Hanstein drove a Porsche Typ 356 B 1600 GS Carrera GT to victory in the 1960 Targa Florio, together with Antonio Pucci.

OPPOSITE Once again, Paul Ernst Strähle and Herbert Linge teamed up for an assault on the 1960 Tour de Corse in their 356 B Carrera 1600 GT. Here, they are shown en route to another overall and class victory.

1960 Carrera GT

Carreras were initially built for both road and track use although when the 356 B debuted in September 1959 at the Frankfurt Motor Show, Porsche had dropped the road-going Carrera GS de Luxe from the model line-up. In the interests of keeping their motorsport aspirations alive and their many loyal privateers happy, Reutters produced a batch of 40 competition spec 1600 GT lightweight racers. Available initially with the existing 115bhp Typ 692/3 1.6-litre unit imported directly from the four-cam 356 A, these came in at almost a 1,000 dollars below the Carrera Abarth from Turin (see later in this chapter).

The 1,587cc Typ 692/3 motor ran to 6,500rpm and, with two twin-choke Weber 40 DCM/3 downdraught carburettors, this car had a top speed of 130mph (209km/h) and zero to 60 sprint time of a little over eight seconds establishing it as the quickest 356 yet.

Weight reduction came about through the fitting of lightweight bumpers (without overriders) as well as aluminium panels for the front lid, doors and the engine cover. Two additional sets of six cooling vents were slotted into the engine cover and the sports muffler system came without baffles to block the flow of exhaust gases. The cabin featured bucket seats and leather window retaining straps replaced the winding mechanism while lightweight plastic side and rear windows were substituted for the heavier glass.

These Reutter lightweight Carreras tend to be overlooked in the light of the exotic Abarth Carreras which were produced around the same time, but importantly, these lightweights kept the flag flying for the 356 family.

The 356 B Carrera 2 (1961)

Available in either street or competition trim, the Carrera 2 was launched at the 1961 Frankfurt Motor Show, the most significant improvement over the existing models being an exciting new engine, making it the fastest road 356 to date. Missing from the model line-up for two years, the

**PORSCHE 356 B CARRERA 2 2000 GS
DETAILS AND SPECIFICATION**

Engine:

Type	587 B4
Displacement	1,966cc
Valve train	2 valves/cylinder, DOHC
Fuel feed	2 Solex 40 PII-4 Carburettors
Gearbox	4-speed manual

Performance figures:

Power	130bhp (97.0kW) @ 6,200rpm
Top speed	124.3mph (200.0km/h)
Acceleration	0–60mph in 9.0sec
Weight	1,010kg (2,226.7lb)

ABOVE The 356 B Carrera 2 2000 GS Coupé de Luxe (1961).

ABOVE RIGHT The business end of the Porsche Typ 356 B Carrera 2 2000 GS Coupé (1962).

Carrera name was reintroduced as the top model in the 356 B range and was targeted towards the racer and elite Porsche buyer. As with previous Carrera models, it was the engine that made one's heart beat faster, but Porsche still felt their Carrera engine needed more torque and the easiest way to achieve this was by increasing the engine displacement. Reintroduced as a 'GS' model, it was destined to become the ultimate road-going development of the 356 and it packed an enlarged version of the Typ 587 four-cam motor first introduced as the Typ 547 back in 1954. This 2.0-litre plain-bearing four-cam (587/1) was first designed by Fuhrmann before he left the firm in 1956.

The 1,966cc Carrera produced in the region of 130bhp at 6,200rpm and the '2' was quicker than any of its road-going predecessors, despite weighing a hefty 185kg more. It was the first Porsche road car to be fitted with disc brakes and would be available throughout the 1964 Model

Year, bearing a 356 C model designation in that final version. The Carrera 2 also boasted larger front and rear windscreens and an enlarged engine cover and could be identified by its brass Carrera 2 scripting on the engine lid.

The Carrera 2 became the top-of-the-line customer model, and was available as a coupé or cabriolet. Two twin-choke Solex 40 PII 4 carburettors gave the 356 B 2000 GS-GT Carrera 2 Coupé a top speed of around 130mph (209km/h) and a 0–60mph sprint time of just over eight seconds. The Carrera 2 was not as fast as the Jaguar E-type, which was also announced in 1961, but its sizzling performance, made it a more than worthy contender in international markets. The prototype Carrera 2 was a 356 B Cabriolet originally built for Ferry Porsche with a 1.6-litre 4-cam engine, but replaced by the first 587/1 engine in 1961 it remained Ferry's personal choice of transportation, even when travelling with a chauffeur. Porsche planned to produce only 100

COMPARISON BETWEEN THE MAJOR FOUR-CAM ENGINE REVISIONS

Engine type	Typ 547	Typ 692	Typ 587
Years	1953–61	1958–61	1962–64
Models used	550 Spyder	356 A and B Carrera,	356 B Carrera 2,
	356 A Carrera	Abarth Carrera GTL	356 C Carrera,
	718 RSK, RS60,		Dreikantschaber,
	RS61 and F2		Carrera GTS 904
Engine capacity	1,498cc	1,588cc	1,966cc
Power output	100bhp–150bhp	105bhp–135bhp	130bhp–155bhp

This table contains only the basic engine configurations as there were many variations of each engine type.

BELOW Always looking for a PR angle, Porsche director of public relations Fritz Huschke von Hanstein, together with a passenger, set off on another journey in their 356 B Carrera 2 GS Cabriolet (1962).

BOTTOM This studio shot shows the fine lines of the Porsche Typ 356 B Carrera 2 Cabriolet (1962).

but eventually made 436 cars (310 B and 126 C models) between 1961 and 1964 and it remains one of the rarest and most desirable of all Porsches.

Carrera 2 GS and GT

By comparison with the road-going version, the lightweight GS and GT versions (both fitted with engine Type 587/2) produced 140bhp and 155bhp at 6,200rpm and 6,600rpm respectively. Bristling with a pair of Weber 46 IDM/2 twin-choke downdraught carbs, their top speed was in excess of 135mph (217kmh) while the zero to 60mph dash took little more than seven seconds, this hike in performance being attributable in part to a straight-through racing exhaust.

The lightweight GS and GT came in Coupé form only and were raced successfully all over the world. The Carrera 2 won the 1963 Midnight Sun Rally of Sweden, but in reality this model was still too plush for it to be turned into a true track star as racing had become too specialised for this dual-purpose GT ideal.

The 356 C (1963–65)

With the arrival of the 356 C, announced in July 1963, customers were given the opportunity to acquire what was to be the final version of the 356, a model that had brought Porsche an internationally respected name both on the road and the track. The company had grown to be so successful that in March 1964 it took over the Reutter body works, which changed its name to Recaro, and concentrated on the manufacture of

ABOVE Donau Rallye, 1964 – Herborn/Altmann, winners in the GT class in their 356 B Carrera GT, check in at a time control in Budapest. (Castrol/ Archive Marinello)

car seats. The final version of the 356 body came with the introduction of the T-6 in 1961 (356 B) and so changes on the C were relatively few as Porsche considered that the model had been developed as far as possible and that no alterations to the bodywork were necessary as it was already an aerodynamically efficient design.

After a production run of 16,678 units, the 356 C was finally discontinued in 1965 to make way

for the six-cylinder 911. Karmann at Osnabrück ceased 356 production on 21 January and the Porsche-owned Reutter factory finished work on the model on 28 April while the Zuffenhausen works also said farewell to the 356 on the same day with the production of the final 356 C Cabriolet.

Farewell to the 356

For all its desirability today, the Carrera wasn't a tremendous sales success at the time. It carried a hefty price premium compared with the pushrod-engined car and acquired a reputation for unreliability due to its complex overhead camshaft feature – ironically, the very reason that had helped lift the model to such prominence in the first place.

Production of the 356 model had taken place at various sites including Karmann at Osnabrück in northern Germany as well as Drauz with the total number of 356s being 77,766 units. However, the bulk of the model's production had taken place at the Porsche-owned Reutter factory in Stuttgart-Zuffenhausen. Officially, the last 356 was manufactured in September 1965 at the Zuffenhausen plant, but in 1966 a batch of ten Cabriolets was produced as a special order for the Netherlands police force.

Time and again, the 356 was praised for the quality of its finish, panel fit, engineering integrity and, towards the end of its life, its remarkable road-holding capabilities. In the 15 years, between 1950 and 1965, the 356 had established the name of Porsche all over the world, which is no mean feat for a small manufacturer.

Other four-cam developments

Porsche 356 B 1600 GS Carrera GTL Abarth (Typ 756) – a difficult birth

Motorsport is a funny old game. The moment you appear to have the opposition licked, they change the rules and for Porsche, America had proven to be a land of mixed blessings on the race track. The Sports car Club of America (SCCA) had up to 1959 run its production-car races based on engine displacement limits, playing nicely into the hands of the 356 A Carrera

---

REUTTER

When the Reutter's company (Karosseriewerk Reutter & Co. GmbH) was taken over by Porsche in 1964, some Reutter staff were appointed to the manufacture of car seats, and thus was born the Recaro company, famous today for sports car seats. This name was made from the joining together of the 'RE' from Reutter and 'CARO' from Karosserie to form – Recaro.

Other Reutter craftsmen were retained for the manufacture of bodies, but through the takeover of the Reutter's company not one member of staff was lost as they were all absorbed into the Porsche organisation. Some of those original Reutter employees are still with Porsche today.

Herbert Linge remembers: 'They made some experimental cars; these were all made with Reutter people within our own bodyshop. The Reutter people, they all came to Porsche.'

On 22 March 1993, the old Reutter's works was declared a historical building by the Stuttgart Council which meant that Porsche was unable to alter it or demolish it in the future to make way for any expansion. Rather fittingly, the assembly of the new V10 Carrera GT engine is carried out in this building, where more than 50 years ago the first Carrera bodies were manufactured.

1,500cc which had dominated affairs in Class F. With the advent of the new 356 B scheduled to appear in 1960, the whole homologation issue was raised again by the SCCA, when they failed to approve the new car under the existing engine displacement criteria, despite running with the same-size motor.

The 1960 SCCA homologation policy had changed from a displacement to a performance-based benchmark, moving the Carrera into Class C together with the big guns such as the Ferraris and Jaguars. Against all expectations, the Carreras dominated the class and they were promptly reclassified into Class B the following year, but against the powerful Corvettes there was little they could do. Racing in America was just not the same as in Europe, where the factory and the engineers were familiar with the FIA rules and set-up.

To a large extent, the Abarth came into being as a result of a loophole in the FIA rules which prompted Porsche to propagate the idea of a lightweight racer. These rules defined a car, in 1959, on the basis of its chassis and the running gear, rather than on its body. If Porsche could mate the 356 B chassis, running gear and trusty four-cam Carrera engine to a specially designed lightweight aluminium body instead of the production steel body, then they could stay a step ahead of the competition.

European racing was becoming much more competitive within the classes, with rival makes such as Lotus and Alfa Romeo pushing each other harder and harder with each passing season. Although still dominant in their class, Porsche was nevertheless beginning to lose its edge on the competition and they wanted to prevent the smaller engined race cars from encroaching on their space, a strategy which they themselves had so successfully accomplished earlier. In order to remain competitive, Porsche decided that just such a plan for a lighter, more streamlined body was necessary and two companies were invited to submit bids for the manufacture of 20 lightweight bodies to fit the 356 B floorpan. These two companies were Wendler, who made the Porsche Spyder bodies, and Zagato of Turin.

ABOVE The Porsche 356 C had matured into a sophisticated luxury sports car as shown by this 1964 Cabriolet. Although not in the official Porsche colour chart, this 'lavender' C is attended by Evi Butz, secretary to Huschke von Hanstein in the Porsche press office. She was later spotted by Dan Gurney and whisked off to America to become Mrs Evi Gurney.

Zagato's reputation in successfully crafting streamlined, lightweight bodies for the likes of Alfa Romeo and Lancia in European competition was attractive and, as a result, it was the Turin firm which was given the green light. This decision was itself not without its difficulties as it was these very same Italian cars which competed with Porsche on the race tracks and in the showrooms, raising a potentially thorny issue for Zagato with its existing Italian customers. In order to divert attention away from Zagato's involvement, Carlo Abarth was called in as a middle man and it was he who received the 'official' order to build the lightweight bodies, while the task of penning them fell to Franco Scaglione, a former Bertone designer. Although the initial order was for the 20 vehicles, consideration was to be given for a continuation order if the project proved acceptable to Porsche.

With the main goal being greater performance, the Carrera Abarth, or GTL ('L' being for Leicht) as it was known, was fabricated in aluminium.

The body was a full five inches (127mm) lower than the 356 GT and almost as much was cut out of the width which resulted in a favourable reduction in the frontal area, of 15 per cent. The total weight saving was down by about 100lb (45kg) on the Reutter GT. In true Abarth style, a small air scoop on the engine lid could be opened by way of a control mounted in the cockpit, which assisted with engine breathing, should the 48 louvres already punched into the engine cover not be sufficient.

When the GTL was announced to the racing fraternity, all of the first batch of the race cars were snapped up in no time, despite a price tag of DM25,000. In fact, Porsche's problem was not selling these cars to the racing world, it was rather more a problem of supply, which was painfully slow.

The GTL's styling, if not a traditional Porsche look, was arguably one of the most attractive race cars of its day. The unmistakable Italian, and more specifically Fiat, influence can be seen in the smooth but tightly rounded rump, a car that looks

BELOW Although the finish of the 1962 Porsche Typ 356 B Carrera GTL Abarth may not have been to their usual high standard, this car set the Porsche designers thinking.

just as menacing at rest as it does at full speed. The Carrera Abarth, however, did most of its talking on the track as it proceeded to clean up the competition in its class all over Europe. Between 1961 and 1963, Nürburgring, Le Mans, Targa Florio, Sebring and Daytona all bore witness to the speed and agility of the fabulous lightweight from Turin and numerous victories were notched up during this time.

Although the GTL project was the first time that Porsche had gone outside of its traditional and trusted body builders, and despite huge successes on the track, Porsche was nevertheless unhappy with certain aspects of the car. By reducing the roofline so drastically, it was uncomfortable for many drivers of modest height to drive and Porsche had to fit lowered, custom seats to alleviate this problem. Poor panel fit and leaky seals let rain water in and the wheelarches had been so tightly trimmed so as to restrict the steering radius. Despite the reservations of the factory engineers,

the GTL embodied, in every way, the company's philosophy of creating lightweight performance machines, capable of running against cars of much greater capacity.

Indeed, the GTL ran with a number of different four-cam engines, five to be precise, and all in the space of a few short years. Initially, the Carrera Abarth was fitted with the improved version of the 1,600cc four-cam motor, pushing out from 115bhp up to 135bhp, while the later 2.0-litre version (which was retro-fitted to this motor by many privateers) delivered between 155bhp and 180bhp. Amazingly, down the Mulsanne Straight at Le Mans, Herbert Linge was clocked in the 128bhp 1,600cc GTL at 138mph (222km/h), and he was later heard to say that this was at a point before the car had reached its top speed. All this in a car that was introduced with drum brakes on all four wheels. This type of performance was clear evidence of the good aerodynamic work carried out by Abarth and Scaglione.

BELOW A Porsche 356 B 1600 GS Carrera GTL Abarth outside the Porsche works, Stuttgart (1961).

Due to the low number of Abarths manufactured, they were not found on many race tracks on each continent. Clearly, they were raced in Europe, England and North America, but one car did find its way to South Africa where it was campaigned by Ian Fraser-Jones in the racing series there. This car competed in Lorenco Marques (in the former Portuguese colony of Mozambique) and also in the Krugersdorp Hill-climb, a well-known event just outside Johannesburg.

Once again, due to the low production numbers, a high rate of recycling was carried out by the factory during the years that the 20-odd cars were under Stuttgart's control. When they had done their duty for the company, the cars were sold off to privateers whereupon several were fitted with the more powerful 2.0-litre engine developed for the Carrera 2. The Porsche 356 B 1600 GS Carrera GTL Abarth, to give the car its full title, undoubtedly played a vital role in the development of the Porsche name on the track, even if it is regarded by some purists as a bit of an outsider

to the family. Manufactured in 1960 and '61, only the original run of lightweight specials was produced, and unfortunately no continuation order was issued to Abarth.

PORSCHE 356 B 1600 GS CARRERA GTL ABARTH (TYP 756)

ENGINE DETAILS:

Type	692/3 and 692/3A
Displacement	1,588cc
Valve train	2 valves/cylinder, DOHC
Fuel feed	Carburettors
Gearbox	4-speed manual
Power output	115bhp @ 6,500rpm with *Serienauspuff*
	128bhp @ 6,700rpm with *Sportauspuff*
	135bhp @ 7,400rpm with *Sebringauspuff*

OPPOSITE Paul Ernst Strähle at speed in his Porsche Typ 356 B 1600 GS Carrera GTL Abarth in the 1962 Targa Florio.

BELOW Ian Fraser-Jones at speed in his Carrera Abarth, Lourenco Marques (Maputo), Mozambique, in 1962. (Automotive Research)

ABOVE The sharp angular features of the Dreikantschaber can be clearly seen in this photograph, taken outside Werk 1, Zuffenhausen 1963.

Porsche 356 B Carrera Dreikantschaber, or 'Scraper' (1963)

Although strictly a racing car, this model deserves a mention because it ran the Fuhrmann four-cam motor using the 356 B as the basis for its construction. Designed by F. A. Porsche, this 2000 GS Carrera 2 only ran in competition in 1963, but was very successful in the hands of the Porsche drivers.

As so often happened within the Stuttgart workshops, the mechanics gave this special model their own rather unusual name, the Dreikantschaber, which literally translated means, triangular scraper or frost scraper, referring somewhat poignantly to its sharp, angular features. It was far from being the most attractive shape to come from the pen of F. A. Porsche, the 'Scraper' as it became known in English, and finished third overall in its debut event, the Targa Florio in May 1963, in the hands of Edgar Barth and Herbert Linge. In the same month, the pair also secured fourth place in the 1,000km race at the Nürburgring.

The Dreikantschaber was based on a 356 B chassis for reasons of classification in the GT class as the rules allowed the manufacturer to change the body, but not the engine and suspension, and

therefore under the skin it closely resembled the Carrera Abarth. Powered by the 1,966cc Fuhrmann four-cam engine putting out 155bhp, the lightweight aluminium racer could top out at 146mph (235km/h).

Placing it alongside the Porsche 904 will reveal some striking similarities, as the Dreikantschaber already carried the front fenders and the hood of the 904. Herbert Linge explains: 'This was already in the design department, so we used this design for the front as we wanted to make it lighter than the Abarth which was, as you know, very badly made.'

The idea behind putting the new and untried nose of the 904 on a 356 B chassis, was to see if this shape was any better than the Carrera Abarth. Despite reports of a second car, Herbert Linge insists that only one was built at this time, while three other similar-looking cars were built on the RS60 frame and ran with the eight-cylinder engine – these were referred to as the Le Mans Coupé cars.

Although the 'Scraper' only ran as a factory car for a year, it nevertheless served as a valuable test bed linking the Carrera Abarth with the car that followed – one of the most graceful sports cars of all times, the Carrera GTS.

Carrera GTS – the 904 (1964)

It was increased competition from the Italians on the race tracks, with their Fiat Abarth and Alfas, that can once again be cited as the inspiration behind Porsche's next racer. Porsche engineers learned quickly what worked and what didn't, and all the while technology was moving ahead, rapidly. This development caused Porsche to rethink their long-term motorsport programme and to consider which of their sports cars would satisfy this requirement. Selecting carefully the disciplines in which they wanted to compete, Porsche soon realised that with the huge advances being made by their competitors, a more advanced Carrera would be needed to meet the demands of a new racing generation.

A perfect blend of both form and function, the Porsche Carrera GTS Type 904, entered the racing world in 1964 aimed at the FIA 2.0-litre Grand Touring category, which in itself requires a little clarification. A Grand Touring car, or GT, is a car that satisfies the requirements of Appendix J, Group 3, of the International Sporting Code, which describes these vehicles as: 'built in small series for customers who are looking for better performance and/or maximum comfort and are not particularly concerned about economy.'

Comfort in a sports car is a fairly relative term, but in the case of the 904, Porsche certainly built it with long-distance endurance racing in mind, as the car even featured a heater and had an adjustable steering wheel. In accordance with the regulations, this also meant that the vehicle must be fully equipped to carry a passenger and even have some luggage space. The 904 could indeed carry a passenger although not very comfortably, while the luggage space was there just to conform to the rules.

One of the other requirements was that at least 100 identical examples of the car had to be built. Such a quantity would have to include a road-going version, because Porsche was unlikely to sell 100 full-blown racers. In order to free up the much-needed resources for this project, Porsche's Formula 1 activities were curtailed as the company reasoned that they would earn back their investment in this new project through the sales of the Carrera GTS, while their Formula 1 cars were not sold, but merely generated exposure for the company.

In creating a new sports car, Ferdinand Alexander 'Butzi' Porsche had to start with a clean sheet as the spaceframe construction used on previous race cars was too expensive and time consuming to build. It transpired that the only similarity with earlier racers was the mid-engined

BELOW Car No. 31, driven by Edgar Barth and Herbert Linge finished 4th in the 1963 Nürburgring 1,000km event, in the Dreikantschaber. Pictured here in the pits, the front end shows a strong 904 resemblance, the racing model which replaced this car.

layout and the use of the 587 four-cam 2.0-litre engine which had been well proven in the Carrera Abarth conversions and the 356 C Carrera sports cars. Writing in *Car and Driver* (February 1964), Jerry Sloniger stated that the 904 was a 'hodgepodge mixture of Carrera, Spyder and the new 901.' While he may have been technically correct, that statement does not do the 904 any favours as this car must rank as one of the most handsome and sleek sports cars of all time.

Construction was a combination of a steel ladder frame and a glass-reinforced plastic (GRP) body, which was a first for the Stuttgart manufacturer, and the start of a long line of 'plastic'-bodied Porsche racers. Body production was outsourced to aircraft manufacturer Heinkel, who were able to assemble complete bodies at the rate of two a day, comprising 50 separate body parts, while Porsche produced only one chassis per day. The completed body was then bonded to the frame, which resulted in a chassis far more rigid than the spaceframe chassis used in their previous racers.

Testing, using three cars, was completed by November 1963, after which production of the required 100 cars for the Privatfahrer commenced

immediately. Suspension was coil over shocks on all four wheels and disc brakes were standard from the outset. Costing a hefty DM29,700, the first cars were shipped out to America where, in its debut outing in the Sebring 12-hour race, the 904 romped home first in class in the hands of Briggs Cunningham and Lake Underwood.

Road & Track, in its test assessment of the 904, said that while it was a more than capable contender in its class, it was not the out-and-out racer that was hoped for. Then again, the 904 was a very effective bridge between the outgoing 356 Carrera, with its Abarth variant, and the planned and dedicated 906 which was introduced in 1966. It was intended that the 904 would receive the new 901/911 six-cylinder boxer engine, but this was not ready in time for the car's introduction and so the trusty 587 four-cylinder four-cam was used. In its original form, the four-cam motor developed an impressive 115bhp and, through constant improvement, the 2.0-litre unit produced a mighty 180bhp at 7,000rpm in the 904, and was even further tweaked to push out a rumoured 200bhp. That is almost double the initial output of ten years earlier.

Rubbing salt into the wound, in what was undoubtedly a highlight of the start of the 904's race career, Baron Antonio Pucci and Colin Davis took the outright victory in the 1964 Targa Florio, Porsche's fifth victory in this prestigious event. This was the one and only time that the 904 was raced by the factory with the four-cylinder boxer engine. Their standard specification 904 was up against competition which included Porsche eight-cylinder prototypes, Shelby Cobras and Ferraris. The Carrera GTS remained successful throughout the 1964/65 season with further victories at Le Mans, the Nürburgring 1,000km race, the Tour de France, and even snatching second spot in a snow-covered Monte Carlo Rally of 1965.

Herbert Linge recalls: 'The factory raced the 904 only once [with the four-cylinder four-cam motor], in the Targa Florio in '64, and from there on the factory raced the 904 with the six-cylinder, and two cars with the eight-cylinder. But with the six-cylinder in the 904, it already showed that we needed

PORSCHE CARRERA GTS (TYP 904)

DETAILS AND SPECIFICATION:

Engine:

Type	587/3 B4
Location	Mid, longitudinally mounted
Displacement	1,966cc
Valve train	2 valves/cylinder, DOHC
Fuel feed	2 Weber twin-choke carburettors
Gearbox	5-speed manual

Performance figures:

Power	180bhp (134.3kW) @ 7,000rpm
Top speed	159.7mph (257.0km/h)
Acceleration	0–60mph in 5.30sec
Weight	650kg (1,433.0lb)

something special for racing. The 904 with the six-cylinder was a fantastic car, but that showed us that for international racing, it was no longer possible to just convert a production car into a race car.'

Eventually, 120 Carrera GTS cars were built and to this day it remains as one of the finest and most successful Porsches ever constructed. It kick-started a programme of 'plastic' racers that would include the mighty 906, 907, 908, 910 and ultimately the all-conquering 917. The Carrera GTS also holds a unique spot in the company's history as the only real dual-purpose sports car Porsche ever built.

BELOW Carrera GTS cars lined up in Werk 2, Zuffenhausen, ready for distribution to customers (1964).

Carrera 6 (1966)

Apart from their Formula 1 cars, the gullwing-door Carrera 6 Typ 906 was Porsche's first all-out race car, whereas the 904 was intended for both race and road use. As mentioned at the outset, it is not within the scope of this study to explore the myriad Porsche race cars as this would in itself fill another volume. However, it is important to mention the Carrera 6 here as it was the model which carried on the Carrera name, albeit on the track.

Herbert Linge reflects: 'No, it was not a road car, but even this we called the Carrera just to show that this was the top car in the Porsche family.'

TOP RIGHT The formidable Carrera 6 outside the Porsche headquarters, Stuttgart-Zuffenhausen in 1966.

BOTTOM RIGHT Heini Walter and Rudolf Jenzer teamed up to drive a Carrera GTS in the 1964 International ADAC 1,000km race at the Nürburgring.

CHAPTER FIVE

What? No Carrera!

'At a recent press conference given to introduce the Series 911-912 Porsches 'officially' to the American market, a Porsche executive blandly said that he was afraid these new-model introductions were becoming a habit with Porsche – they had had one just 15 years ago.'

Road & Track' February 1966

The introduction of the four-cam 547 motor in the 550 cars in 1954 is probably one of the most significant milestones in the company's history, even to this day. At the time, it simply launched the company into the stratosphere, setting Porsche on the road to instant recognition. Although they didn't win the Pan Americana event outright, to the factory and to the rest of the world it seemed as though they had, and their third overall placement in 1954 garnered instant respect for the small German firm. This respect came not only from the spectators and competitors but also from other major manufacturers and teams as they quickly realised that here was an infant sports car manufacturer that knew how to get its drivers onto the winner's podium, a mere five years after introducing their first model.

To have given the name of their 1954 Mexican 'victory' to the four-cam motor that got them there in the first instance was no small public relations coup. Wrapped up in all that emotional aura of one of the toughest road races at the time was the recognition of what a remarkable achievement it

had been for the emergent Stuttgart company. Mention the name 'Carrera' to any motoring enthusiast and they think almost automatically of the famous Mexican race.

Having already been victorious in Europe, success in Mexico meant a lot for the factory as Ferry Porsche had now succeeded in making a name for his company on the doorstep of the largest automobile market in the world at that time, namely North America.

When Dr Ernst Fuhrmann first considered installing the four-cam motor in his personal 356, little could he have realised what a success that engine would turn out to be on the international motorsport stage. In fact, little did he realise what a perfect combination the 547 motor and the road-going 356 model would prove to be for the company, not only in generating much-needed sales for all the other models in the range but also by providing valuable opportunities for greater public exposure. The emotional tie between the name Carrera and the infant company's success in Central America would live on for decades, but the

OPPOSITE Standing ready at the 1959 Nürburgring 1,000km, (from top to bottom) Porsche 718 RSK, 356A 1500 GS Carrera GT and a 356A 1600 GS Carrera GT.

full extent of this achievement could not have been foreseen back in 1954.

Just as Dr Ferdinand Porsche had predicted in 1938, ahead of the ill-fated Berlin–Rome race, that the VW engine was well suited to endurance racing at sustained high speeds, so too was the complex four-cam 547 motor equally well suited to the tough world of international motorsport.

There are not many motor manufacturers in the world today, and for that matter throughout automotive history, who can boast of having world-class racing drivers on their permanent staff. For Porsche, such names as Herbert Linge, Huschke von Hanstein, Jürgen Barth, Roland Kussmaul (Paris–Dakar Rally driver in Porsche 911 and 959, and later the technical project manager on the Carrera GT project) and others, all had permanent jobs within the company. They were not just paid faces, but were mostly in engineering and also in other areas such as public relations. These were not weekend racers, but

rather drivers who had competed in the Carrera Panamericana, raced at Le Mans, Targa Florio, Sebring, Mille Miglia, Nürburgring and other similar world-famous race events, and who had also helped Porsche to set countless world speed records at different times.

Racing drivers and racing mechanics who can bring back first-hand experience from the track are an absolutely priceless asset for any sports car manufacturer, and this enabled the Porsche engineers to find solutions to technical problems far quicker than most. They would exchange their racing overalls after the weekend's race for their workshop clothes on the Monday, and proceed to work on the cars they had raced just the day before. The factory driver could then discuss the suspension, cornering problems or mechanical maladies with the racing director and chief engineer in the workshop directly following the race meeting, which was very different from any other company. For this group of skilled drivers

BELOW Evocative 'Carrera' scripting on the Typ 356 B Carrera T5 (1961), the only right hand drive 'B' Carrera Cabriolet made by the factory. (Author)

and engineers, there was simply no better way to understand the behaviour of a race car except by feeling for themselves the reactions of the car under proper racing conditions, and this gave them a considerably greater advantage over other manufacturers in implementing improvements.

Herbert Linge, in an interview with the author, told of how he worked for the Hoffman organisation in New York by servicing customers cars during the week, and then attending races on the weekends as technical support for competition customers. Linge worked with Hoffman in America from 1952 to '56 and his work pattern remained this way throughout these four years, which went a long way towards establishing a reputation for the firm in America. No other foreign car manufacturer offered this level of personal service for their vehicles, and customers warmed to the fact that they knew their car, an exotic foreign import, would be looked after in the event of a problem.

However, it had been hoped from within the corridors of the Zuffenhausen head office that the phenomenal Porsche racing achievements, and especially those of the Carrera-engined cars, would result in significantly increased sales of the road-going 356 Carrera and other Porsche models. Despite selling more Carrera cars than initially anticipated by the factory – and they were notorious at underestimating expected sales – this quantity was not meteoric for the famed Carrera car. Unfortunately, the four-cam Carrera had developed a reputation in the market place for not being an easy motor car to live with on a daily basis due to its need for a high-revving driving style. Maintenance of the complex motor was not without its problems and, frankly, if you weren't going to race the car, why have all that potential performance sitting under the engine lid in the first place?

If it was comfort the customer was after, there were other more comfortable Porsche cars in the model range to choose from. With the American market being the prime target, buyers preferred a more softly sprung car and the Carrera was just not the right motoring package for *les poseurs*, or the posing brigade. Despite all the corporate talk of only going racing to further the technological

boundaries of the company, the bottom line was that Porsche wanted to sell cars. It had to in order to survive.

It was the 547 four-cam motor that had started the ball rolling, but it was this 356 Carrera which had tied the Carrera name to Porsche's high-performance road cars between 1955 and 1963. But, while the anticipated rise in sales did not materialise to the extent hoped for, the reputation created by the name 'Carrera' generated such respect for the Zuffenhausen firm that they could not have come close to those levels of exposure even with the most perfectly planned advertising and promotional campaign. No amount of public relations effort or money could have bought the company the same reputation that they had earned on the track with the four-cam motor, as they continued to rack up victory after victory.

The value and heritage of the name 'Carrera' cannot be overestimated at this stage, as it gave the small Stuttgart company an identity and a position in the market place. In the words of Herbert Linge: 'It means a whole lot because the Carrera was not just a number. I think the name for a car like the Carrera was something special, not just another Typ.'

ABOVE Out with the old, in with the new. The outgoing 356 C (left) with the incoming 901 (right, cropped), displayed for the first time together at the IAA in Frankfurt (1963).

No 911 Carrera – 1963 to 1972

'The critics said the 356 is so beautiful already why do you bother with a new car? But there was the need to make more space in this car', recalls Klaus Bischof.

The gung-ho days of raucous engines, thrashy cams, constant high revs and harsh ride were beginning to change. With a more demanding, more sophisticated car-buying public to contend with, Porsche took the opportunity to consider where their next model range would be heading and what dynamics the consumer would require. Buyer sophistication came by way of a demand for quieter engines, smooth power delivery from a well-mannered engine, passenger comfort, and the ever-present need to satisfy increasing safety regulations and noise reductions. Contemporary trends indicated that manufacturers would have to give far more attention to the growing demands of the performance car customer if they wanted to sell their cars.

For a company like Porsche, the end of one model line and the introduction of another completely new one as its replacement is not an operation to be taken lightly. A great amount of uncertainty surrounded the introduction of the new 911, but by the same token, the company realised that they had to separate the new generation from the old. 'The 911 should have a completely new independent identity', explained Klaus Bischof. The 356 was still being manufactured in 1964, as the company was unsure of the acceptance of the newcomer as a worthy replacement in the market by Porsche's sometimes critical customers.

The six-cylinder production engine, which eventually powered the 911, was in fact developed in parallel with the racing version of the same motor which powered the 904 Carrera GTS in the Nürburgring 1,000km in 1964. Apart from running a dry sump, racing camshaft, a different clutch and a competition exhaust, the racing engine was otherwise almost a standard 911 unit.

Although the new 911 was introduced at the IAA in September 1963, the racing engine was ready first and ran in three 904 Carrera GTS cars at the Nürburgring in mid-1964. With sales of the new sports car commencing later in the year, the new engine had already had a taste of competition life.

The launch of the 911

Following the introduction of the Porsche 901/911 at the Frankfurt Motor Show in September 1963, actual production models were only available to the public in late 1964, due to normal production preparation. A problem that only surfaced with the introduction of the new model at the Frankfurt Motor Show was that Peugeot objected to the use of three-digit model descriptions with a zero in the middle, '901', as they had the naming rights to such a numerical sequence. The simple solution was to replace the offending '0' with a '1' so as to ensure plenty of room for expansion of numerical model identification before reaching four-digit model numbers. Nevertheless, when the vehicle arrived, it was well received by most and over time it just grew on the sceptics who had initially said it wasn't fit to be a 356 replacement.

With the demise of the 356 B in 1963, the Carrera road car, to all intents and purposes, 'dropped from the radar' with the exception of a limited number of racing vehicles for the factory, and certain racing customers. However, along with the announcement of the 901/911 came another bombshell for the Porsche driver – there was to be no production Carrera in the new model range.

The winds of change

Designed by Butzi Porsche, the 911 first appeared while the company was experiencing a period of family and management restructuring. A 'changing of the guard' at Porsche saw the younger generation moving in to replace the older management team as the younger family members took charge of managing development projects and occupied leading positions in the company. Ferdinand Alexander Porsche, known affectionately in family circles as 'Butzi', assumed the daily management responsibilities of the company, but later went on to establish a new

design consultancy of his own, Porsche Design GmbH, in Stuttgart in 1972, with a staff of four. He moved his office closer to the family home, Zell Am See, in 1974. Hans-Peter Porsche, who had joined the company in 1963, became production manager in 1965. Ferdinand Piëch, Ferry Porsche's nephew and son of Louise Porsche and Dr Anton Piëch, began his professional career at Porsche in 1965 as the manager of the engine development department and in 1966 he replaced Ing. Tomola.

These changes to the long-established structures and hierarchies within the company affected the complexity of the history of the origins of the Porsche 911. The final years of Komenda's time at Porsche were marked by conflicts with members of the Porsche family within the company over the development of the Porsche 904 and 911. (Komenda was going to be sidelined in the 911 design process because he wanted the car to follow a different style, but when this dawned on him, he became more flexible in his approach and fell in with Butzi's plan.)

Although the 911 represented a rather radical departure from the by-then familiar 356 shape, in its own way, the newcomer was nevertheless just as

BELOW The newcomer, Typ 901/911, certainly created a stir at the 1963 IAA in Frankfurt.

distinctive a car. The same Porsche design principles were present, as was the simplicity of shape, performance and power which had come to be expected from the Stuttgart-Zuffenhausen manufacturer.

The Typ 547 four-cam Carrera motor introduced in 1953 had been intended principally for competition use and therefore little thought was given to regular maintenance since this would be largely carried out by factory mechanics with the engine unit removed. It was only when the 547 four-cam motor was subsequently installed in the 356 road-going model that these problems became evident, but the factory thought it had done enough to alleviate the problem by training up the dealership mechanics. It took a skilled Porsche engineer one week to rebuild the complex Carrera engine, and a highly tuned racing version needed rebuilding all too frequently. With the introduction of the 911 model in 1963, Porsche offered a model which could be used as a more than competent autobahn cruiser, while at the same time it was just as happy to potter around town at low revs, without the complications inherent in the Typ 547 four-cam-engined Carrera. The 901 engine also represented the first Porsche power plant with chain-driven camshafts.

By the time the 911 was launched, Porsche was clearly going down the route of producing two streams of cars consisting of dedicated race cars for the circuit and a separate range of road-going cars for their normal but performance orientated customers. With the benefit of hindsight, this development was inevitable as the company had realised the problems associated with using the 356 body for both road-going and lightweight racing cars. These were good cars both on the road and the track, but no longer the best in either spectre – there comes a point where you must do one or the other, you cannot effectively satisfy both needs with the same basic vehicle.

As a result, during the 356 years, the Carrera Abarth GTL was produced which had limited success, but this development in itself had highlighted the need for a dedicated race car. This meant that when the 911 came on the scene, in the minds of the Porsche engineers there was less of a need to have a high-performance derivative of

LEFT An early press photograph of a 2.0-litre Porsche 911 Coupé in a typical daily touring scene (1966 Model Year).

ABOVE Hans Herrmann (driving) and Wolfgang Graf Berghe von Trips powered their way to a sixth place overall and first in the 1,500cc Sports car class at Sebring in 1956.

this new model at launch to go racing with, as the 904 was born around the same time. The race-bred Carrera GTS, or 904, in turn inspired a whole host of glass-fibre and composite race cars which followed in its footsteps. It was a case of 'race cars' were developed for racing and 'road cars' were developed for the road. While that outlook made perfect sense to the marketing people, there was nevertheless a group of very staunch Porsche weekend racers who were champing at the bit to get behind the wheel of something a bit more powerful.

In the words of the well-known author, Denis Jenkinson, writing in *Motorsport* (February 1973), 'Ever since the 911 Porsche series began in 1964 I have felt that the car was too big for the engine.' No doubt echoing the thoughts of many, he went on to say: '. . . and although the 911-series went ahead in ride, steering, road-holding and braking, it lagged on sheer performance, and other cars set the performance standards for the mid-1960s.'

The truth of the matter is that Porsche had enough on its plate with the introduction of the 911 not to add to the workload by producing a high-performance Carrera version of their new

model, as this would have necessitated further testing to meet homologation requirements if the car was to be raced. As mentioned above, Porsche had decided not to go this route as they rolled out the lightweight 904 for GT racing in 1964, followed by the dedicated Carrera 6 race car two years later. The timeline of the Carrera name spanning the introduction of the 911, was that the last 356 C 2000 GS Carrera 2s were officially manufactured up until December 1964, with a few still coming through in early 1965. The Carrera GTS (904) was manufactured between January and October 1964 and raced through into the 1965 season, while the first 911s were delivered to customers in September 1964. The first race for the 906 was the 1966 Daytona which ran in January, and according to Herbert Linge they worked on the car in November and December of 1965 to get it ready, which means that the name of Carrera was not really dropped for very long, if at all.

The Carrera badge may have been missing from the road-going model range, but it was carried with pride on the race cars, the arena into which the original Fuhrmann racing engine had been born about ten years earlier.

Competition for the new Porsche 911

Fuhrmann's philosophy was similar to that of Ferry's – to produce road and race cars that closely resembled each other so as to exploit the potential marketing link between them.

On the track

In the earlier chapters on Porsche's success with privateer racers, such as Glöckler, Sauter and others, and in the 1953/54 Carrera Panamericana, Targa Florio, Mille Miglia, Le Mans and the race tracks of America, it is patently clear that the company's philosophy, of developing small and light cars, was a successful one. Even without the huge financial resources of the other bigger manufacturers, Porsche was able to make changes to its cars quickly. Motorsport rule changes were constantly being introduced and Porsche responded with new engines, new cars and revisions where necessary, as fast as they were required.

In 1965, with the factory's attention switched to the new six-cylinder 911, Porsche entered the new coupé in that year's Monte Carlo Rally claiming a top five finish. Although the 911 would go on to make a name for itself in rallying – including winning at Monte Carlo on multiple occasions, and did well in road course action also, development of the 911 as a race car was largely ignored by the factory until the 1970s.

Even so, in private hands, the 911 did well throughout the world, winning its class at Le Mans as well as in the prestigious North American Trans-Am Championship, and in the International Motorsports Association's Camel GT. In 1967, Piëch's engineers put together the 911 R (see later this chapter) as a technical exercise, the only real factory attempt at producing a lightweight 911. This was the closest thing to a Carrera that the 911 would get to for another five years. Never built in

enough numbers (again, there were only 24 made), the 911 R, which featured a stripped interior and glass-fibre fenders, doors and deck lids, was forced to run as a 'prototype' in competition. Nevertheless, it provided a taste of what might have been, and that established a foundation for later racing 911 models.

Late in 1969, the factory produced around 35 lightweight bodyshells. These would be used to build up both circuit racing and rally 911s through until 1972. Although Porsche never gave these lightweights their own designation, referring to them only as '911 S', unofficially they were dubbed '911 ST'. In their final form, in 1972, they were raced with 2.5-litre flat-sixes, which used many parts from the Carrera 906 programme. Perhaps, more important than their record was the fact that they served as a foundation for what came next, the Carrera RS.

BELOW Assembling at Werk I prior to departure for the 1965 Monte Carlo Rally, from left to right: Pauli Toivonen, Rolf Wütherich, Eugen Böhringer (seated in 904), (person leaning forward not known), Peter Falk and Herbert Linge. The factory entered a 904 and a 911 in the event.

that there was no other vehicle in their class at that time that could be compared with the Porsche 356 and 911 for performance or value. Tested on the tracks, Porsche put the lessons learnt in competition to good use in their road cars.

The vehicles in the table below represent a wide range in terms of specification, price and availability, and gives an idea of some of the makes that Porsche was up against in the international market.

Over the years, the fortunes of Porsche have fluctuated like any other specialist motor car manufacturer. During the 1970s, especially around the time of the oil crisis, Porsche suffered some sales losses – in the words of Rolf Sprenger: 'But in relation to the market, I think that Porsche always grew through these years.'

ABOVE The early 911 series was extremely popular around the world. Here, an original-looking 1968 Porsche 911 T 2.0-litre shows off its clean lines. (Author)

On the road

Having studied how successfully Dr Ferdinand Porsche and later his son, Ferry, agreed on the optimum performance package for their cars, that is a rear-engine rear-drive layout, it can be argued

The missing link

In order to get a better understanding of the events that led from the introduction of the 911 (1964) up to the legendary 911 Carrera RS 2.7 (1973), it is important to explain the role that certain other

EARLY 911 MODELS COMPARED WITH OTHER SPORTS CARS ON THE INTERNATIONAL MARKET AT THE TIME

YEAR	MODEL	ENGINE	POWER OUTPUT	MAX. SPEED
1964	Porsche 911 Coupé	2.0-litre, 6-cyl boxer	130bhp	125mph
	Ford Mustang Coupé	4.7-litre, V8 (289ci)	200bhp	120mph
	Jaguar E-type	4.2-litre, straight-six	265bhp	150mph
1965	Chevrolet Corvette	5.3-litre, V8 (327ci)	250bhp	140mph
1966	Porsche 911 S Coupé	2.0-litre, 6-cyl boxer	160bhp	140mph
	Chevrolet Camaro Z28	5.7-litre, V8 (350ci)	360bhp	126mph
	Lamborghini Miura	4.0-litre, V12	350bhp	175mph
	Maserati Ghibli	4.7-litre, V8	330bhp	154mph
1968	Mercedes Benz 280SL	2.8-litre, straight-six	170bhp	121mph
1969	Aston Martin V8	5.3-litre, V8	380bhp	170mph
	Datsun 240Z	2.4-litre, straight-six	151bhp	125mph
1971	Alfa Spider 1750	1.8-litre, 4-cylinder	135bhp	124mph
	Lamborghini Countach	3.9-litre, V12	375bhp	175mph
1972	BMW 3.0 CSL	3.0-litre, straight-six	200bhp	135mph
	Porsche 911 S Coupé	2.4-litre, 6-cyl boxer	190bhp	144mph
1973	Porsche 911 RS 2.7 Carrera	2.7-litre, 6-cyl boxer	210bhp	149mph
	Jaguar E-type V-12	5.3-litre, V12	282bhp	142mph

models played in this development. It must have come as quite a shock to enthusiastic Porsche competition drivers that when the four-cylinder four-cam 2.0-litre Carrera motor was eventually culled, it was pushing out a healthy 180bhp in the 904 race car, with reputedly even higher output in some cars.

However, at the 1963 launch, the competition boys were without a real performance car and the racing fraternity hankered after another Carrera-like model in the 911 range. That development, unfortunately, was still some time away. With the introduction of the 2.0-litre 901/911, the new six-cylinder power plant pushed out 130bhp in the road-going version and by 1965 the competition version still only developed a conservative 160bhp by comparison.

For some it may seem that the nine years between the launch of the 911 and the introduction of the next true-blooded Carrera RS 2.7 road car in 1972 was a long time. According to Herbert Linge, this was necessary as the company was concentrating on the Sports Car Championships and with the 906, 907 and 910 they had cars with which to capture such laurels, and, as such, a road-going Carrera was not seen as necessary to supplement the 911 range.

The absence of a Carrera road car was perfectly logical for another reason. To build a race car out of a production model is very often not possible due to the motorsport regulations at the time that govern the class into which the racing version was intended to fit. Because Porsche knew that the customers buying any new Carrera model would want to go racing, this had to be taken into account. They also took the view that in order to break even they would need to target around half of their sales at the road-going buyer and the other half at the competitive driver. Unfortunately, around this time, the motorsport rules governing a potential race car based on the 911 production car prevented that from happening, and so it was deemed not to be commercially viable to introduce a Carrera at the time of the 911 launch.

The 911 S

'With the introduction of the 911 S, the Porsche people say the current 900 series of Porsches is now complete in the same manner as the line-up of the 356 models. That is, there's now a direct parallel to each of the 356 models (Normal, Super and Carrera) in the 912, 911 and 911 S.'
Road & Track, April 1967

A vague parallel there may have been, but the 'S' could hardly be called a Carrera. Early in the 911's competition career, Porsche entered a 160bhp 2.0-litre 911 in the 1965 Monte Carlo Rally. Piloted by Peter Falk and Herbert Linge, this car finished a credible fifth overall which showed that, with some development, the new model certainly had the potential to become another giant-killer.

On 25 July 1966, two years after the new 911 began rolling off the production line, the 911 S derivative was announced by the factory.

BELOW An official Porsche poster showing the 911 S. The driver dressed in a suit suggests that this model is aimed at the sophisticated end of the market, as well as the sport-minded.

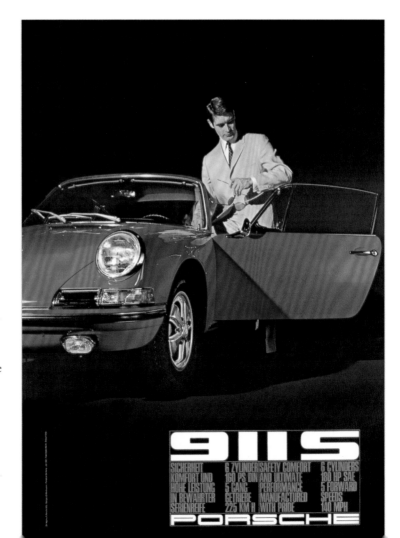

ABOVE A contemporary press picture of the 2.0-litre Porsche 911 S Coupé (1967 Model Year).

LEFT The engine room of the 1968 Porsche 911 S showing the 2.0-litre motor (1969 Model Year).

OPPOSITE TOP AND BOTTOM Introduced to the media at the Hockenheim circuit in December 1967, the 911 R was every bit the race car.

This new car had a more powerful version of the by-now trusty 1,991cc flat-six motor developing 160bhp instead of the conservative 130bhp. This engine, the 901/02, had been used very effectively in racing during the 1965 season and had shown a high degree of reliability.

A leading American auto journal, *Sportscar Graphic*, cited the main difference between the standard 911 and the 911 S as follows: '...the former is a quality sports car and the latter is a high-performance GT that retains all the practical and luxurious attributes, yet offers far more enjoyment to those that view car-driving as an art.' Improved and uprated versions of the 911 S continued to be developed for the more professional racing drivers in competition.

Featuring a slightly higher compression ratio (9.8:1), larger valves, modified carbs and exhaust plumbing, top speed was raised by an impressive 9mph (15km/h) over the standard 911, to 140mph (225km/h). Improvements in acceleration speeds over the standard car were phenomenal to say the least, with the 0–100km/h (62mph) sprint down by 1.2 seconds to 7.4 seconds for the 911 S. In August 1969, the 2.0-litre engine gave way to a new 2.2-litre unit (2,195cc) developing 180bhp which powered the S through 1970/71.

An interesting feature of the 911 S was that it was the first model to be fitted with the famous Fuchs alloy wheel rims. Fuchs, the German word for 'fox', manufactured these wheel rims for Porsche and for the Model Year 1967 the whole wheel rim was in the silver alloy finish, whereas all the later Fuchs alloys had silver centres and were painted black around the outside. These well known Fuchs alloys stayed with the 911 right through until 1989.

For 1972, Porsche again improved the 2.2-litre power plant in line with sporting regulations which allowed engine capacity to be increased to 2,500cc. As the original 901 engine had been deliberately designed with future capacity increases in mind, the engineers could now take advantage of this without increasing the stroke, which all sat rather well with the planned development of this unit, right up to 2.7 litres. The uprated 2.4-litre engine in 1972, officially known as the 911/53, was now up to 2,341cc and pushed out 190bhp although there was no significant increase in top speed over the smaller 2.2-litre models. The 911 S had shown that increased engine capacity had not affected reliability at all, and that there existed further scope for development of this unit in the future.

The 911 R

Manufactured in the spring of 1967, the 911 R was a very important vehicle in the development of a factory competition model in the 911 range. With only 24 cars built, similar in number to both the Abarth Carrera GTL and the lightweight 356s, the 911 R acted almost as an experimental model that showed the Porsche engineers that a lightweight 911 could certainly deliver the goods. With such a low production run, the 911 R was never homologated as a GT car and could therefore only compete as a prototype. The R was not intended to be a production-based race car, but it served to show just how much weight could be saved, should such a vehicle be needed.

two inches (50mm) and Koni racing shocks fitted, but priced at DM45,000, this car was only for the discerning racer.

Externally, this model is easily distinguished from other 911 models by the small, twin round tail lights and the 'Porsche' lettering along the bottom of the doors, which played a role in setting the Carrera RS 2.7 apart from the rest of the pack a few years later. The smaller tail lights, which in a distant way resembled the early 356 roundels, were essentially a weight-saving tactic, shaving about a pound (0.45kg) off the weight of the standard 911 units. With a few exceptions, most of the 24 911 Rs were painted white.

With hindsight, the 911 R very nearly became what the RS 2.7 was to become five years later. Huschke von Hanstein suggested that a limited run of 500 cars be made, but it was the conservative approach of the marketing department that put the lid on that one, fearful of not being able to sell that quantity of specialised vehicles. However, the 911 R was undoubtedly instrumental in the development of the Carrera RS 2.7 in the early 1970s.

However, in 1967, and once again using the banked circuit at Monza, a 911 R was used to break a whole host of world records in the hands of Rico Steinemann (later to become von Hanstein's successor) and his team. Amid grave concerns by some of the factory engineers, a race-prepared engine was dropped into a 911 R and driven to Monza for the record attempt, together with a second car destined as spares for the first car. By the end of the session, the Porsche 911 R had claimed five world records and 14 international records in the 2.0-litre class, averaging 130mph (209kmh) for 96 hours.

The 911 R was campaigned by the well-known British Porsche driver, Vic Elford, but it was at the hands of Gerard Larrousse that this car scored its most important victory, by winning the 1969 Tour de France. In the following year's event, the 911 R, again piloted by Larrousse, came home third behind a pair of Matra prototypes.

The 1969 version of the 911 R developed 230bhp, but unfortunately this model was not listed in the Porsche catalogues for 1970. The 911 R had unquestionably initiated some thoughts of

Fitted with the Carrera 6 engine (901/22) and weighing in at only 830kg (1,830lb), the 210bhp R was very basic in the comfort department, while the body boasted glass-fibre doors, front and rear lids, front wings and bumpers, with most windows finished in Perspex. A severe weight watcher's diet resulted in a completely stark interior featuring Scheel racing seats and a roll bar, with the window mechanisms removed, and even the floor was drilled to reduce weight. To round off the package, the ride height was lowered

ABOVE In the hands of Gerard Larrousse, this 911 R won the Tour de France in 1969.

OPPOSITE This 911 R, chassis No. 307671, is the third prototype (R3) and one of only four factory prototypes. This actual car was driven by Jochen Neerpasch, Hans Herrmann and Vic Elford to victory in the 1967 Marathon de la Route at the Nürburgring. The 911 R was fitted with a 901/22 2.0-litre engine as found in the Carrera 6, and for this tortuous 84-hour event, this car was fitted with a Sportomatic gearbox. This very significant and historic car is pictured here at the 2005 Porsche Festival, Brands Hatch, England. (Author)

producing a lighter and higher performing 911, but no matter how hard the factory tried, they could not get the 911 homologated as a saloon car as the back seats were deemed too small to carry passengers.

As the 1960s drew to a close, the company looked back to assess the market and how the 911 had fared since launch. Both the 911 S and 911 R were important models for the company, recalls Herbert Linge, 'because it showed us how many [911] customers would like to have a race car.' With some owners wanting to drive the car only on the road, an all-out 911 race car was not feasible as there was always the risk that they might not sell cars for competition. So it was important that any future racing version of the 911 would be fully road legal, but also competitive enough for the track.

With the return to Porsche of Dr Ernst Fuhrmann in September 1971, he gave the go-ahead for the 911 to be geared up for GT racing. October 1972 saw the introduction of the Carrera RS and, for homologation purposes, Porsche built an initial batch of 500 coupés in road trim. They were snatched up so fast that they had to build a second batch, but more about that in the next chapter.

CHAPTER SIX

Carrera – the sound of the future

'Keeping up with the pace of tomorrow means accelerating today.'

Porsche AG

Professor Ernst Fuhrmann returned to Zuffenhausen as technical director in September 1971, fully aware of the substantial number of victories the 911 had amassed in private hands in the preceding seasons. With numerous GT wins in events such as the Nürburgring 1,000km, Spa and Monza, Le Mans and the Targa Florio, the 911 had made its mark in the GT world, with first the 2.2-litre and then the 2.4-litre motors.

Such illustrious victories, at a time when sports car racing was at its peak during the late Sixties and early Seventies, inspired Fuhrmann to bring their race programme back in line with the production cars, drawing to an end the ruinously expensive, although highly successful projects, such as the 906, 907, 908, 909, 910 and 917 programmes. For many of their racing customers the step up from the 904 to these dedicated race cars was outside their financial means, and so a model was required to bridge the gap between the production cars and the professional race cars. The 911 Carrera RS 2.7 was intended to be just such a model.

Relaunch of the Carrera legend

The 911 Carrera RS 2.7 Coupé (October 1972)

It now seems almost inconceivable that Porsche did not continue with its Carrera model as their top-of-the-line production model, or indeed that they did not continue with any form of top road-going performance model when the 911 was introduced. In a world when the Mustang was born, 1964, and with the whole advent of the pony car era, this was surely a world hungry for high-performance cars. Following the introduction of the 911 in 1963, it was a full nine years before a true road-going performer was introduced, or 'hammer' as the factory called it. This was a period during which the appetite of the consumer for higher performance cars continued to grow, right up into the 1970s. It would surely not have taken very long to produce a 'hot' 911 for a market that was longing for more performance – just as its customers had done with the launch of the 356, until a privateer, Walter Glöckler, had taken the first steps to design his own sports car body for better performance.

Part of the answer undoubtedly lies in the fact that Porsche has always sought to grow slowly, and in the beginning, with the 356, the company saw itself as a manufacturer of grand touring cars rather than racing cars. However, it could not have been difficult to have read the signs in the market that pointed to a performance-hungry car-buying public. When eventually the company did produce a limited number of 911 'supercars' in October 1972, they once again underestimated the demand

OPPOSITE The business end of the Carrera 2.7 RS. (Author)

ABOVE The 911 S was first produced as a 2.0-litre model in 1967. (Author)

in the market. For Porsche, the effects of the fuel crisis which hit the industry the following year, in 1973, was perhaps negated to a certain extent by the fact that they had several cars in their line-up which were not that thirsty, thereby ensuring a smoother ride through the crisis than some might have expected.

On Rolf Sprenger's arrival at the factory in 1967, the 911 model range was still fairly new and little had been done to develop the car to any competitive level. 'I remember when I arrived, we had the T and the S as carburettor cars and then we split them – the T, E and S and the output was relatively close together. There was no, how should I say it, no "hammer", no very special strong engine, because we needed to develop the fuel injection', Sprenger recalls.

Once again Porsche was pushing the technology envelope with fuel injection, because at that time it was fairly new, there being no other air-cooled engine on the market with fuel injection. One of Sprenger's first tasks was to adapt and develop the fuel injection system for the six-cylinder 911, just at the time when there was talk of increasing the engine capacity to 2.7 litres. Sprenger again: 'When it came to the 2.7-litre, I developed the

power curve as well for the 2.7 with this very special torque curve, and when we drove the car, the engineers, I am sure Mr. Porsche and Bott and Piëch, everybody in the upper levels, said now it is time we have another "hammer", its time to use the name Carrera again.'

Success with the 911 S in competition had convinced the Porsche engineers sufficiently that a lightweight version of this car could achieve even greater success. However, the sporting regulations at the time limited the extent to which the 'S' could be modified for homologation purposes, and so the decision was made to produce a run of 500 specials, which was included as an extra model to the range. Once it had been decided to develop the engine to its maximum capacity, it took surprisingly little time to complete the work as Rolf Sprenger recalls: 'It was actually a period of no longer than twelve months, to develop that engine.'

Available only in coupé form and developed as a lightweight version of the 911 S, the Carrera RS debuted at the Paris Salon in October 1972. Considering that a 911 S Coupé could be bought for DM31,180, the basic Carrera RS was almost a gift at DM34,000, but the price was deliberately kept this low as the Zuffenhausen sales department was still nervous about the possibility of not being able to sell them all.

There was no mistaking the newcomer to the Porsche family, with its bold side lettering and revolutionary rear spoiler, but the improvements to the car ran far deeper than mere external embellishments. The extent of the surgery that was carried out ensured that the Carrera RS 2.7, made it eligible for homologation in Group 4, the GT racing category (for improved cars) that Porsche was to dominate so convincingly in the future with this new weapon.

The fact that Porsche wanted to homologate the Carrera RS tells us that they intended this car for competition use, but in order to ensure the sale of all 500 cars, they had to be offered as manageable street cars. Powered by an enlarged version of the 2.4-litre 911/53 engine used in the 911 S, the 2.7-litre motor (designated 911/83), was identical to the engine from which it was derived except for the cylinder bore increase (from 84mm to 90mm), and the material from which the cylinders were constructed. For the 911/83 engine, the cylinders were electrolytically coated with Nikasil which greatly improved the frictional qualities of the cylinders, thereby increasing power output.

Many lessons learned by Porsche in their motor racing activities found their way into the production cars and the Nikasil-coated cylinders were a feature of the indomitable 917. The increased bore pushed the engine capacity to 2,687cc and by retaining the same stroke, the general engine dimensions remained unaltered. With fuel being delivered by mechanical fuel injection, output was increased from the previous 911 S's 190bhp to 210bhp, and, combined with various weight-saving measures, the Carrera RS topped out at 149mph (239km/h) while the 0–60mph dash was achieved in an impressive 5.5 seconds.

Originally the Carrera RS 2.7 was developed basically as a homologation series and a car for customer competition. Working closely with the RS project, Rolf Sprenger explains: 'Actually, the project was more a kind of competition project for those customers who wanted to do smaller competitions, but we also knew there are some rich people who didn't want to drive so fast but they liked to have more comfort, and for that reason the M472 "Touring" was made.'

The Porsche Carrera RS 2.7 has become one of the most recognisable sports cars of all time. As a manufacturer, Porsche had never been prone to putting any decoration on their cars that wasn't absolutely necessary. Norbert Singer, creator of the Carrera RS 2.7, reckoned that the car needed gluing down at the rear when at speed, and as usual, he was right. Sporting a distinctive rear spoiler which significantly improved rear down force, this appendage was not initially popular with the top management at Zuffenhausen. 'Butzi' Porsche, designer of the 911, felt that it did not do

BELOW The Porsche 911 Carrera RS 2.7 was first introduced to the public at the Paris Salon in October 1972, but was not available until the following year.

the styling of his original 911 any favours, but there were those who thought that the rear spoiler gave the car a menacing, more aggressive attitude. Steps to improve airflow over and under the car included the fitting of a deep front air dam, to reduce front end lift at speed, and the installation of the now famous rear spoiler, or duck tail, which helped to put the power on the road at the rear, and keep it there.

Klaus Bischof remembers the early comments about the spoilers well: 'It was the very first production car which had been fitted with such aerodynamic aids. That was a trendsetter for the whole world. Today, we take it for granted. And this car was the first one.'

For the body, 0.7mm sheet steel was used in place of the normal 1.0mm, and the windows were replaced with lightweight Glaverbel glass. The engine lid with rear spoiler was fashioned from glass-fibre and, in order to accommodate the wider tyres, the fenders were widened to take the 6-inch (front) and 7-inch (rear) Fuchs alloy wheels.

The interior was a spartan workplace for any driver, as all comforts had been stripped out in the interests of saving weight. Soundproofing and even underbody corrosion proofing was omitted, although the lack of the latter item did cause these cars to rust quite badly later on in life. By the removal of soundproofing, corrosion coating and electric windows, around 250lb (113kg) was saved in the Carrera RS Racing. The sales department was not upbeat about the sales prospects of the RS 2.7, and right up until the last minute were still debating as to whether to install a wind-up window, a heater and even a radio. The competition department insisted on the leder strap for the window, while the other items were available as optional extras.

With the inclusion of this top performer, the model range had now grown, which had not been the intention of the company at the outset. By already having to provide different spec cars for the US market, the company wanted to limit the

model range to three, and with the launch of the Carrera, some realigning of the model range had to take place. The 911 Coupé replaced the old 911 T, the 911 S Coupé became the middle model (replacing the 911 E) and the Carrera became the top performer once again. And so the company had come full circle with the Carrera name rightfully filling the top spot in the range of road-going cars.

Developing 190bhp, to make full use of the previous 911 S's 2.4-litre motor, Porsche owners were advised to keep the engine revs above 5,000rpm and rapid overtaking manoeuvres often required changing down a gear in order to get past a slower moving vehicle. However, in the Carrera RS, the increased torque made it unnecessary to change gears if the revs did not drop below 4,500rpm. This basic 2.7-litre motor remained in production with very few changes until the end of the 1975 Model Year.

The big advantage for Porsche competition drivers up until this point was that even the Carrera RS 2.7 still ran on regular-grade fuel, the engines not requiring high octane or racing fuel to deliver high performance, thanks also to a relatively low compression ratio of 8.5:1. This of course had made it a relatively simple job to run your Carrera around town without the concerns of plug fouling and a stuttering engine when driving at low speeds in traffic. The Carrera RS came in three guises, two street legal models and the full racing RSR. The Touring option (M472), was by far the most popular as it featured all the creature comforts found in the 911 S and was understandably heavier, while the Sport option (M471) was basically a stripped version of the same car. The racing version (M491), known as the Carrera RSR, was dealt with as a separate model by the factory as this car could not be registered for street use. The basic price for the Carrera RS 2.7 was DM34,000 in August 1972 and the options shown in the table right reflect the additional cost for each option listed.

The product model year at Porsche had always run according to the company's summer holidays. Thus, a model would be produced up until August in any year, at which time the factory would cease production for the holidays while the assembly line

PORSCHE 911 CARRERA RS 2.7 – SPORT, TOURING, RACING VERSIONS

Model	Description	Price
M471	Carrera RS Sport. Fuel tank – 85 litres; Recaro sports seats; rear seats removed; sound insulation removed; rubber mats replaced carpets; basic door trimmings; dashboard clock removed; passenger sun visor removed; 300km/h speedo.	DM34,700
M472	Carrera RS Touring. Interior furnishings and trimmings similar to the 911 S, adding 115kg to weight; 1,308 Carreras had Touring finish including interior clock, carpets, hood lining, sun visors, full door trim; steel rear bumper.	DM36,500
M491	Carrera RS Racing – known as the RSR. Engine capacity increased to 2,806cc, 300bhp; available only with 5-speed gearbox.	DM59,000

BELOW The perfect 'his' and 'hers' combination – one for the road and one for some serious fun on the track. The Carrera RS 2.7 shows the early positive scripting along the sill.

OPPOSITE TOP This 1973 photograph shows the 911 Carrera RS 2.7 (left) next to its big brother, the 911 Carrera RSR 2.8.

OPPOSITE BOTTOM The 'Renn Baron', Huschke von Hanstein age 62 years, after his record-breaking run in the 911 Carrera RS 3.0, 28 July 1973.

was changed in anticipation of the new model to commence production in September, the new production year. Thus, for the sake of consistency, a model manufactured from September onwards would be known as the following year's model.

Herbert Linge remembers: 'We figured, we had sold about 175* Spyders which is unbelievable for a race car, so we estimated that 200–250 cars would go racing, the other half to be used on the road.' (*This was a rough estimate, with the total number of 550s being 137.)

According to Georg Ledert, head of Porsche advertising at the time of the RS 2.7 introduction, their advertising campaign stressed that only 500 men would drive the new Carrera, as they didn't bargain on any female customers. When Porsche was questioned as to why only 500 were produced, because by then demand had surpassed even their wildest expectations, Ledert laughingly recalled that their response to the media was, 'Oh no, that is only 500 for Germany.'

The first batch of Carrera RS 2.7 sports cars was produced in the original 911 bodyshell with the first cars (1973 Model Year) being delivered by the factory in October 1972. This early series was produced up to July 1973. As it happens, there is always a model that bucks the system and the factory has no record of Carrera RS 2.7 deliveries in August 1973, and so July marks the end of this early series. Following the Paris Salon launch, all of the first batch of 500 produced for homologation purposes were snapped up within a matter of weeks, even before a single one had been built. As a result, a second batch of 500 cars was then approved for production and when they too were swallowed up by the market, yet more production was approved and by the end of this ten-month period a total of 1,590 Carrera RS 2.7s had been completed. The vast majority of Carreras during this time were built in left-hand-drive form, with only a hundred or so right-hand-drive cars for the British market. However, the Carrera RS 2.7 was not sold in America.

Clearly, not every RS 2.7 owner wanted their car to be a road legal track car, and being desirous of some comforts, around 550 cars went back down the production line to be fitted with full 911 S trim and equipment. With the bulk of the total production (just over 1,000 vehicles) being finished as lightweight models, the Carrera RS 2.7 was actually homologated in Group 3, for standard Production GT cars.

Von Hanstein has been responsible for many motorsport and publicity achievements and had earned great respect in the process. However, there cannot be many manufacturers who can boast that their director of motorsport and public relations has actually participated in famous international races and world record-setting events. These accomplishments earned von Hanstein the title of the Renn Baron or 'Racing Baron'. In 1973, at the age of 62, he took part in Porsche's record attempt for the '10 Miles' and '10 Kilometres' from a standing start. Driving a Carrera RS, the Renn Baron claimed these records for Porsche because they were there for the taking, once again maximising the potential publicity generated by this record attempt.

September 1973 kicked off with an altogether new Carrera RS 2.7 sporting a smoother body, American 'safety bumpers' and the distinctive reflective red strip now joining the two back light clusters. Safety regulations introduced in America delivered what was thought to be a crippling blow to the typically sleek lines of sports cars around the world, when the authorities there declared that all cars were required to be fitted with 5mph (8km/h) impact absorbing bumpers. Integrated into the bumper construction of the Porsche, were impact-absorbent pistons that not only complied with the safety regulations, but they even looked stylish. While several prominent sports car manufacturers simply attached black rubber blocks to their bumpers as overriders, Porsche took the challenge in its stride and actually made a feature out of the problem.

Whereas the first Carrera RS 2.7 had only been offered in a coupé body, for the 1974 Model Year it was offered in both coupé and Targa bodies.

This new series, known by the Porschephiles as the G-series, was available from September 1973

ABOVE For the American market, the 911 Carrera 2.7 Coupé (left), 911 2.7 Coupé (centre) and 911 2.7 Targa (right) models were available for the 1975 Model Year.

OPPOSITE An early promotional poster expounding the attributes of the 911 Carrera RS 2.7.

until July 1975, and could still push out a healthy 210bhp. The 2.7-litre engine with its mechanical fuel injection was retained for the Carrera for markets other than the USA. Cars bound for America were fitted with the 911 S engine now also in 2.7-litre format producing 175bhp and featuring K-jetronic electric fuel injection to meet emission regulations.

As has been the tradition with Porsche engineers, nothing stays static for very long, and soon there were moves to provide greater engine power and flexibility.

The history of the famous Carrera script

'The nomenclature – the giving of the word', says Tony Lapine, when asked to explain the essence and character of the Carrera name. Immediately, at the start to our conversation, it becomes apparent that Lapine, head of Style Porsche from 1969 until 1989, appreciates the value in accurate communication and the meaning of model identity for the customer.

Anatole Lapine, born in Riga, Latvia, spent many years working for General Motors in America on the Corvette, under the watchful eye of Harley Earl and Bill Mitchell. In his position at GM, a good understanding of the American

market was crucial and so when he joined Porsche in 1969, lessons learned Stateside proved invaluable to the German manufacturer.

Porsche's badging has always been discreet, conservative and low-key, until the arrival of the Carrera RS 2.7 that is – just like its performance on the road, the Carrera's embellishments were equally loud. Why was the Carrera RS 2.7 treated so differently by the factory? According to Klaus Bischof, manager of the Porsche Museum, 'It was decisive, that that was the first motor over 200PS and it was very definitely different even in the construction of it. It was even more a racing version than a production engine.'

Making a good car is one thing, marketing it and presenting it to the public successfully is quite another matter. In the case of the Carrera, carrying on the image that had been etched in the minds of the faithful followers of the Zuffenhausen marque and nurturing the emotion that had been stirred by those early memories of the Carrera successes was going to be no easy task.

Serving as race mechanic at Porsche from 1968 to 1981, Klaus Bischof worked on all the major race cars as well as on the Safari Rallye. He was then with the Jöst team and later worked on the 956/962 series, followed by ten years as an engineer with Norbert Singer (1981–1990). Only at Porsche, can the museum manager be as highly qualified as this. He remembers the introduction of the RS 2.7 well: 'It was therefore not all about engineering, it was also a special design characteristic. This Carrera writing, he [Lapine] really liked it and he put it on the side of the car in red, blue or green, depending on the colour of the car. And that was a very important point. The time for marketing had come.' The weight of this statement must not be lost at this point, as it confirms that the company realised, in order to continue to appeal to the market and to grow with popular demand, product marketing was going to have to play an increasingly important role for them. No longer would it be simply motorsport achievements that got their cars noticed, but some much-needed marketing and public relations would also be required. The 1970s was all about being noticed.

Deutschlands schnellster Seriensportwagen!

210 PS
245 km/h
5,8 sek. von 0 - 100

ABOVE LEFT This 911 Carrera RS 2.7 shows the bold, in-your-face 1970s style and presentation.

ABOVE RIGHT An early example of some 'Carrera' and 'Porsche' colouring and scriptology being considered by the styling studio.

The department in Stuttgart charged with overseeing the visual identity of the Carrera RS 2.7, was known as Style Porsche, the design studio. Indeed, the scripting of the original Carrera name was down to one man, Herr Ploch. Already working at Style Porsche when Lapine arrived on the scene, Ploch was responsible for script styling as well as being the fabrics and colour co-ordinator – a 'one-man-show' according to Anatole Lapine. However, well-known graphic artist and designer, Eric Strenger, who worked for the agency responsible for Porsche's racing posters from the early 1950s right up until the early 1970s, is thought to have helped Ploch with the Carrera lettering, according to Georg Ledert, head of Porsche's advertising department during those years.

Far from being a script taken from a book, the studio was responsible for the famous lettering of the Porsche company, where each elongated, stout letter in this name is longer than it is tall. The scripting of the famous 'Spyder' and 'Carrera' names, as well as the Porsche crest, came from the pen of Herr Ploch. The method of styling the Carrera script according to Lapine, was typical of the day, where Ploch would write it out by hand, view it, put it away, the next day perhaps working on one of the letters again, until eventually, the scripting was acceptable.

The importance of the Carrera script was no less significant when, in 1972, the Carrera RS 2.7 was born. Of course, by this time, styles had moved on from the 1950s when the first Carrera scripting was penned, but the critical task in 1972 was to retain the heritage of the name while modernising the visual image of the Carrera car. Lapine picks up the story again: 'Well that was using the "Carrera" script such as it already existed and then we decided to use it down at the sill area underneath the door which was a popular thing to do. The Ford GT40s chose that as a good place to advertise the name Ford and so that was why we did it.'

Asked why the lettering was first used on the sills in the 'positive' form and then the 'negative' form, he says, 'Just fun, just fun. It kind of shook people up, if you stood very close to the script, it was blurred, it didn't make sense it was just a lot of areas of lines and colour. But when you stepped back you could read it clearly.' Again, this styling was from the desk of Ploch, and, according to Lapine, there was no problem in getting this radical, very '70s style of 'in-your-face' messaging approved by management, which is in itself quite surprising for a naturally conservative company.

Georg Ledert said: 'At first it [Carrera lettering] was positive, all the cars had been in white. The colour of the lettering was red, blue and green and the customer could order the car with one of these three colours. That is why it was positive and not negative.' He went onto say: 'Later on, it was changed.'

One of Porsche's customers, Kremer Racing, borrowed this lettering style in 1973 and had the Kremer name styled along the bottom of his car doors in the same manner that the Carrera name was done.

In recognition of the pioneering and brave step that the company had taken, Bischof says with fondness: 'That was so typical of Anatole Lapine. He was very much ahead of his time with regards to the writing and painting.' Lapine wanted to make the car unique – he succeeded admirably.

The location of the lettering on the sills came very much from the race track, and, according to Lapine, it was always good inspiration to follow. 'Whatever you see on racing cars and participating in speed events, you get a good deal of inspiration from that', he added.

As regards the body colouring of the Carrera RS 2.7, the story starts much earlier. A differentiating characteristic of early racing cars was that they were traditionally painted in their national colours, red for Italy, British Racing Green for England, white (or silver) for Germany and blue for French cars. Bischof again: 'And for him [Anatole Lapine], the RS was a racing car and therefore it had to be white.' According to Klaus Bischof, the classic RS was white with green lettering, but some customers wanted the scripting in blue or red.

Carrera RSR 2.8 (1973/74)

Meanwhile, around 60 Carrera RSRs were developed from the lightweight base model of the RS 2.7. Taken from the main assembly line and

BELOW This early press shot (1972) illustrates the positive 'Carrera' scripting along the sills, as well as on the base of the engine cover. Note also the central and high position of the 'Carrera RS' lettering on the rear spoiler; this was later moved lower down and to the right.

RIGHT This studio photograph shows the more popular negative 'Carrera' scripting along the sills.

BELOW The 911 Carrera RSR 2.8 (Prototype 3.0) on test around Weissach in 1973. From the left: Paul Frère, Helmuth Bott, Manfred Jantke and Norbert Singer.

reworked in the customer service department in the old Werk 1 building, their engines were modified with new cylinder liners and high-domed pistons to give a 10.5:1 compression ratio with an engine capacity of 2,806cc. This was the largest bore possible (2mm larger than the 2.7-litre motor) in the existing magnesium crankcase. The cylinder heads were revised with extra-large valves and the cams modified to run in four bearings each.

'With the 911 RSR, we didn't call it 911 Carrera RSR, actually we shortened it and said 911 RSR', Sprenger explains, and that RSR stood for 'Racing Sport "Racing"; we needed to have another name', he adds with a grin.

In terms of its engine, the Carrera RSR was fairly standard stuff, not differing much from the basic unit except for an increase in displacement. Despite its similarity to the specifications of the 2.7-litre unit, the combination of increased compression ratio, recalibrated fuel injection, improved porting and some radical cam timing ensured that this motor developed a stonking 300bhp at 8,000rpm. This was a real stormer.

Developed under renowned Porsche engineer Norbert Singer in 1972, after Piëch had left the family firm, the Carrera RSR was the first true effort at creating a 'production-looking' 911 that could dominate the racing arena. Although it was lighter in weight than previous 911s, it did not go to the same extremes as the 911 R with its drilled floors, but it nevertheless featured a number of glass-fibre panels including bumpers and deck lids. In fact, the front 'bumper' was little more than a low spoiler which also housed the centre-mounted oil cooler. The cabin featured a roll bar, sprinkler fire extinguisher system, 110-litre (29-gallon) fuel tank and a racing seat with four-point seat harness.

The Carrera RSR was only available with a five-speed gearbox and the transmission had its own pressure lubrication system and oil cooler. Front and rear suspensions were both beefier than the road-going version and power was transferred to the tarmac by way of the widest possible wheels allowed by the regulations. The fenders incorporated stylishly modified wheelarches, widened by 2in on either side, which served to reaffirm the no-nonsense attitude of this racer. Up front the 9-inch rims carried Dunlop 230/600-15 tyres, while the 11-inch rims at the rear were fitted with 260/600-15 rubber. Brake discs, radially vented and cross drilled with four pot calipers, came straight from the 917 CanAm car to ensure massive stopping power.

In a report by *Road & Track*, the road-test team was staggered by the drivability of the RSR, despite its phenomenal potential and scary statistics. The magazine timed the RSR from 0–60 mph in 5.6 seconds with a top speed of 178mph (286km/h). Despite the price of DM59,000, nearly double that of a standard RS, these cars sold quickly because they were built ready to race. At the time of the car's introduction, Californian Porsche dealer and racer, Alan Johnson, hinted that the Carrera RSR represented the closest thing to an off-the-shelf race car that one could get. That was all down to the high standard of the test facilities available at the recently completed Weissach Research and Development Centre, just north of Stuttgart.

RACING THE CARRERA RSR

Although it has not been the intention to dive into the vast ocean of Porsche's racing achievements, it is important to draw the connection between the Carrera RS and Carrera RSR. With the RS being built as a road-legal car, it is all the more impressive when you consider the impact of the first victory of the Carrera RSR at the Daytona 24-hour event on its debut outing in February 1973. Against full-blown prototypes such as the Matra, Gulf-Mirage and Lola cars, Peter Gregg and Hurley Haywood achieved the unexpected, finishing a whopping 22 laps ahead of the second-placed Ferrari GTB4.

An astonished Helmuth Bott, Porsche Development Director, said after the race: 'Actually in Daytona, we only wanted to absolve a long-distance test of our engines.'

The company press release went on to say: 'The first of eleven races for the World Championship of Makes was unexpectedly won by a Porsche. Even for the optimists in the factory in Stuttgart this victory was a surprise, coming as it did in the first competitive event for the new Carrera RS.' Besides the win by the Gregg/Haywood Carrera RSR, there were five more Porsche 911 Ss in the top ten finishers at Daytona that year.

The irony is that the car could not be entered for the Daytona race in Group 4 as homologation under that class was only due to take effect the following month, and so the cars were entered in Group 5 for prototypes. It also wasn't a matter that once the big players had fallen by the wayside that the Porsches could coast to victory, as there were two opposing Porsche teams competing for the laurels with identical machinery – Roger Penske Racing and Brumos Porsche – and no quarter was given by either team.

Once homologated in Group 4, they ran away from the opposition in Europe, with the works entering two cars under Martini sponsorship. In 1973, Herbert Müller's extensively modified Group 5 car finished fourth at Le Mans. Another great victory was achieved in 1973 when Müller and van Lennop outlasted all the other prototypes to win the last of the great open road races, the Targa Florio, with four other RSRs in the top ten. Clemens Schickentanz crowned a great season by taking the European GT Championship, while Gregg took both the TransAm and IMSA GT championships in America with his RSR against far more powerful Corvette and Camaro opposition.

BELOW A well-known photograph of a well-known car. This 911 Carrera RSR 2.8 took first place in the Targa Florio as well as the Daytona 24-hour; both events in 1973.

ABOVE For 1974, the Carrera RS 3.0 was introduced with a bigger 2,994cc engine developing 230bhp.

The Carrera RS 3.0 (1974)

For 1974, the Carrera RS 3.0 was introduced, sporting a bigger version of the 2,687cc engine (the stroke was lengthened from 90mm to 95mm). Pushing out 230bhp, the RS 3.0 at DM64,980 was almost double the price of its predecessor, which cost DM34,000 the year before. There was more than just the slight increase in engine capacity that accounted for this huge jump in price.

Porsche began the production of a series of 100 of the new 3.0-litre cars in the autumn of 1973, with the first 15 of these earmarked for the IROC (International Race of Champions) series in America. These were identically prepared RSRs, each with the 1974 3.0-litre engine and larger turbo-style whale tail, although the contours were not as aggressive, giving the car a more 'production' look.

A company press release, dated 12 November 1973, highlighted the changes to the following year's model: 'The main features of the RS 74 are a Carrera engine with capacity increased to 3.0 litres,

a modified and more effective rear spoiler, wider wheels and tyres, but an unchanged weight of 900kg (1,985lb).'

Getting the 1974 Carrera RS 3.0 homologated was not as much of a problem as it had been for the original RS 2.7 back in 1972. The new model was described as 'an evolution' of the original Carrera RS 2.7, and therefore the company only had to produce 100 of the uprated cars (although 110 were eventually produced). But nothing is ever quite what it seems and the oil crisis of 1973 intervened, which sent shivers of fear into the management as they envisaged themselves sitting with a load of high-powered, but unsold inventory. This anxiety was short-lived however, as after more racing victories came their way, the cars just sold themselves.

Other victories included the IMSA Camel GT and European FIA GT championships during that period, as well as a host of individual race triumphs, including the Targa Florio in 1973. Daytona proved to be a happy hunting ground for the Stuttgart firm, winning the 24-hour event there three times outright, before the car ended its racing career in 1977.

911 Carrera RSR Turbo 2.1

In 1974, Norbert Singer took things a step further, producing a turbocharged RSR with revised aerodynamics that included a raised rear roof and a huge rear wing – this was the only turbo-powered 911 ever to be called a Carrera. The Martini-backed 911 Carrera RSR Turbo 2.1, to give it its full title, finished second at Le Mans in 1974, the highest placing ever for a Carrera RSR. Developing 450bhp from just 2.1 litres, this giant beater was a one-of-a-kind vehicle. The reason for this coupé's existence was the upcoming so-called 'silhouette' prototype formula that was to be instituted in 1975 for the World Makes Championship.

The 3.0 Euro Carreras (1976/77)

For Porsche, the 1970s was a period which saw many changes. Professor Ernst Fuhrmann returned as the technical managing director of the company in the autumn of 1971 following the withdrawal of the Porsche family from key management operations, and taking over as chairman in 1976. The mid-1970s saw the introduction of the first production turbo model and, in 1976, Porsche was the first motor manufacturer to use an all-steel hot-galvanised body on a production car. This process gave a considerable boost to the company's marketing effort as the cars could be sold with a six-year guarantee against corrosion.

Announced at the 1974 Paris Salon, the Porsche Turbo 930 set the sports car world ablaze. In a world where business and economic prospects were not at their brightest and the Cold War was in full swing, other sports car manufacturers were struggling, to put it mildly. Aston Martin went under at the end of 1974, although a few partially completed cars were finished in late 1975, but production didn't really restart again until January 1976. Jaguar only sold 1,245 of their XJS model in 1975 and Ferrari sold a total of 1,337 cars worldwide that year.

Introduced as a 1975 model, the Turbo sold for DM65,800 which was almost double the Coupé price of DM33,450. The Turbo had a special place

BELOW The only Porsche Turbo to be badged a Carrera. This Porsche 911 Carrera RSR Turbo is driven here by Manfred Schurti/Helmut Koinigg in the 1974 International ADAC 1,000 km race at the Nürburgring.

in the company's model range and took over as the top performer of the road-going cars. Known in the European market as the 911 Turbo, this car used the 2,994cc engine introduced in the Carrera RS 3.0 in 1974. In South Africa, the Turbo became known locally as the 930 Turbo while in America, the biggest export market, the car was known as the Turbo Carrera. Although no other road-going turbo-engined Porsche was ever called a Carrera, the marketing department of Porsche North America wanted to maximise the value and heritage of the Carrera name.

The 911 Carrera 3.0 was introduced in 1976, using the same basic 2,994cc engine as in the Turbo, but without the turbo assistance. Apart from some minor differences, this basic motor remained in production virtually unaltered from September 1974 until August 1977. The Carrera RS 3.0 (1974) used mechanical fuel injection, whereas both the Turbo (lower compression ratio) and the later Carrera 3.0 used the K-Jetronic fuel

injection system. The Carrera 3.0 was somewhat heavier than the original Carrera RS 2.7 from which it had grown, the increased weight somewhat blunting the potential performance advantage of the bigger engine.

Known simply as the Carrera 3 in Europe, or the 911 S in America, this model could be ordered with the option of a 'Comfort Pack' for the US market which included softer Bilstein shocks and 14-inch alloy wheels, but these cars were limited to 130mph (209km/h) because of these tyres. For the more competitive drivers, one could order the 'Sport Pack' which was made up of wider tyres, wheels and arches and a five-blade cooling fan to allow for higher revs.

The Carrera 3 could really be driven by owners of diverse driving ability. Available normally with either a four-speed or a five-speed manual gearbox, the owner could now also opt for the Sportomatic 'box which undoubtedly took some of the edge off the performance and economy figures, but still

BELOW This press picture shows the 911 Carrera 3.0 Targa (1976 Model Year) featuring Porsche's 2,994cc engine.

offered a typical Porsche drive. With an eye on the US market, Porsche reasoned that this option would broaden the saleability of the range and at the same time would satisfy the American idea that a floor gear shift was really for the youth market. With the benefit of hindsight, the Sportomatic was actually a very sensible alternative to the more demanding drive of the traditional Carrera, especially as Porsche's market was mostly made up of more mature owners who could afford the luxury of owning a Porsche. The Sportomatic thus offered smoother driving, but still allowed the Porsche owner to strut their stuff if they so desired.

The 911 Carrera 2.7 and 3.0 Targa models were the first Carrera cars to be given the body style name of Targa. Normally, the Carrera name was reserved for the top performer in the model range, but Porsche saw fit to break with this tradition. The 911 Carrera 3.0 Coupé and Targa models (manufactured August 1975 to July 1977) were the last 911 cars to be known as Carreras, until the introduction of the Carrera 3.2 in 1983.

For the 1975 Model Year (H-series), Carreras dropped to their lowest power output levels yet in North America. Carreras were still outlawed from running their 210bhp 2.7-litre engine in America, and had to be fitted with a '49-State' motor, while the Californian legislation required even tighter emission controls. In order to meet the stringent emissions regulations in the USA, Porsche had to produce two distinct engines specifically for this market, these being the 165bhp '49-State' (911/43) and the 160bhp (911/44) California-only unit. These two engines were based on the regular European 175bhp S engine.

Rolf Sprenger had joined Porsche in 1967 after a spell in England where he had developed his skills as a fuel injection specialist at Simms Group Research and Development. It was while working for this company that Sprenger also did work in this field on Rolls-Royce injection systems.

It was somehow inevitable, in a company like Porsche, that a service such as the Sonderwunsch-Programm would be provided. With the demand for personalised improvements and modifications to all manner of Porsche cars being placed on the factory's repair shop, a dedicated facility would have been required sooner or later. Located in

ABOVE The 911 Carrera 3.0 Coupé (MY 1977).

Werk 1, this facility was started in 1978 to cater for the personalisation of customer's cars, in satisfying the 'special wishes' of those who wanted certain optional extras fitted to their car, or some other mechanical or body enhancements to be carried out by the factory.

'I actually started for Porsche at the end of the 1970s, the Sonderwunsch-Programm. I am the father of the what you call today the Exclusive Program Tecquipment, to make Porsche cars special, very personal', explained Rolf Sprenger, whose rather enviable responsibilities included making fast cars go even faster.

SCs 1978–83 (August 1977)

Although they shared the same 2,994cc engine as the Carrera 3.0, the SC was not a Carrera. Sometimes incorrectly called the 'Super Carrera', 'Sport Carrera' or 'Special Carrera', the SC was actually the 911 S version in the C-Programm of the 911 family. It was the SC that saw the demise of the much-loved and respected name of Carrera from the model range, and it was to be another six years before a Carrera badge would again adorn the engine lid of a rear-engined Porsche.

Porsche 924 Carrera GT (August 1980)

When it was launched in 1980, not all Porsche enthusiasts were convinced that the 924 was a worthy custodian of the Carrera badge. After all, this was a front-engined car which carried a motor made by another manufacturer, Audi.

The 924 had started out as a development project for the Volkswagen Audi Group (VAG), which had wanted a front-engined sports coupé to fit into their Audi model line-up. In 1974, just as it was reaching the pre-production phase, VAG pulled the plug on the project due to the uncertainty in the performance car market and the Group's own dire economic position. The project was then offered back to Porsche who gladly took the fledgling model under its own wing as the future of the air-cooled 911 at that point was not considered feasible beyond 1980, due to increasingly stringent noise and emissions regulations.

BELOW The Porsche 924 Carrera GT badge lifts this model into esteemed company. (Author)

With the 924 having been planned for the Audi line-up, it was natural that an Audi power plant would be fitted under the bonnet and so VAG offered Porsche a choice of engines. The 1,984cc unit, which was to power the new Audi 100 model, was selected and the Stuttgart engineers opted for the FR (front engine, rear-wheel-drive) layout with a transaxle system that included a combined gearbox and rear axle for better weight distribution.

Launched in the spring of 1975 (1976 Model Year), the 924 was considered underpowered by the critics right from the outset. In true Porsche fashion, however, the 924 was continuously improved and in November 1978 the Turbo was introduced, lifting power from a lowly 125bhp to 170bhp in the new model. The following year, at the Frankfurt Motor Show, Porsche introduced a 'styling exercise' showing the 924 in an altogether more aggressive light, a car which clearly showed the company's sporting intentions with this model.

Tony Dron, international sports car driver, remembers: 'I won the 924 Championship which they ran for one year in 1978, Andy Rouse was second in the Championship and the two of us were invited to drive at Le Mans in works 924s in 1980 as a result.' The 924 Championship was run in Britain for the 1978 season which served to generate publicity for the model launch here. These cars were standard 924s and clearly many lessons were learned from this race series.

The difference between the 924 Carrera GT and its predecessor, the 924 Turbo, was increased performance. Fitted with the same 1,984cc Audi engine unit as used in the first 924 (1975), by increasing the compression ratio and installing a new digital ignition timing system, power was boosted to 210bhp, giving the car a top speed of 150mph (240km/h). At a time when the 3.0-litre 911 SC Coupé cost DM48,750, the 924 Carrera GT in the early autumn of 1980 came in at a hefty DM60,000.

The intention of the company through the introduction of the 924 Carrera GT was two-fold. First, to move the 924-series upmarket through the use of the 'Carrera' nameplate and secondly to serve as a platform with which to go racing. In order to homologate the 924 Carrera GT for racing in Group 4, the company was required to produce 400 cars. According to a company press release in June 1980, all these cars were earmarked for the European market with half of this number staying in Germany, 75 right-hand-drive cars were destined for the UK and the balance were to be distributed in other European countries.

Distinguishing the 924 Turbo from the Carrera GT is a fairly simple matter as the latter car was fitted with a rather bold air intake on the bonnet and the front spoiler was deeper and faired into wider wings, which housed much larger, 215/60 rubber. Body rigidity was improved through the windshield which was now bonded to the body

BELOW Fifty 924 Carrera GTS cars lined up outside Werk 2, Stuttgart-Zuffenhausen awaiting distribution in 1981.

and weight was saved in the glass-fibre construction of the widened wings.

The GTS, GTR and GTP cars meanwhile were all produced by the Weissach competitions department. From as far back as the days of the first 356 Carrera, Ernst Fuhrmann had endeavoured to draw a strong visual link between the competition cars from Porsche and their road-going counterparts. It had always been his belief that success with cars on the track which could be identified by customers, was more likely to translate into sales of road cars. The development of the 924 Carrera GT racing programme was intended to do just that.

For the 1980 Le Mans 24-hour event, the factory entered three works 924 cars, designated GTPs. These three cars were suitably piloted by a team from Germany (Jürgen Barth/Manfred Schurti), Great Britain (Andy Rouse/Tony Dron) and the USA (Al Holbert and Derek Bell, who stood in for the injured American, Peter Gregg).

In preparation for this race, the 924s were given a 36-hour shake down at the Paul Ricard circuit in France. With Norbert Singer in charge, drivers Tony Dron, Andy Rouse and Derek Bell were to

RIGHT The 'American' 924 Carrera GT driven by Al Holbert/Derek Bell (Bell stood in for the injured Peter Gregg) at Le Mans, 1980. They finished in 13th place overall.

run their car flat out for the duration of the test, but problems were encountered with cylinder head temperatures and valve survival.

Although the valve and head problems were supposed to have been sorted out before the Le Mans event, the British duo of Dron/Rouse and the American pair, Holbert/Bell, developed problems with the cylinder head and valves after 18 hours. Following the repair of these two cars, both teams were sent out again. However, as Tony Dron remembers: 'They were convinced that they had solved the problem but sadly they hadn't. We still finished a good twelfth, Andy and I, although for the last six hours of the race we had to run with reduced power. It was still reaching the same speed down the Mulsanne Straight, but it just took much longer to get there, so we were losing sort of 15 seconds, 20 seconds a lap.' The Barth/Schurti car came home sixth overall and the Holbert/Bell car one place further back. Dron calculated that had the cylinder head and valve problems not plagued them, they might have finished as high as fourth, which is amazing for an engine whose basic block could be found in many other models throughout the VW range at the time.

924 CARRERA GT AND DERIVATIVES

Model	Introduced	Max. speed	Power output	0–62mph	Quantity produced	Price
Carrera GT	1980	150mph	210bhp	6.9secs	406	DM60,000
Carrera GTS	1981	155mph	245bhp	6.2secs	59	DM110,000
Carrera GTR	1981	180mph	375bhp	4.7secs	20	DM180,000
Carrera GTP	1981				6*	n/a

*Although the production numbers ran from 001to 006, not all of these ended up as full cars.

In the 1981 Le Mans race, the Jürgen Barth/ Walter Röhrl combination managed seventh place overall in a works GTP, powered by a 2,479cc version of the 924 Carrera GT engine. This combination was the forerunner of what was to become the 944 road car.

These 'successes' by the 924 did much to lift the model which had not yet enjoyed full acceptance in the market, nor with of some Porsche insiders. Tony Dron again: 'When the 924 got the Carrera name, it was no fake, it was the business and from the way people treasure them now, the way they are seen now, anyone who was opposed to the use of that name was actually misguided at the time.'

The Carrera 924 GTR was developed for both rally and race applications, but the Rallye car was dropped in the face of stiff opposition from Audi. Having received such a lukewarm reception back in 1975, by the time the model ran out in 1988, over 150,000 of all 924 derivatives had been produced.

For a car that was perhaps not fully appreciated by the market, Tony Dron sums up, 'What I do remember that car for, is the wonderful integrity of its chassis, an extremely stiff chassis and the handling of the car was extraordinarily good. One of the best handling cars I have ever driven, I really liked the feel of it.'

BELOW The view that most drivers saw of the 924 Carrera GT. This 1981 model developed 210bhp from its turbocharged 1,984cc engine, and had a top speed of 150mph (240km/h).

TIMELINE:

1984	**1987**	**1988**	**1989**	**1990**
911 Carrera 3.2 introduced.	911 Carrera CS introduced.	Carrera Speedster introduced.	Four-wheel-drive 964 Carrera 4.	964 Carrera 2. Porsche

CHAPTER SEVEN

Carrera lives on

'Some manufacturers will design a car in order to satisfy a popular trend, which is basically fashion. By nature, fashion changes frequently. Classic lines, however, are timeless.'

Author

Increasing environmental constraints had led Fuhrmann to the conclusion that the company's future models lay in the front-engine layout, a view that did not sit well with 911 enthusiasts, but more importantly it did not please Ferry Porsche. Continuing tensions between the two leaders resulted in a parting of the ways and Fuhrmann was to leave the company.

It was announced to the press late in 1980 that the new chairman appointed to succeed the outgoing Ernst Fuhrmann, would be Peter Schutz. German-born but raised in America, Schutz quickly established his supporters, and more worryingly, his opponents, within the corridors of Zuffenhausen.

Following the uncertainty surrounding the long-term survival of the 911 at the end of the 1970s, many saw the naming of the whole model range 'Carrera' in the early 1980s as a strong signal that the 911 would be around for some time still. History would judge whether this was the right move or not, but it certainly fired some debate amongst the Porsche staff and loyal enthusiasts at the time. However, this potential new phase in the life of the 911 served to strengthen the position of the new chairman, even if his attitude towards the rather formal and more traditional Swabian way of doing things was somewhat dismissive.

The 911 Carrera 3.2 (1984)

The introduction of this model, known simply as the 911 Carrera, signalled a change in company thinking whereby all 911s were to be called Carrera, and from that moment on, that 'hallowed' name was no longer reserved solely for the top performer in the range. In retrospect, this move was justified by the marketing department at the time as an attempt to boost flagging sales which had suffered as a consequence of a strong Deutsche Mark, as well as a sports car hangover in the market as a result of the oil crisis. The strong German currency made the car substantially more expensive in America, the company's chief export market, but it was felt by Schutz that in using the name of 'Carrera' across the whole 911 range, it would lift the model's image and with it, the company's fortunes.

In the words of Rolf Sprenger: 'We produced very expensive cars and we didn't earn the money we should earn on each car. It [the name Carrera] is so strong, that actually we needed it, we had to say Carrera. The Carrera had a value and a strength.'

Whatever the reasoning behind the new naming policy, Porsche had to get on with the business of selling production cars. Now in its 20th year of production and the most profitable model in the

OPPOSITE An American spec 911 Carrera 3.2 Targa – model year 1984.

arrived at by lengthening the stroke by 4mm and compression was increased to 10.3:1, while ignition and injection were controlled by a Bosch Motronic system for maximum efficiency.

Introduced in 1984, the Carrera 3.2 was available as the Coupé, Targa or Cabriolet, and just to confuse things slightly, this model was also offered as the Coupé Turbolook and Targa Turbolook, while the Cabriolet Turbolook was introduced the following year. Externally, the Carrera 3.2 had front fog lamps integrated into the front air dam with its most recognisable feature being the new rear wing. Together, the deep front spoiler and new rear wing contributed substantially to high-speed stability. If ordered, the Turbolook package included the wider 911 Turbo fenders with its distinctive rear wing as well as beefier brakes and suspension.

The Carrera 3.2 was the last model to be equipped with the familiar, and by now much-liked, Fuchs alloy wheels, the reason being that it was not technically possible to have ABS fitted with these wheels. The Fuchs alloys were first fitted to the 911 S in 1966, so this was a significant departure for the company, not to mention its customers who had grown to like that style. The 1984 Carrera 3.2 was then the first 911 to get the

company, the basic 911 received an extra power boost through the enlarged 3,164cc engine, or 3.2-litre in marketing language. With the maximum output up to 231bhp, the 0–62mph dash was achieved in an impressive 6.1 seconds, going on to a top speed in excess of 150mph (240km/h). The additional engine capacity was

ABOVE Porsche racing driver, Stefan Bellof, collects his 911 Carrera 3.2 Coupé, 1985.

RIGHT Three 1984 models for America, from left to right: 911 Carrera 3.2 Targa, Coupé and Cabriolet.

new-look Telefon wheels which had been fitted to the 928, although the Fuchs alloys were also available up until the model's demise in 1989.

In keeping with the demands of an increasingly sophisticated market, the folding top of the Carrera Convertible went electric in 1985. The seats, too, came in for electric actuation and all this additional equipment resulted in the 911 becoming heavier, although with little difference in performance. It's a strange anomaly in the sports car world that owners seem to be happier to pay more for less. Just as the 911 Carrera was being upgraded with all manner of luxury fittings, the company offered a stripped-out version of the same car called the Clubsport, or 911 Carrera CS.

GLOBAL SALES OF PORSCHE 911 MODELS (BY MODEL YEAR)

Year	Model	Sales
1975	H-Series	8,189
1976	J-Series	10,677
1977	K-Series	13,793
1978	L-Series	10,684
1979	M-Series	11,543
1980	A-*Programm*	9,874
1981	B-*Programm*	8,698
1982	C-*Programm*	10,735
1983	D-*Programm*	13,229
1984	E-*Programm*	13,669

BELOW The stylish 1984 911 Carrera 3.2 Targa fitted with Telefon alloy wheels instead of the familiar Fuchs wheels.

The response of the sales department at Porsche, which had received numerous requests to do away with all the luxury trappings, was to make a simple sports car again. Always willing to provide the right car for the market, Porsche rolled out the Carrera CS in 1987, which had lost a good deal of weight and had gained slightly in power output. With the 0–62mph sprint down to 6.1 seconds and with an exhaust note that would not be out of place at a drag strip, the motoring purists were in their element.

The end of the 1980s was an extremely busy time for the Stuttgart manufacturer. One faction within the company was set on reviving another old name, the Speedster, while another had their sights set firmly on the future – four-wheel-drive.

The Carrera Speedster (1988)

Back in 1955, Porsche had produced the 356 Speedster (see Chapter 3) because customers had demanded that style of car at the time. The recipe for this model was simple – a lightweight, no-nonsense, devoid-of-any-luxuries type of car for those who wanted a Porsche, but could not afford the fully equipped model. Almost thirty years later, in 1982 to be precise, Helmuth Bott, director of Porsche research and development, decided to revive a model name deeply entrenched in the company's history, and close to the heart of most sports car lovers – especially the Porschephiles.

The classic shape of the 356 Speedster is one of the most copied in the field of replica cars, not that

we want to delve too deeply into that subject, but suffice it to say that this trend has developed as a result of the success of the pure and simple lines of this classic.

With the company's recently completed Cabriolet, Porsche were able to develop a Speedster prototype that was ready early in 1983. Unfortunately, the pressure from another important project, namely the all-new 964 model, sidelined the Speedster concept and the car stood idle for three years, only being revived again in 1986. During this time, the playing field had changed somewhat and the original idea of having a low windscreen that the driver could see over, rather than through, had to be revised along with several other key points.

However, the Speedster idea was reworked and made ready for the 1987 Frankfurt Show, where the car was shown to the public to gauge their reaction. According to a company press release at the time: 'The Speedster represents unalloyed joy in sporting, top-down driving at Porsche. Thanks to its versatility this permits an easy conversion from road use to club sport competition – more so than the more comfortable Cabriolet can.'

What the company intended to produce was a modern version of the boulevard cruiser of the 1950s, which could be converted into a weekend racer with minimum effort. The windscreen was easily removable and could be replaced by a smaller aero screen and the car only offered two seats, making it 70kg (154lb) lighter than the Cabriolet on which it was based. The convertible hood was

BELOW The Porsche 911 Carrera 3.2 Speedster 'Turbolook' – only 2,103 of these distinctive models were made (1989 Model Year).

unlined and folded completely away beneath a plastic cover and the windscreen was set five degrees flatter than on the Cabriolet. The car ran on the same mechanicals as the other Carrera models of the day.

The market introduction of this car was set as a 1989 Model Year, although it would have been launched in late 1988, appropriately marking the 25th anniversary of the launch of the 911. Only 2,274 Speedsters were produced in 1989 which makes this a very special model in the company's history.

The four–wheel drive story (1989)

Porsche's involvement with four-wheel-drive propulsion stretches back as far as 1899, when Dr Ferdinand Porsche built the Lohner-Porsche, a revolutionary four-wheel-drive vehicle with an electric motor located in each wheel hub. It was only much later, in 1947/48, through the famous partnership with Piero Dusio that the company built the fabulous Porsche Typ 360 Cisitalia with a four-wheel-drive system controlled by the driver. Through a mechanical lever in the cockpit, the driver could transfer drive to the front wheels in order to transmit this car's considerable power to the road.

In 1955, Porsche built the Jagdwagen, a four-wheel-drive vehicle based on the 356 chassis, which was to be used by the German border patrol, although only civilian units of this vehicle were ever built. Porsche studied the Ferguson tractor all-wheel-drive system as used in the British Jensen FF of 1967, but this method was protected by patents in the UK. It was the all-wheel-drive system of Audi's Dr Ferdinand Piëch that attracted the attention of the Porsche engineers. Piëch, grandson of Dr Ferdinand Porsche, rose to fame with the Audi Quattro in 1981 after he had moved to the Ingolstadt firm a decade earlier, following the family and management reshuffle around that time.

Changes in the racing regulations permitted greater flexibility in the development of standard-looking vehicles for circuit racing in Group B. Under Helmuth Bott, the Porsche engineers set about building a new race car based on the 911,

but with the possibility of also being adapted for normal road use. The result was the superb all-wheel-drive 959 which was shown to the public at the 1983 IAA. The 959's first competition victory was in the 1984 Paris–Dakar Rally in the hands of Frenchman René Metge. The following year, the 959 won the Pharoahs Rallye in Egypt and in 1986, the Porsche 959 took first, second and sixth places in the Paris–Dakar event.

The potential advantages of the all-wheel-drive system envisaged by the engineers were expected to far outweigh any negative perceptions due to the increase in price for the Porsche owner. Not only did this system ensure 100 per cent use of the vehicle's weight to transmit drive torque but it also improved straight line stability in cross winds. The full advantages of all-wheel-drive would become obvious when accelerating in a curve, especially on a more slippery surface, while wheel spin at pullaway would also be eliminated.

However, it was not a simple matter of adapting the existing bodyshell to receive a four-wheel-drive system along with a host of other necessary improvements. Essentially, the 911 was a car that had been introduced back in 1963 and, at that time, nobody had considered or even had the foresight to take into account what technical advances would be made over the ensuing quarter of a century. For starters, the current wheels and

ABOVE The 1984 Porsche 911 Carrera 3.2 4x4 Paris–Dakar car being put through its paces at a test ground near Munich.

steering set-up could not accommodate ABS braking needs and the air-conditioning unit that had become a modern-day necessity, could also not be contained within the old bodyshell.

Due to the more pressing production requirements of the 911 Cabriolet, further development of the 911 all-wheel-drive vehicle was put on hold. Valuable lessons had been learnt from the 959 model and one thing that had become apparent was that an entirely new floorpan was needed for a 911 all-wheel-drive vehicle, requiring considerable development and engineering resources. Indeed, the engineers were in a tough position because the question was: how do you better what had been achieved in the 959? The more important question facing the company was, however, how to apply all that valuable knowledge and experience gained through the 959 project – that valuable expertise just couldn't lie unused on a shelf in the factory. Although a 911 Cabriolet all-wheel-drive prototype had been built as early as 1981, it wasn't until March 1984 that the Porsche

BELOW The 1990 line up of the 911 Carrera 4 3.6 range consisted of: Cabriolet (front), Targa (middle) and Coupé.

board issued the development order to begin work on an all-wheel-drive 911 Carrera, under the Typ number 964.

The 911 Carrera 4 Typ 964 (1989)

In no uncertain terms, the 911 Carrera 4 represented one of the most significant steps forward for the company technically, for many years. One could be forgiven for thinking that the 964 looks like a 911 which has just undergone an annual face-lift, because the only real external changes were to the wheels and details below the bumper line, designed to improve aerodynamics. Even the interior looked familiar, but beneath the surface lay an altogether new model, capable of providing a platform to support a whole new generation of 911 models.

Introduced in the 25th anniversary year of the original 911, Project 964 was the first attempt by Porsche to market an all-wheel-drive production car for the everyday Porsche driver. Although the

company had by now had some considerable experience with four-wheel-drive systems, substantial changes were needed in order to prepare this model for normal assembly line production. The 964 introduction comprised two models, the Carrera 4 and the Carrera 2, and although developed simultaneously, the latter was held over until the following year so as not to overshadow the significance of the new all-wheel-drive model. The decision was also taken to introduce the Carrera 2 the following year due to the additional workload in the factory in producing what was essentially two new models simultaneously.

A totally new floorpan had to be developed which allowed the driveline that transmitted drive to the front wheels to be installed in the assembly process from below, rather than from inside the vehicle, thereby also easing any future maintenance requirements. Considering that the wheelbase and track dimensions are virtually unchanged, the Stuttgart company had worked wonders in introducing an almost entirely new vehicle, which shared as little as 15 per cent of its components with its predecessor.

In the all-wheel-drive system employed in the 959, the rear axle is driven directly from the gearbox while the front axle is driven from the rear axle via a controlled centre clutch. This is referred to as a clutch-controlled all-wheel-drive system. Even in a top-of-the-line sports car such as the Carrera 4, this system would have been too expensive to produce and so a somewhat cheaper mechanical differential was developed for the 964. In this unit, the drive torque in the C4 is first directed to a centre transfer case, and from there, under normal driving conditions, drive is distributed in a 31:69 ratio to the front and rear axles. As driving conditions change, the unit adjusts this distribution automatically without the driver even being aware of the change, except through an indicator light on the dashboard. This torque split was best suited to the Porsche rear engine layout, as with most of the weight over the rear wheels a 50:50 torque split would have produced the characteristics of a front-wheel-drive vehicle. The objective of the all-wheel-drive system was not only to provide improved traction but also better handling, especially in the wet and on slippery surfaces, as this is where the four-wheel-traction would produce its greatest gains.

The all-wheel-drive system added over 100kg (220lb) to the overall weight of the car, necessitating the installation of power steering as standard on the Carrera 4. This was the first time that power steering and ABS brakes were included as standard features on a 911. To carry this extra weight around, more power was needed and so at the time of its launch, the Carrera 4, fitted with a bigger 3.6-litre engine, was the most powerful naturally-aspirated model in the 911 range. Developing 250bhp and giving a top speed of 162mph (260km/h), it covered the 0–62mph sprint in just 5.9 seconds. This increase in capacity was achieved by increasing both bore and stroke, which necessitated the development of an entirely new crankcase.

As discussed earlier, Porsche has always strived to maintain a very strong 911 family resemblance over the years, and this approach has set the

BELOW As a result of customer demand, the interior of the Porsche 911 Carrera 4 3.6 began to take on a far more luxurious feel. This is a 1992 American model.

ABOVE The Porsche 911 Carrera 4 3.6 Coupé retained much of its original 1963 styling – this is a 1989 model.

marque apart from other manufacturers. With the 964 model, this was achieved despite 85 per cent of the car's components being totally new when compared with this model's predecessor. Altogether, 33 prototypes were built and tested during the development phase of the 964, with a large proportion of the test time being focussed on handling on wet and slippery surfaces.

While the interior came in for some mild upgrading, it was the underside of the car that received a radical makeover. Just like the model that inspired the all-wheel-drive technology, the 959, the new 964 road car was fitted with a full-length belly pan providing several benefits. One of the main advantages was a reduction in engine noise in compliance with European regulations, as well as reducing the noise to the cabin occupants. While noise reduction was regulated by the authorities, this did not necessarily please the Porsche enthusiasts who craved the sound of that sweet six-cylinder boxer engine in full flight. The belly pan also ensured that the engine compartment as well as the engine itself became partially encapsulated, resulting in one of the cleanest engine bays of any road-going car, while at the same time, inherent underbody smoothness

further improved aerodynamics under the car.

A revolutionary new rear spoiler automatically extended from the engine lid at speeds above 50mph (80km/h), and retracted again when the speed dropped below 6mph (10km/h). This extendable rear spoiler was no gimmick as the company explained in a press release in 1988:

'Porsche led the way with the introduction of today's common additional spoilers for nose and tail. The extendable spoiler of the Carrera 4 now underlines the functional character of an aerodynamic lift-reduction aid, something Porsche would never see as an optically-fashionable attribute.'

Key to the introduction of this extendable 'lift-reduction aid' as it was called was that the company did not want a fixed rear spoiler as seen in the Carrera RS 2.7 or the later Turbo 930, as they wanted to retain the unspoiled, original 911 silhouette. In addition, through the extendibility of this spoiler, it almost doubled the area of the air intake without compromising the body lines of the car.

The inclusion of the all-wheel-drive transaxle system interfered with the forward trunk capacity, which required some clever trickery in maintaining the original lines of the car. As a condition of the entire project, the engineers had to retain the front luggage space as in the traditional 911. With the drive housing for the front wheels naturally located towards the front, the customary flat trunk space had to be altered but a similar overall capacity was retained without any change to the frontal area. Due to the overall aerodynamic improvements to the car, the drag coefficient was reduced from 0.39 to 0.32, resulting in better overall performance.

In developing the 964 concept, feedback received from dealers and selected customers, who were aware of the impending new model with its groundbreaking all-wheel-drive system, was that the engineers and designers were not to mess with the original 911 shape. These groups were emphatic that the factory maintain the strictest adherence with the traditional 911 silhouette. To build an entirely new concept, housing new technology and a new engine, retaining traditional brand and image qualities, while at the same time modernising an old shape sufficiently to support the next generation model, is no small task for any team. In fact, not only did the 964 meet these stringent parameters, it clearly surpassed them in many respects and the Carrera 4 went on to become an unmitigated success, receiving the accolade of the 'best 911 ever' up to that time.

At the August 1988 introductory price of DM114,500 (1989 Model Year), the Carrera 4 Coupé represented good value for money with its all-wheel-drive system, comfort, ride and handling, and with Porsche's renowned build quality. Even at launch, the entire first year's production of the Carrera 4 had already been sold, but was this car a success in everybody's eyes? The sales numbers may suggest otherwise, but there is one factor which cannot be denied, and that is that the Carrera 4 served as a crucially important platform on which to build future generations of 911s, but more of that in the next chapter.

Porsche Panamericana – concept study (1989)

In a press release issued at the introduction of the Panamericana at the 1989 IAA, the company announced: 'Porsche presents a study of unusual shape and technology based on the Carrera 4.' They weren't kidding.

Based on the 964 Carrera 4, the Panamericana was intended to demonstrate a forward-thinking attitude by Style Porsche, the company's design studio, and was presented to Dr Ferry Porsche as a gift on the occasion of his 80th birthday. 'Future-orientated thinking, long-term conceptual certainty, creativity and competence in technology' – these were all words used to enhance the Panamericana concept in the corporate press release.

Loved by some and hated by many, the Panamericana nevertheless represented an important step in Porsche's thinking at a time

BELOW An American 911 Carrera 4 3.6 Coupé (1992 Model Year).

when Ulrich Bez and Harm Lagaay had just arrived at the company. Hired to breathe new life into the 911 following a rather disappointing phase in the company's sales history, the Bez/Lagaay Panamericana was probably intended to test public reaction more than anything else.

Through this announcement, the company wanted to draw on the strength and endurance associated with the Carrera Panamericana road race of the 1950s to demonstrate the creative alternatives in automobile construction in providing 'answers to the demands of the times in the future, using path-finding technology and intelligent detail solutions'.

Dramatic it certainly was, beautiful it certainly was not, as the Panamericana was stylistically a mixture of several schools of thought. The sweeping roof line which tapered down to the rear fenders offered an interesting alternative for consideration and could have won over some critics in time. Front end treatment smacked of some 928 design cues with its sunken headlamps, while the rear end similarly looked a little confusing, if not un-Porsche-like. The least attractive aspect of the car was the rather aggressive open wheel styling, which made the car look more like a beach buggy on steroids than anything else. Various roof configurations were possible – hardtop, Targa, convertible and coupé – offering a versatile style of driving.

BELOW The Porsche Panamericana was certainly controversial in its styling – the concept did not progress.

As an overall concept, it provided much food for thought although some of the styling touches looked out of place on any vehicle that was hoping to offer up some ideas as a future 911. Having said that, as a design study it certainly had merit and, perhaps, with a sympathetic hand it may have gone further.

The 911 Carrera 2 Typ 964 (1990)

If the Carrera 4 had been a success, its younger brother was an even bigger success. For many, the Carrera 2 represented a purer form of Porsche motoring, with its traditional rear-engined, rear-wheel drive layout. If this is what a customer wanted in their car, then they had the added bonus of a car which weighed 220lb (100kg) less than its all-wheel-drive brother, and at an introductory price (August 1989) of DM103,500 it was a full DM13,100 cheaper as the Carrera 4 had increased by over DM2,000 since its launch in August 1988.

Including all body shapes, coupé, Targa and cabriolet, the Carrera 2 sold 32,766 units while the Carrera 4 sold only 19,484 examples in a twelve-month longer period, a situation which was no doubt influenced by some of the factors mentioned above.

On the question of body aerodynamics, the company had this to say: 'On the subject of aerodynamics of the 911, lift is just as important as drag. Reducing lift via the use of front and rear spoilers as well as special modifications to the underbody is of paramount importance.'

Through the measures adopted by the engineers, the drag coefficient of the Carrera 2 and 4 was reduced from 0.395 to 0.32, a significant reduction.

Introduced on the Carrera 2 was a brand-new automatic gearbox with manual override called the Tiptronic. Taken from a company press release at the time of the car's launch, 'The new Porsche Tiptronic that was designed especially for the 911 Carrera 2 opens up new dimensions in 911 motoring.' This new piece of technology relied on the experience gained with the Porsche dual-clutch (PDK) used in the successful 962 C competition model.

The console-mounted shifter is operated along one of two parallel channels. In fully automatic

mode, with the selector in the left channel, the car can be driven in the normal and familiar P-R-N-D-3-2-1 sequence. In this mode, the adaptive program control of the Tiptronic senses the way the car is driven, avoiding the drawbacks usually found with automatic gearboxes, particularly with unwanted upshifts when cornering, as all shifting operations are carried out under load. By slipping the shifter into the right channel, the driver could operate the automatic 'box manually, by simply tipping the shifter forward for upshifts, and backwards for downshifts. This offered the driver the best of both worlds, as one could languish in heavy traffic relying on the automatic mode and saving on the clutch-work, or feel the power in a conventional way by only changing gear when the driver needed to.

The Carrera 2 made use of the same double ignition power plant as the Carrera 4, as was inspired by Porsche's aircraft engine technology. Externally, the Carrera 2 is indistinguishable from its all-wheel-drive brother save for a prominent '2' or '4' next to the Carrera lettering on the engine lid.

In essence, some supporters in the Porsche two-wheel-drive camp saw the Carrera 2 as the spiritual successor to the Carrera 3.2 of 1984. While you could argue the pros and cons of two-wheel versus four-wheel-drive format on the same vehicle for many hours, the truth is that the Carrera 4 represented a major technological step forward for the company, which served to elevate the Porsche marque into the top echelons of the sports car world. If you didn't want that, then you could buy the Carrera 2 and save yourself some money in the process!

The 911 Carrera RS Coupé (1992)

Made only in the Model Year 1992, the Carrera RS boasted an even more powerful version of the same 3.6-litre boxer engine, classified by the media as a 'lightweight super sports version of the Carrera 2'. Tracing its roots back to the legendary Carrera RS 2.7 of 1972, this rear-wheel-drive Carrera RS amounted to little more than what could be called

a street-legal 'Cup' model, which in marketing terms was the base model for their homologated GT race car.

In Porsche terms, less normally means more, because if the car contains less by way of comfort and luxury, then it is more likely intended for sporting purposes which translates into higher performance and higher spec, and therefore more money. Carrying a price premium of DM26,330 over the C2 Coupé in March 1992, the Carrera RS came in at a weighty DM145,450. For your money, you got the same blueprinted engine as in the Cup model, producing 260bhp (10bhp up on the C2), and the same gearbox as the 964 C2, but it came with an uprated limited slip differential as used in the 911 Turbo. The RS was fitted with the Turbo's larger ventilated and perforated brake discs and the race-proven brake system of the Cup car. There was no underbody protection, no sound proofing, no rear seats and the interior trim was limited to a cloth covering with floor mats.

FAR LEFT Carrera 2 3.6 featuring the optional Tiptronic gearbox (1990 Model Year).

FAR LEFT BELOW The 911 Carrera 2 3.6 Cabriolet 'Turbolook' was very popular in America. This is a 1993 model, capable of 160mph (255km/h).

BELOW The potent 911 Carrera RS 3.6 Coupé (1992) which now developed 260bhp.

The Carrera RS weighed in at about 10 per cent less than the Carrera 2, being fitted with a lightweight aluminium front lid and rear bumper as well as thinner side glass, it tipped the scales at 2,712lb (1,230kg), a saving of around 386lb (175kg). Porsche referred to this diet as 'dispensing with extra comfort elements'. The extendable/retractable rear engine cover spoiler was retained as this had proven advantages for engine cooling and aerodynamics. The bodyshell was seam-welded for extra rigidity.

Although the increase in engine output appears marginal at best, combined with the remapping of the engine management, a lightened flywheel, wider 17-inch Cup-design magnesium wheels and lower profile rubber, performance was significantly enhanced. The top speed was 162mph (260km/h) and 0–62mph was achieved in just 5.3 seconds (Carrera 2: 5.7 seconds).

The road-going Carrera RS obviously did not carry a roll cage and steering had no power assistance, while a more comfortable 'Touring' version of this model offered power-assisted steering. The suspension in the base model was the same as fitted to the Cup car and the ride height was a full 40mm lower than the standard C2 car, enhancing the sense of speed by being lower to the ground. With the stiffer suspension and lack of soundproofing, road noise was amplified in the cabin, thereby enhancing the sporting intention of the Carrera RS.

The Porsche Carrera RS made its world debut at the Birmingham Motor Show in September 1991 and although the company originally planned to build 1,800 cars, over 2,000 of this model were built in total through the summer of 1991 and into 1992. The Carrera RS was aimed at the Group N GT class for the 1992 season.

Media reaction to the car was mixed. Some did not like the harsh ride saying that for a road car it was unacceptable on the country roads of Britain, while others said that it was a pity that the production numbers were to be limited. *Performance Car* probably summed it up best, reporting that during the 20 years of Carrera development since the introduction of the first

BELOW A pair of 964-series 911 Carrera RS Coupés. (Author)

911 Carrera, Porsche had turned a 'wild ride into an even wilder ride, but the handling was more developed and forgiving.'

The 911 Carrera 4 '30 Jahre 911' (1993)

To commemorate the 30th anniversary of the 911, Porsche launched the 'Thirty 911 Years' model in 1993, based on the Carrera 4 with Turbo attributes. This combined the technical advantages of electronic and dynamically controlled four-wheel drive together with the widened body of the Turbo model and 17-inch Cup wheels, to underline the sporting elegance of the model.

The fixed rear spoiler of the Turbo body was replaced with the extendable spoiler of the Carrera 2/4, retaining the classic 911 silhouette. Performance figures of the 3.6-litre boxer engine remained the same at 250bhp and a top speed of 158mph (255km/h) with the 0–62mph sprint being covered in a sporting 5.7 seconds.

The exterior was given a new anniversary body colour, viola metallic, specially created in the Porsche Design Studio for the occasion. Below the silver '911' engine cover badge was the wording '30 Jahre', unmistakably setting this limited model apart from the normal range.

The interior also came in for an upgrade, fitting for an anniversary model. Full leather trim in a new anniversary interior colour, Rubicon Grey, included steering wheel and gear knob, while the dial facings were also finished in grey to match the leather. Embossed on the folding rear seat backs was the '911' script in celebration of this special model. A metal plaque set on the rear parcel shelf carried the number of each car built in this special series – a total of only 911 cars in anniversary trim were built. Other cars with combinations of these individual attributes would make up the series total of 1,500 vehicles.

The 911 Carrera RS 3.8 Coupé (1993)

Just when everyone thought the flat-six boxer engine had reached its limit at 3,600cc, the Porsche engineers did a little bit more stretching, which, for an engine that started life as a 2.0-litre

ABOVE A Porsche 911 Carrera 2 3.6 Cup car for the Carrera Cup Championships (1991).

ABOVE Ferry Porsche with his oldest son, Ferdinand Alexander in 1993. On the left is a 1963 2.0-litre 911 Coupé and on the right, a 3.6-litre 911 Carrera 4 Coupé (1993 Model Year) representing 30 years of 911.

with planned development up to 2.7 litres, is some achievement. With motorsport never very far from the minds of the Porsche engineers, it was inevitable when they produced the Carrera RS 3.8 that it would end up on the race track, and it was therefore fitting that this model was developed and built by hand at the Porsche Race Sport Department. With the 1993 Carrera 2 as the starting point, Porsche had to make at least 50 road-going cars in order to qualify this new model for the German ADAC GT Cup, which served as the basis for a motor racing variant to come, the Carrera RSR 3.8.

While retaining the same stroke of 76.4mm, the bore was increased to 102mm to produce an engine capacity of 3,746cc, or 3.8-litre in marketing terms. Power output was up 15 per cent on the 3.6-litre RS, coming in at a storming 300bhp, and this boost was not achieved by means of a simple boring out exercise on the workbench to increase capacity, as it involved a rather more intricate engineering solution. An improved intake system with six individual throttle flaps combined with larger inlet and exhaust valves and a slightly higher compression ratio all resulted in a much more powerful engine. The RS 3.8 pistons were

lighter than those in the 3.6 engine, and a new Motronic engine management system developed by Bosch improved the timing of ignition and fuel metering, with the RS 3.8 laid out to use 98 octane or 'Super Plus' quality fuel.

Gone was the extendable rear spoiler of the C2 and C4 models, and mounted in its place was a veritable armchair of a spoiler, rising almost to roof height and ensuring that the back end stayed firmly planted on the road, with the bold inscription 'RS 3.8' impressed on its side supports. The Carrera RS 3.8 could do the 0–62mph dash in 4.9 seconds, topping out at 169mph (272km/h). Front brakes were taken from the 911 Turbo 3.6 while the rear units came from the racing version of the 1992 Carrera RS. The brake calipers, visible through the wheels, were painted red to indicate their high performance potential. The Carrera RS 3.8 was shod with massive 235/40 ZR 18 rubber up front and 285/35 ZR 18 at the back.

The 1993 RS 3.8 shared some of the suspension modifications of the Carrera RS 3.6, but the Turbo-style wide-fender body received lighter aluminium doors, and despite heavier brakes and larger tyres, it weighed in just less than the earlier model, at 1,210kg (2,668lb). Inside, comfort was restricted to a pair of Recaro bucket seats, thin carpet trim and fabric looped door pulls and out went the central locking, alarm, electric windows, door trim and sound insulation, while power-assisted steering was also omitted. The options list, however, included an airbag and a radio, although the latter seemed pretty pointless given the absence of any soundproofing. The standard Carrera RS 3.8 Coupé was offered at a monstrous DM225,000 and at that price, understandably, there weren't many made (estimates range from anything between 55 and 100 cars).

For those wishing to use their car competitively, a more sporty Club Sport version was available which included a roll cage, six-point racing harness, a fire extinguisher system and competition brake pads.

The early-mid 1990s saw a resurgence in GT racing which had sadly been lacking for the best part of a decade. With increased competition from Ferrari, McLaren, Lotus, Lister and Jaguar, Porsche needed to have a worthy mount on the grid in order to be noticed at these events around Europe and in the UK.

Enter the Carrera RSR 3.8, which was nothing other than an all-out racing car. Prepared by the factory, the RSR 3.8 could be delivered to the track in a race-ready, 'just-add-driver' form. Just such a car won the GT class at Le Mans in 1993 and the Spa 24-Hour race of the same year. The pure-bred Carrera RSR 3.8 was an altogether different animal, with a racing chassis and fully adjustable Bilstein shock absorbers, Turbo S brakes with retuned ABS and competition brake pads as well as cockpit-adjustable anti-roll bars. The engine of this car was further tweaked and fitted with racing cams, the output varying from 325bhp to 375bhp, depending on track requirements. The top speed was a mighty 181mph (291km/h) and the 0–62mph blast took just 4.7 seconds. Production of this awesome racing machine in 1993, ran to just 45 cars.

The 964 – pinnacle of 911 development?

Many 911 supporters, both within the Zuffenhausen works and outside, felt that with the 964 the end of the line had come for that much-loved and most recognisable of sports car shapes. Packed to the gunnels with new innovations, all-wheel-drive technology and aerodynamic efficiency, there were those who thought that the immortal 911 had lost some of its original charm in its quest for high-tech advancement.

On his arrival as head of Research & Development, Ulrich Bez was faced with the challenge of convincing the Supervisory Board at Porsche that the 911 had indeed not reached its development ceiling, but that there was further potential possible for the model. In fact, the 964's successor, the 993, would usher in a whole new generation of development for the Porsche 911.

BELOW The awesome 911 Carrera RS 3.8 Coupé (1993) developed a magical 300bhp and had a top speed of 170mph (270km/h).

TIMELINE:

1993	**1995**	**1996**	**1998**	**2000**	**2003**
993-series launched October.	Carrera RS 3.8 introduced January.	996-series launched October.	Dr Ferry Porsche dies.	911 Millennium model.	911 40th anniversary model.

CHAPTER EIGHT

Carrera – a new beginning

'Life itself, in so many ways, is a race. None of us seems to have enough time to accomplish what we would like to do. And if you are not ready, if you are not prepared, life will go on. You will be left behind. Sadly, the finish comes all too soon, and we are left to reflect on our victories and failures. And what we might have done differently.'

Porsche Cars North America Inc.

The decade of the 1990s was undoubtedly the period which saw one of the fastest growth spurts in the popularity of the super sports car. A large proportion of those people who bought into the sports car culture then, were younger buyers who had made it big during the years of prosperity at the end of the 1980s and the start of the 1990s. Between the years 1988 and '90, the world saw a boom in the field of investment cars and rare vintage cars, during which time the price of a previously rather ordinary Jaguar saloon rose from £3,000 to £30,000, while the price of a 911 Carrera RS 2.7 reached the dizzy heights of £120,000, which in 1990s money, was a staggering amount.

The car park of a stock brokers' firm contained more super cars than any sports car dealership could ever hope to have on its showroom floor, and if you attached the word 'classic' to a car you were selling, you could almost be assured of fetching a substantially higher price for it. This trend reached fever pitch in the early 1990s before tumbling inevitably, down to relative normality once again. However, many previously conservative drivers, through perhaps a higher than normal income level at this time, were now able to consider other higher performing cars on the market, than they might otherwise have done in the past. Names like Ferrari, Lamborghini, Porsche as well as some British and American makes were suddenly to be found on doctors' and lawyers' driveways and the attitude towards sports cars became one of investment, rather than just leaving these cars to the performance-orientated driver.

As a result, far more 'ordinary' folk, young and old, men and women included, as opposed to only motorsport-minded enthusiasts, began to drive performance cars and the manufacturers had to be mindful of this, because not everyone had the driving ability that was needed to handle these powerful machines. Technical features such as anti-lock brakes (ABS) were found on more and more

OPPOSITE Porsche 911 Carrera 3.6 Cabriolet, 1995 model year.

149

vehicles, and Ferraris even had electric windows
and electric seats. Although the Porsche 911 had
offered these features for some time, the number
of business executives driving these high
performance vehicles began to increase in the early
1990s, thanks to the boom years of the late '80s.
As the profile of the sports car owner continued to
change, manufacturers of high-performance
sports cars had to offer increasingly more creature
comforts, a feature that had previously been
foreign to cars in this market segment.

For Porsche, the latest model in their now
30-year old 911 family line, represented by their
new 993 model, saw the company responding
to a new breed of Porsche owner, a far more
demanding and sophisticated driver of the 1990s.

The 993-series (1994–98)

911 Carrera

For the Stuttgart manufacturer, the Porsche 993
represented, once again, a significant step forward
for the trusty 911. Still sporting the tried-and-

tested 3.6-litre boxer engine, the engineers
produced a model which was more of the right
stuff as far as the Porsche enthusiast was concerned.

Introduced in October 1993 at the International
Automobile Exhibition (IAA), Frankfurt, the new
993 Carrera (1994 Model Year) could be had first
in coupé form and then in cabriolet style, from
March 1994. The 911 Carrera Coupé as it was
officially known, had a reduced front fender
height, sculpted wheelarches, widened body with
the headlights flatter and raked back, while the
front of the car bore a striking resemblance to the
legendary 959. The engine had a revised intake
system, free-flow exhaust, hydraulic lifters, new
electronics and a multitude of internal changes
boosting power output to 272bhp.

Initially, the 993 Carrera as it became known
to the outside world before long, was introduced
only in rear-wheel-drive format. This model was
the first recipient of the all-new multi-link rear
axle concept featuring the LSA system (light-
stable-agile) and it also boasted the revised ABS 5
anti-lock brake system. For the first time in a

Porsche production model, the 911 now came standard with a six-speed manual transmission. Airbags were standard for both driver and front passenger and newly developed ellipsoid headlights were styled in the traditional round, 911 style.

A more powerful version of the 911 Carrera, the Exclusive, was introduced in 1994 with power up to 282bhp, and the Porsche Motorsport Weissach model which developed 300bhp, thanks to a larger, 3,746cc engine.

It proved to be a busy time for the staff in Stuttgart in 1994 with the introduction of the 911 Carrera 4 Coupé and Cabriolet in August of that year (1995 Model Year), both of which used the same 3.6-litre engine as the earlier 911 Carrera. Power was up to 285bhp from the same motor, but of course, the all-wheel-drive capabilities of the Carrera 4 were well known. The Coupé was priced at DM132,950, while the Cabriolet was pegged at DM150,800.

Although the Cabriolet was substantially more expensive than the Coupé, it occupied an important place in the range. Incorporating an ingenious electrically folding roof, the Cabriolet was popular in the all-important American market. Even at its top speed of 168mph (270km/h), with the convertible hood raised, extra body strengthening ensured the car remained stable, providing the occupants with a comfortable ride.

Crucially, the Cabriolet could now be offered as a 2+2 thanks to a new passenger restraint system

BELOW The rear seats of the cabriolet now featured seat restraints (1993), in response to demand for this, largely in the USA. This model is a 911 Carrera 2 3.6 Speedster.

installed in a belt dome in the rear. A convenient draught stop was offered as an optional extra and could be positioned automatically when the top was lowered.

The fully automatic power operation of the folding top meant that the roof could be raised or lowered in a matter of 13 seconds, although this procedure could not be carried out while on the move. Extensive work was carried out on the lines of the folding hood to ensure that when raised, the silhouette of the Cabriolet resembled that of the Coupé as closely as possible.

The 911 Carrera RS 3.8

Introduced in January 1995, the 911 Carrera RS, called a 'street-legal two-seater' in company literature, could easily be used in amateur motorsport activities. The basis for this car was the 911 Carrera, but at 1,270kg (2,800lb), the RS was a full 100kg (220lb) lighter. In typical fashion, the engineers stripped out all unnecessary clutter such

as electric windows and mirror adjustment, central locking, headlight washing system and loudspeakers. Even the windshield washer bottle came in for some dietary treatment, being trimmed from 6.5 litres to 1.2 litres, while driver and passenger airbags were optional. A further 5kg (11lb) was saved by fitting thinner window glass, the front aluminium luggage compartment lid saved 7.5kg (16lb) while the two bucket seats were 30kg (66lb) lighter.

The bore of the boxer engine was increased to 102mm, resulting in a capacity of 3.8 litres which produced a healthy 300bhp. Once again, the RS was suitably lowered to improve handling and the dynamic limited slip differential, which was optional on the Carrera, was standard on the RS. Despite a weight of 7kg (15lb), power-assisted steering was retained as this provided easier handling, while the 18-inch wheels were of the RS Cup design.

The Clubsport version of the RS was also road-legal, but obviously better suited to the track. One hundred units of this version were produced, which was the requirement for homologation into international FIA GT2 class events. Selling for DM170,650, the Clubsport featured a welded roll cage, special bucket seats, a six-point seat-belt system, main battery switch and a fire extinguisher. The engine and running gear were otherwise identical to those of the basic 911 Carrera RS, if that could be called basic. For the more serious racer, there was the 911 Carrera Cup RSR, a 3.8-litre 350bhp monster built for the tracks of Europe, and designed also for running in the SCCA and IMSA series in America.

The 911 Carrera 4S – the Business Coupé

In keeping with the opening paragraphs of this chapter, Porsche had to increasingly provide features to satisfy an ever-more demanding customer base. Entitled the 'Business Coupé' in the company's media literature, the Carrera 4S provided an exclusive blend of speed, comfort and luxury, while at the same time ensuring safety for the occupants through its all-wheel-drive system. The 4S incorporated Turbo wide-body features,

BELOW This red 993-series Porsche 911 Carrera Cabriolet was pictured in a Paris city street. The high-line third brake light was an optional extra, found mostly on American models (1994/95 Model Year). (Author)

but without the larger fixed rear spoiler, using instead the extendable Carrera spoiler.

Introduced in November 1995 (1996 Model Year), this 3.6-litre car was only built in coupé form. Positioned between the Carrera and the Turbo, the 4S represented a high level of sporting character, exclusivity and comfort, and at DM158,100 it was DM16,100 more expensive than the standard Carrera 4 Coupé.

Interior appointments, which set this model apart from the others in the 911 range, included a Porsche CR21 radio with a sound package consisting of a six-channel 150-watt amplifier and six speakers, and air conditioning sufficient to cope with everything from Arctic temperatures to tropical conditions. Importantly in this market, the 4S came equipped with a car telephone as standard (either portable or permanently installed)

as well as electrically adjustable leather seats which featured a folding, adjustable backrest and power height adjustment.

The features mentioned above confirmed that Porsche recognised the changing profile of the sports car driver in the market during the mid-'90s. No longer just a sports car for the enthusiast driver, this model had also become a tool with which the owner could conduct his or her business affairs, while at the same time conveying their status in society which was becoming an increasingly important facet of life for highfliers at the top of their profession. Porsche could not afford to sit by and watch the other supercar manufacturers pandering to the needs of this market segment without participating in it themselves, and by insisting that their cars were only aimed at the sports orientated driver. They

ABOVE Capable of 173mph (277km/h), the 911 Carrera RS 3.8 Coupé (1995) was for the serious motorist or motorsport enthusiast.

had a product which filled this niche more than adequately and, with a few simple modifications and accessories, the Carrera once again fulfilled a very important role in the 911 model range.

The 911 Carrera S – Varioram induction (1997 Model Year)

For the start of the 1997 Model Year, the 911 Carrera S was fitted with the wider front and rear bodywork of the Turbo, with a distinctive split in the extendable rear spoiler, and was also recognisable for its full-width rear light panel. One of the most important features, however, was the new Varioram induction system. Through this variable induction system, the Porsche engineers were able to boost mid-range torque, in that crucial area between 2,500rpm and 4,500rpm, by an average factor of 15 per cent. While retaining the same 3.6-litre engine capacity, power output was increased to 285bhp but with no adverse effect on fuel consumption.

From as early as the 1990 year model, the 911 engine has featured a hinged resonance flap, which

at low speeds, divides the intake system into two halves, while at engine speeds over 5,800rpm it opens, effectively doubling the volume of the system. The Varioram system further enhances this operation with sliding sleeves on the six intake pipes. Over 5,100rpm, these sleeves are pushed upwards, each uncovering an air gap and effectively shortening the length of the intake pipe, thereby changing the characteristics of the intake air. Together with a modified cam and larger intake valve sizes, the power flow was smoother than before, improving the car's everyday usability.

The owner was given the choice of a six-speed manual gearbox or the Tiptronic with optional steering wheel toggle shift. The standard model was priced at DM137,500.

Unsurprisingly then, the 993 Carrera has become one of the most sought after of the 911 classics, and for good reason. It offers the owner up-to-date technology with comfort and power in good supply with reliable performance that has been continuously developed over more than 30 years. For the purists, this has become one of the most collectable models of recent years due in no small part to the fact that it was the last of the air-cooled generation.

The 993-series ran out in 1998 which was a significant year in several ways for the Stuttgart manufacturer. Importantly, it was the company's golden anniversary which carried with it all kinds of memorable milestones, both joyous ones as well as sad ones. What had started in a timber shed in a small Austrian mountain village not long after the cessation of hostilities, and during what were very uncertain times, had not only survived but had flourished in the face of many difficulties. Porsche had conquered the motoring giants on the track more times than the competition would like to remember, silenced its critics in the market and in the process created many firsts in the automotive industry.

The tiny 1,100cc air-cooled engine of 1948 had increased over the years to a mighty 3.8 litres while retaining its unique feature. After 34 years in the market, the air-cooled boxer engine was about to be confined to the history books, as technology and European engine regulations had decreed that

it was too noisy. On the horizon, however, was a new generation of Porsche sports cars and engines to follow on the great tradition.

Evolution of the species – photographic profile of the Porsche Carrera

This brief photographic account tells a story of the development of the Porsche shape and style from the late-1950s through to the late-1990s. In the top view of the cars, it can be clearly seen how the length of the vehicle has increased over this period, as well as the width and general bulk of the car. In 1959, the 356 B Carrera had a 1,600cc four-cylinder engine developing around 100bhp, but by 1993 this had more than doubled to 3,600cc while the power output had nearly trebled to 272bhp. The latter car was packed with modern passenger safety equipment, better suspension and much greater interior space for the more sophisticated buyer of the 1990s

Comparing the rear-end shots of each model, the width factor is even more evident as much wider tyres provided unimaginable levels of lateral

BELOW The 1998 Porsche family line up – front row, left to right: 911 Carrera S 3.6, 911 Carrera 3.4 Coupé and 911 Targa 3.6. Back row, left to right: 911 Carrera 4S 3.6, 986 Boxster 2.5 Roadster and 911 Turbo 3.6.

BELOW Top view of
Porsche models from
1959-1993: 356 B 1600
GS Carrera GT (1960),
911 2.0 Coupe (1963),
911 Carrera 3.2 Coupe
(1987), 911 Carrera 2 3.6
Coupe (1989) and 911
Carrera 3.6 Coupe
(1993).

OPPOSITE Rear and side
view of Porsche models
from 1959-1993: 356 B
1600 GS Carrera GT
(1960), 911 2.0 Coupe
(1963), 911 Carrera 3.2
Coupe (1987), 911
Carrera 2 3.6 Coupe
(1989) and 911 Carrera
3.6 Coupe (1993).

grip and stability when compared with its older relative from 1959. Modern safety regulations have resulted in an increased glass area as well as rear light clusters, but the heritage is unmistakable. It is interesting to note the small and high-placed rear windshield on the 356 B Carrera, and the much larger windshields on the later models.

Perhaps the side view highlights the same basic body theme which runs through all the models, even better than the other two illustrations. A common factor between the first and last of the models shown is the curved front fender line and also the slight curve which has been brought back into the profile of engine cover. With an increase in bumper height, this has simultaneously raised the height of the rear light clusters for improved visibility.

Importantly, these five Porsche models represent the history of the air-cooled era, one of the foundations on which the company was established back in 1948. All-in-all, when one considers that the 993-series was manufactured until 1998, almost forty years separate these five generations of cars. It is even more amazing to think, when one looks at all three photographs in this study, that in all that time, the same basic shape has been retained – and that is because it was just so good, right from the outset. The aerodynamic efficiency of the 356-series has been carried through into the new millennium which

says so much for its founding father, Ferry Porsche, and indeed his father, Ferdinand Porsche as well.

The 996-series Porsche 911 Carrera (1997–2004)

The Typ 996, or 911 Carrera, was introduced to the European market in October 1997 and a year later in America to allow for both Coupé and Cabriolet to be launched there simultaneously. First offered in rear-wheel-drive Coupé form only in 1997, the cabriolet body was introduced at the 1998 Geneva Motor Show.

Following the launch of the original 901/911 in 1963, most of the subsequent 911 developments had been an evolution or upgrade of the previous model being replaced. Admittedly, the 964 and 993 Carreras had both been significant upgrades, but even the 993, which was a big step on from the 964, had been an evolutionary development. When the design engineers at Porsche were considering the styling of the 993 in the early 1990s, the desire was there to create a new car, not just an upgrade of the old 964. For various reasons that never happened. However, with the requirements that any future model in the Porsche model line-up would have to have an entirely new engine with plumbing for water cooling and not air cooling, now seemed as good a time as any to totally redesign and reconfigure the 911 model.

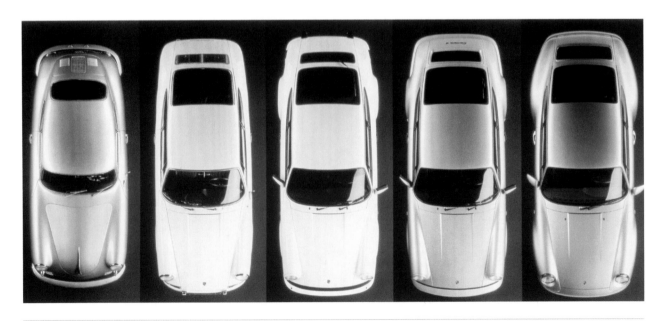

ABOVE The launch of the Porsche 911 Carrera 3.4 Coupé – IAA Frankfurt, 1997.

The demands placed on the design engineers, and indeed all the engineering disciplines involved with the new model, were made more complex by the requirement that the new car must still be easily recognisable as a 911. Financially, this placed huge pressure on the company as they were busy with a second model development at the same time, the Boxster (Typ 986), and together these two models would stretch resources to their absolute limit.

In order to accomplish this, the first aspect to come under review was the management of the two projects, and so a new approach called Simultaneous Engineering was developed to cope with these challenges. This integrated network process brought together all engineering and production faculties at the company including some of their external suppliers, in an effort to streamline supply and production even further. This development, which was really the application of improved management principles, but extended into the production domain, shaved almost 20 per cent off the production time for the new 911 model. One of the areas in which it was possible to do this was by shortening the assembly lines at Stuttgart-Zuffenhausen by getting parts

supplied as complete assemblies, such as a fully assembled front axle instead of all the components being delivered separately for assembly on the main production line.

While the new 911-variant would not utilise any of the components from the outgoing 993, the new 911 Carrera Typ 996 would have to share some of its engineering and component costs with the other project, Typ 986, being developed at the same time. This requirement in itself would also provide its own challenges as the Typ 986 was to have a smaller engine, totally different configuration (mid-engined) and appeal to a totally different market segment, and, as a result, was in a different price budget.

Although being developed simultaneously, there was no question that the 911/996 would not take priority as the lead project, should the need to apportion resources arise. Despite this announcement by the factory, it was the Typ 986 Boxster that made it to the showrooms a full year earlier (October 1996) than the Typ 996. Porsche cited 'commercial reasons' as the rationale for this development, although good Boxster sales would certainly help in the final development of the all-important new 911 Carrera.

Nevertheless, the two models shared many components and panels in the early stages as the engineers rose to the challenge of developing two models simultaneously, and this is why the front ends looks so similar. But that is where the similarity ends, as from the A-pillar rearwards, the 996 is a totally different animal. The brief was to recreate the classic 911 in a modern style, but in order to do this the body had to be lengthened, widened and made higher than any previous 911. Normally that would mean that it would also be heavier, but in actual fact the 996 was 80kg (176lb) lighter than its predecessor. With interior comfort improved due to the large overall dimensions, the rear parcel shelf could also be extended further backwards thanks to the absence of the cooling fan over the engine.

Correct body dimensions were crucial to the success of the new 911, because not only did this have to satisfy stricter passive passenger safety requirements but in achieving this it could not be

any less aerodynamic than its predecessor. Ultimately, the length was increased by a substantial 185mm and the width by 30mm, and yet amazingly, the drag coefficient was down from 0.34 to 0.30. This was only the second time that the 911 had been 'stretched' during the course of its 34-year history (up until 1997), the first such occasion being in August 1968 (1969 Model Year) where 57mm was added to the wheelbase to improve straight line stability.

The roof line of the 996 peaked over the driver's head instead of where it joined the windscreen as in the 993 and all other 911s before it, allowing a windshield angle of 60° instead of 55°. Fender curves were bigger but smoother than on previous models, eliminating that 'stuck on' look, which helped with the streamlining of the 996 body. The lines of the longer car called for a higher tail-end design which aided drag reduction and gave more room in the engine compartment. This move allowed for a more modern rear light arrangement

BELOW The first press photograph of the new 911 Carrera 3.4 Coupé (Typ 996), pictured in Spain, February 1997.

featuring higher placed individual light clusters which replaced the slimline style that had been with the car since the '60s.

The extendable rear spoiler operated in the same way as it had done on the 993, except it now raised at speeds above 75mph (120km/h) and not 50mph (80km/h) as before. Although the chassis and suspension were fabricated largely from aluminium, the body was an all-steel construction utilising the hot-galvanising process first introduced back in 1976. Static torsional stiffness was vastly improved on the 996 – up by 45 per cent on its predecessor, thanks also to the bonded-in front and rear windshields, the only robotised process on the Zuffenhausen assembly line.

In the engine room, Porsche developed a new unit of smaller capacity, 3,387cc, but which developed a maximum output of 300bhp, 15bhp up on the 993. With a top speed of 174mph (280km/h), fuel consumption was down by approximately 10 per cent. It had been expected with the new water-cooled engine that fuel consumption would be improved and engine noise would be lower, thanks to the cooling effect and sound-deadening properties of water circulating in the block.

Dispensing with the large and noisy cooling fan, which sat on top of the previous engine, meant that the new engine was far more compact being both 70mm shorter and 120mm lower than its predecessor. The new engine not only satisfied the noise pollution regulations but provided a platform for improved fuel consumption, while for the engineers it also opened the door for the introduction of four-valve technology. Engine management is performed by digital motor electronics (DME) and as this new motor is devoid of any conventional ignition distributor, ignition voltage flows directly from six individual coils to the spark plugs.

Water cooling required the radiators to be located up front, ahead of the front axle. Cars fitted with a six-speed gearbox needed two radiators, located left and right, while cars fitted with the new five-speed Tiptronic S transmission had an additional radiator located centrally to assist with the cooling of the transmission fluid. All this extra plumbing called for a larger coolant capacity, 22.5 litres to be exact, which carried with it a weight penalty.

Right up to and including the Typ 993, the 911 cabin and dashboard had always been a bit plain

BELOW The Porsche 911 Carrera 3.4 Cabriolet (left) and with hardtop fitted (right).

and simple – certainly unadorned, would describe it adequately. And there was good reason for this, because people who drove Porsche sports cars were more interested in the car's capabilities and were therefore more concerned with drivability and performance. But that was up until the mid '90s, when more high-earners began to see the Stuttgart-cars as a suitable alternative in the credibility stakes to some Italian models. The 993 Carrera dashboard certainly showed a marked improvement over its predecessors, but it still possessed that unmistakeable '60s architecture. To move into the supercar territory suitable for high street posing, would require some significant changes, and this the 996 did most impressively.

Two important features have remained as the hallmark of the Porsche 911 dashboard. These are that all-important location of the ignition switch, left of the steering column, and the five circular dials facing the driver, the latter being a requirement set in concrete many years before by Ferry Porsche himself. The dials in the 996 were unmistakably there in their required format, even though a little squashed together, but this was necessary due to the fitment of the Porsche communication management system (PCM)

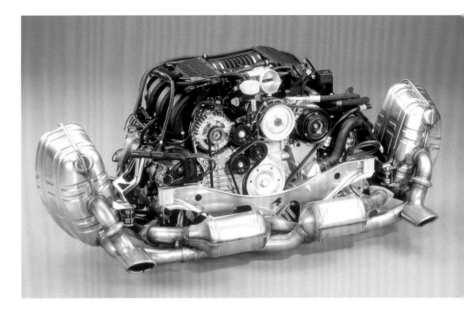

centre stage. Developed in conjunction with Siemens, the PCM served as the communication system for the radio, air-conditioning controls, electronic computer display for fuel consumption and day/date/time information, the integrated car phone system and, of course, the satellite navigation system. Gone was the plain and simple Porsche dashboard of the '60s, and in its place was a

ABOVE The new Carrera 3.4-litre flat-six water-cooled engine (1998).

BELOW The interior of the 911 Carrera 3.4 took on a whole new look as the 996-series had to satisfy a new brand of highly sophisticated consumers (1998 Model Year).

BELOW LEFT The Paris Salon 1998 – in the foreground is the 911 Carrera 4 3.4 Cabriolet.

command and control centre at least equal to, and in many cases better than, most other supercar nameplates. At DM5,900 the PCM was not cheap, but it was everything the sophisticated owner could want in a car that would serve as a comfortable grand tourer, as well as a 'business coupé'.

The 911 Carrera – 1998 onwards

October 1998 saw the introduction of the four-wheel-drive version of the 996-series, the 911 Carrera 4. Fitted with the same 3.4-litre engine, the 911 Carrera 4 was offered in both coupé

(DM147,640) and cabriolet (DM166,160) forms. For their money, cabriolet buyers also received a very striking, graceful-looking, detachable aluminium hardtop. For the first time, the prospective Carrera 4 buyer also had the choice of Tiptronic or six-speed manual transmission. With such a tantalising list of choices and alternatives, Porsche was really announcing to their prospective customers that they could rival anything the other major sports car manufacturers might offer.

As the end of the century approached, the Stuttgart marketers planned to offer the top

FERRY PORSCHE

Sadly, the 996-series Carrera was to be the last model introduction that Ferry Porsche was to witness, as he died on 27 March 1998, less than two weeks after the Geneva Show closed. In some ways it was fitting that he had seen the introduction of the all-new 996, the most comprehensive restyling and engineering exercise carried out on the 911 since its dramatic entrance 35 years earlier. It is fair to say that the 996 was as new a vehicle as the 901/911 was, when it was launched at the IAA in Frankfurt in September 1963.

Ferry had seen countless innovations, upgrades, improvements and technological advances made to the immortal 911 over the years. He had seen sales rise, sales fall and he even presided over the Porsche family voluntarily withdrawing from the operational management of the company that he had helped to establish. Very few industrialists are able to experience the golden anniversary of the company they have founded and helped to shape, and yet Ferry Porsche could be proud of the progress that his company had made during those 50 golden years.

BELOW Ferry Porsche casts an approving look over the awesome 911 GT1 on a visit to Weissach. This is one of the last photographs of the great man (1997).

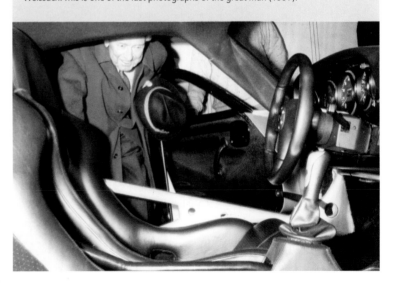

Carrera 4 as a special edition 'Millennium' model. Billed as the 911 Carrera 4 Millennium, this model came equipped with sports suspension and 18-inch wheels. Finished in chrome viola, trimmed with an all-leather interior with dark maple wood touches, only 911 of these special models were produced. Only available in coupé form, this limited edition cost a weighty DM185,000.

From the 2000 Model Year onwards, the 911 Carrera received improved 'tear-drop' front headlamps, a more attractive proposition than the original Boxster lights. But the biggest improvement to the Carrera range early in the new millennium was in the engine bay, when in August 2001 (2002 Model Year) the engine displacement was boosted to 3,596cc, or 3.6-litre in marketing terms. This was achieved by lengthening the stroke to 82.8mm while retaining the same bore dimension of 96mm, and this new

power plant was immediately available in both coupé and cabriolet models. Power in this new engine was up through the magical 300bhp barrier, to an awesome 320bhp with a top speed of 174mph (280km/h). Increased power also came from the innovative VarioCam Plus system of inlet-cam timing and lift, and further optimised fuel consumption.

The summer of 2001 proved a busy time for the factory as they not only introduced a new engine, but in September, the all-wheel-drive 996 Carrera 4 was launched, again in both coupé and cabriolet form. The Carrera cabriolet version had matured into a wonderfully attractive car, which for the 911 was reflected in the higher sales of the cabriolet in both the two-wheel and four-wheel-drive versions. Refreshingly, the Carrera Cabriolet was not just a chopped version of the coupé model like many other cars on the market, rather this was a well-constructed,

ABOVE For the year 2000, Porsche produced a special version of the 911 – the 911 Carrera 3.4 Millennium model.

ABOVE For 2002, the 911 Carrera 4 received a new, bigger, 3.6-litre engine and distinctive 'tear-drop' front headlamps.

The 40th anniversary 911 Carrera (Model Year 2004)

Appropriately, only 1,963 cars of this rather special model were built in commemoration of the year in which the 911 was first introduced to the public. Available only in exclusive GT Silver Metallic, the anniversary model was not only a 'looker', it also had an uprated motor producing 345bhp and a top speed of 180mph (290km/h) with 0–62mph in 4.9 seconds. Amazingly, with this enhanced performance, the '40 Jahre 911' anniversary model still returned a respectable 26mpg (11 litres/100km) on the motorway.

The '40 Jahre 911' anniversary car also featured a 10mm lowered suspension and was equipped as standard with Porsche stability management (PSM). This automatic control system stabilises the vehicle in extreme driving situations by selectively braking individual wheels, and can be manually switched off to allow the driver a more active driving experience if so desired.

Enlarged front air vents with lateral air intake grilles are painted to match the car's special colour finish, while 911 Turbo flared sills and 18-inch Carrera wheels add to the distinctive styling. Inside the cabin, the anniversary edition's sport seats with a two-level seat heater are standard equipment. As part of the deal, your anniversary 911 Carrera came with two exclusive, fitted leather suitcases, handmade in dark grey natural leather to match the car's interior.

For just €95,616, the '40 Jahre 911' anniversary model surely represented a golden opportunity for any self-confessed Porschephile to buy into a piece of the Stuttgart company's history.

Market sentiment

That not everyone would be entirely happy with the 996 was to be expected, but this feeling was not based on a sense that the newcomer was technologically inferior or lacking in any way at all. The idea that the new 996 was 'soft' came from those diehards who still revelled in the unpredictability and the out-and-out sporting character of the air-cooled forerunner, and that unmistakable flat-six sound which they had grown

suitably strengthened, dedicated model that benefited from extensive design and styling work by the Porsche design staff.

Always keen to satisfy the American market, Porsche had found that their Carrera models had consistently sold well when fitted with the 'Turbolook' body. Research revealed that in addition to the much lower price of the non-Turbo cars in the States, popularity for this model was boosted by the substantially lower insurance premiums that went with this car. The wide-bodied Turbolook cars carried that same aggressive, muscular look, but without the same financial burden, and so in December 2001 Porsche introduced a special version for this market, the Carrera 4S Coupé. The 4S was more than just a Turbolook in body alone, as it had a lowered suspension and Turbo brakes to match, which together greatly enhanced road holding. It was not until September 2003 (2004 Model Year) that the Carrera 4S Cabriolet was introduced, and now, with the new European currency in effect, it was priced at €99,792.

fond of. In the 996, the engineers were careful in trying to re-create that distinctive Porsche sound which set it apart from anything else on the road, and to a large extent, they succeeded in satisfying most of the market.

The problem came from the fact that the new 911 Carrera did everything so well that there was less room for 'fun' because the sophisticated electronics kept watch over the driver and prevented them from enjoying themselves too much. The important thing for Porsche though, was that they sold cars, and the fastest growing segment of the market was quite happy to have all the new toys in their Porsches, and that was who the company had to keep happy.

Taking a slightly philosophical standpoint for the moment, the 996 was the car that Porsche needed to take it into the next century. The old 993 had, to all intents and purposes, reached its development ceiling and a new platform was needed to move the 911 on. With the 911 accounting for two thirds of

Zuffenhausen annual production, through the new 996-series, the engineers had a big responsibility to develop a car that could carry the company forward. The success of the new 911 Carrera rested not only on developing a worthy custodian of this weighty heritage, but the 996-series had also to adapt to a changing market with more sophisticated customer demands and ever-increasing technological advances.

From an examination of the media pack distributed to journalists at this car's introduction, the company spoke of its customers being active, success-orientated individuals who like to express their sportiness and communicate their particular lifestyle. In short, Porsche recognised that they had to provide what the market wanted. They saw their customers as looking for a 'business car with sporting qualities' and through the 996-series 911 Carrera, Porsche had provided a car for the 'job' of motoring that was practical enough for everyday driving comfort.

BELOW The 996-series 911 Carrera Coupé '40 Jahre 911' anniversary model (2004 Model Year).

PORSCHE
Carrera

TIMELINE:

1950-54	1955	1964	1972	1990
La Carrera Panamericana in Mexico.	356 A Carrera launched.	Porsche 911 introduced.	911 RS 2.7 launched at IAA.	Carrera Cup begins.

CHAPTER NINE

Carrera heritage – looking back

'There is a saying at Porsche that change is easy, but improvement is far more difficult.'

Porsche Cars North America Inc.

The origins of the Carrera name in Porsche terms is a special topic and fits well with the overall discussion on what this revered name has come to mean for the Stuttgart manufacturer. There are several different views on the origins of this name, but this is one time that the public relations and marketing departments did not play a role in the initial stages of the name selection process.

Traditionally, the naming of a motor car has been left to the marketing, sales, public relations or even advertising people to come up with suggestions. Usually, this task calls for much research, often involving focus groups and countless committee sessions. In the case of a small firm such as Porsche back in the 1950s, there were no such committees, or any public relations agency involvement, as there simply wasn't the money to pay for these services to be carried out externally.

As early as the 1952 Carrera Panamericana, Herbert Linge recalls fellow racing driver, Paul Alfons Fürst Metternich using the name of Carrera in the company of the Porsche technicians, suggesting that this would be a good name for a Porsche type. After this event in Mexico, Metternich suggested to Max Hoffman that the 356 models which had competed in the Mexican event should be given a name rather than merely a model number.

Hoffman had for some time tried to persuade Ferry Porsche to give the cars names rather than a numerical identification as he claimed that Americans preferred this system – numbers did not go down as well in the States as names did. It was only three years after Metternich had first suggested using Carrera as a model name that the 356 A Carrera was launched at the IAA, but at what stage that final decision was taken in the sales and marketing department is still uncertain. Although the pushrod motor had made fantastic in-roads into the record and history books, even Ferry Porsche realised that they needed a replacement racing engine as the old unit had reached its development ceiling.

It is thought that the technicians involved in the Carrera Panamericana began using the Carrera name around the factory when referring to the cars that had competed there, but even the folk within Porsche are today uncertain as to the exact commencement date of the use of this name. It is clear, however, that the name of Carrera was being used by Porsche technicians before the Fuhrmann four-cam engine had been developed. In fact, it was only in the 1954 Mille Miglia, in which Herrmann and Linge finished sixth, that the first Fuhrmann four-cam motor was officially used in a 550 race car. After a busy year of racing on the Continent, the first Fuhrmann-engined 550 was

OPPOSITE 1961 Porsche 356B Carrera Cabriolet, the only right-hand-drive car built. (Author)

ABOVE Constantin Graf von Berckheim (right), driver of Porsche 356 1500 Coupé No. 10, in discussion with a race colleague during the 1952 Carrera Panamericana.

fitted with the Fuhrmann engine, that the factory engineers considered installing the Fuhrmann four-cam motor in a normal 356 production road car. As we have seen earlier, the Fuhrmann-engined 356 A was introduced at the IAA in October 1955 and it seemed prudent at the time, in view of the recent good performance of the four-cam engine in Mexico, to call this model by the Carrera name in recognition of this achievement.

It can therefore be assumed that Carrera became a model name sometime between the 1954 Mille Miglia (May) and the 1955 IAA (September) when the 356 A 1500 GS Carrera Coupé was launched in Frankfurt. Logically, the final decision to call a 356 model by the Carrera name must have been after the Liège–Rome–Liège Rally of 1954, in which a 356 Gmünd Coupé was seen by the factory to be capable and worthy of carrying the Fuhrmann four-cam engine.

then entered in the Carrera Panamericana and achieved a remarkable third place finish. For the sake of clarity, it must be mentioned that at no stage were any of the 550 race cars ever known by the Carrera name.

It was only following the victory in the Liège–Rome–Liège event of 1954, in which one of the aluminium-bodied 356 Gmünd Coupés was

Linge remembers that Hoffman and Metternich, who were both very well known in the factory and who both had the ear of Ferry Porsche, were instrumental in persuading the company to give the four-cam 356 A a name that the public

could identify with. This would make good sales sense for Hoffman in the States where the name Carrera would make a stronger statement to the car-buying public there than 'just a bunch of numbers'. It seemed to make good sense to borrow the reputation recently earned recalls Herbert Linge, 'I remember very clearly that he [Metternich] was saying that the Carrera name would be a good name for a Porsche Typ.'

So began a tradition within the company, that the highest-performing model within the current 356 model range carried the name of Carrera, in recognition of the roots of this high-performance motor.

However, with the launch of the new 911 model in 1963, the company initiated two separate model lines for its cars – road-going cars and pure race cars. It was at this time that Porsche concentrated its efforts heavily on building up its racing pedigree, and with the introduction of the new 911 range, there was no place in this model set-up for a higher-performing road car to carry on the Carrera tradition at that time, although the 904/906 race cars did fly the Carrera flag with pride.

Not wanting to repeat any of the earlier findings already explained in this book, the two most important early factors responsible for moving the company name quickly up the ladder more than any other, were the 550 (thanks to Glöckler) and the 547 Fuhrmann engine. Together, these two products mapped out the road into the future that the company would follow. Without the performance and other racing successes that the Typ 547 four-cam engine achieved, Porsche may have taken much longer to reach international acclaim. Not to take anything away from the achievements of the pre-Carrera boxer motor or those of the later six- and eight-cylinder engines amassed, but it was unquestionably the Typ 547 motor that hit the podium first, enabling those that followed to attain the results that they then went on to achieve.

The Carrera bloodline

Tracing the bloodline of your family name has today become much easier with the advent of the Internet, and there is even software that specialises

in helping to organise your findings. When looking at a normal family, there are records that can be researched, such as birth, marriage and death certificates, that help create a family tree.

When tracing the models of a motor manufacturer, these are not always as clear, as early prototypes are often destroyed or they have served as the test bed for various models over a long period of time, just as the 'Coupé Ferdinand' had done. This task is made all the more difficult when the 'family name' is applied to both road-going and race cars, and as a result there can be some overlapping and blurring of the picture.

What started out as an unofficial name for an engine, eventually became the model name, and one of the most revered badges in the Porsche family tree at that. Following an illustrious period as the top performing model in the 356 range

during which time it built a fearsome reputation as a 'giant killer', it appeared that the Carrera name was dropped with the introduction of the new 911 model line-up in 1963. While this may seem to be the case, the Carrera name was in fact carried on very strongly in the race car line-up, adorning such models as the 904 or Carrera GTS, and the 906 or Carrera 6, which soldiered on into the late 1960s. It should also be remembered that the Carrera GTS was also available as a road car, albeit in very limited numbers. So by no means did the Carrera name disappear from the radar altogether, but the name was carried on in the racing series.

In an interview with Herbert Linge, the reason for the absence of any road-going Carrera models during the middle to late 1960s lay in the rules for the racing of sports cars. Sports car rules at that time would have made it difficult for the company to produce a road-legal sports car which was also eligible for the GT racing series at that time, and so management decided to focus their efforts where they could be assured of the most public attention – in pure GT racing.

As we have seen in earlier chapters, there were several models within the 911 range during the Sixties which did point the way towards the introduction of the legendary RS 2.7 of 1973, and these were the 'S' and 'R' models. Once the company was happy that their top road version of the 911 could be homologated for racing, they proceeded with the development of the RS 2.7, which was itself responsible for a distinguished range of Carrera models that followed.

When the final road-going Carrera RS and RSR bowed out in the late Seventies, the Carrera name did disappear for a few years from both the 911 road going and racing cars. With the introduction of the 924 Carrera GT and its siblings in 1980, some of the Zuffenhausen staff were not impressed that such a name should be given to a front-engined car whose basic power plant came from Audi, but this chapter in the company's history has to be told. In fact, the 924 GTP was placed as high as sixth in the 1980 Le Mans race and seventh the following year, which, with hindsight, goes some way towards allaying those concerns.

The Carrera name was once again dropped from the Porsche model line-up until 1983, when the

respected and much sought-after 911 Carrera 3.2 (G-series) made its entrance in coupé, cabriolet and Targa body styles, to be joined later by the potent Clubsport in 1987. With the introduction of the 911 Carrera 3.2 Coupé, Cabriolet and Targa in 1983, all the 911 variants became known as the 911 Carreras, with the one exception, that being the 911 Turbo. Some of the prominent old guard in Stuttgart-Zuffenhausen did not warm to this development as, in their view, the name of Carrera should be reserved only for the top-performing road model at any time.

To call the whole range by this hallowed name, dilutes its heritage more than just a little, and Tony Lapine agrees: 'Absolutely, in my opinion.' It was during the reign of Peter Schutz as chairman of the board of Porsche AG (1981–87), that this move took place and many felt at the time that this decision was made purely to increase sales, with little consideration for 'Porsche tradition' as another insider put it.

Lapine continues: 'It was just diluting the name, it had a fine ring, it had a place in history with Porsche cars.'

Klaus Bischof agrees: 'But, yes I would always keep the name for special cars.'

Following on where the 3.2 Carrera left off, the 964-series was introduced in 1989 in the form of the Carrera 4, and this car was most certainly

ABOVE The 911 Carrera Targa 3.2 (1984–89 Model Years) had a black Targa bar (instead of the earlier silver bar) and the rear fog lights were integrated into the light clusters rather than below the bumper. This car is fitted with a non-standard steering wheel. (Author)

OPPOSITE TOP
The Porsche Typ 356 Coupé Ferdinand (1950) proved to be a favourite with the factory staff.

OPPOSITE BOTTOM
A Porsche Carrera RS 2.7 on a parade lap during the 2004 Porsche Festival at Brands Hatch. (Author)

worthy of carrying the Carrera name, if any was. Rated as one of the company's finest cars, this model was bristling with technology and superb performance. During the reign of the Carrera 4, the other 911 derivatives were known by their own distinguishing names, such as the Turbo, Targa or simply 911.

Herbert Linge, one of the longest standing Porsche employees and who has served under more Porsche chairmen than most, feels that the name Carrera has a special place in the company's history. 'Because the Carrera was something outstanding, it should always be that way, but that is history, and today history doesn't … [count]', he muses, shaking his head.

The spirit of Porsche

Being in and around the Porsche works in Stuttgart-Zuffenhausen, it is not hard to notice the dedication with which the personnel go about their work. The sense of commitment and pride that goes with working for a company with such a rich heritage as Porsche has, is almost tangible. It is not difficult to understand this sense of belonging by the staff, as they can but admire what has been achieved by those who went before them, and who succeeded against the odds. Being able to rub shoulders or work alongside Le Mans and Targa Florio race winners (and many others besides) and to call them by their first names, can only fill one with admiration.

Porsche must boast one of the lowest staff turnover rates in the industry. 'Many children of our staff come into the company, through apprenticeships for example on the industrial side, or because of their connections to the company through a parent, and they usually stay on. We have a very long average staff membership in our company', comments Dr Heinz Rabe, who started with Porsche in 1955, rising to head of the welfare department in 1970 where he remained until his official retirement on 31 July 1995. Dr Rabe, who is still active in the community today, was destined to work at Porsche, his father being the legendary Karl Rabe, one of Dr Ferdinand Porsche's first engineers back in 1931.

Some people have looked for the hauntingly

elusive concept that makes Porsche a mystical force, but the secret of that achievement lies not in a conservative or traditional attitude. Progress would never be made in the industrial world if new methods were never put to the test, or if new thinking was always shunned in favour of following what was already known to work. Progress is that boundary which certain individuals have to push because they are never happy with the status quo. In the same way that impossible mountain slopes challenge climbers to scale their dizzy heights, so too must the industrial pioneer seek to find a better way, a more efficient way, of making his product better, cheaper, lighter or faster – in a single word, it is called progress. Professor Ferdinand Porsche was such a man, and those genes lived on in his son, Ferry.

One does not have to dig very deep to understand why Ferry Porsche has always had such a good working relationship with the racing and engineering personnel at the factory. He always had a good grasp of racing issues, because he was himself a motorsport enthusiast and understood what a racing driver wanted.

In an interview with the author, Jürgen Barth said, 'Ferry Porsche was also quite a fast driver, like his father. But I think a unique thing you find in the early Porsche history is that we always had Dr Porsche and Professor Fuhrmann standing [with us] in the Le Mans 24-Hours race, all the time, 24-hours long. Today, you don't find this anymore.'

To be the head of your company and to understand the limitations of both man and machine is a rare gift. This does not only refer to the limits of the engine, chassis, gearbox or other mechanical workings of the machine but also the ability of the driver to extract the best out of that race car under current conditions.

The company's senior management were involved in all aspects of the operation, as Jürgen Barth recalls, 'But also the important thing was in the 1950/60s, that nearly every day Dr Ferry Porsche came down to the production line, talking to the guys in there, and even to us apprentices. He came and asked: "How are you", he tried to understand everything.'

There can be little wonder why, with commitment and involvement in every aspect of

the production process by top management, that staff worked in the factory with pride. The Carrera heritage is as important as it is sensitive to the history and continuation of Porsche, and clearly the strength of this name runs through the very fabric of the company.

Today, body panels are no longer pressed on site, so they arrive at Werk 1 from an outside supplier. Body assembly and painting is all carried out in

BELOW Three close friends who worked together for many years, but who have now retired from Porsche, from left to right: Klaus Parr (Head of Porsche Historisches Archiv), Dr Heinz Rabe and Rolf Sprenger. (Author)

TOP A line of Porsche bodies is conveyed across the bridge which joins the two main assembly plants in Stuttgart-Zuffenhausen.

BOTTOM A 911 engine in the assembly process in Stuttgart-Zuffenhausen (2005).

OPPOSITE Porsche 911 Carreras being assembled at Stuttgart-Zuffenhausen (2005).

this building and once completed, the bodyshells are placed on an enclosed conveyor system that transports them high above Schwieberdinger Strasse to the main vehicle assembly plant. Sitting in the company restaurant during mealtimes, or the Casino as it is called, one can view the painted bodyshells as they make their way across the road to the assembly plant. The sides of the conveyor tunnel are enclosed in glass, allowing the motorists below to view the Porsche bodies as they move slowly across from one plant to the other, no doubt many aspiring to own such a vehicle one day.

The main Porsche assembly plant is unique in that it comprises three levels. Most other manufacturing plants are constructed in such a way that the assembly lines are as long and straight as can be accommodated on the site. For Porsche, this has been a problem as the city of Stuttgart has continued to encroach on the plant, until such time as the available ground has limited the works to the site in which it now stands. Porsche has overcome this problem by constructing a turntable or rotating jig at each end of the assembly building, so as the empty bodyshell enters the building on the third floor from the body and paint shop across the road, a lift takes the body down to the next level as it completes the assembly stages on the floor below.

Research has shown by turning the cars around to face forwards as they are lowered to the assembly line on the floor below, that for the workers, this has a positive psychological effect on the manufacturing and assembly process. It is better to work on a car which is moving forwards rather than backwards – a small example of the extent to which management has gone to ensure high manufacturing standards. This is not usually a problem with plants that have long, flat production lines. Workers in the manufacturing process are rotated frequently, as this increases corporate responsibility by individual workers to the total production process. By doing this, Porsche feels that assembly line staff will realise the impact of sub-standard work in another part of the process, as he or she might be working there at that workstation in the future.

It takes one mechanic two hours to assemble a 911 engine, as he travels together with each engine

on a moving platform at a speed of four metres per hour. Complete engines used to be signed by the mechanic who assembled them, but this was stopped in 2004 as the company found that customers from all over the world would ask for a specific mechanic who had assembled their last Porsche engine to 'please assemble my new one' – this was not always possible and so it was stopped.

With around 80,000 vehicles manufactured per annum by Porsche, only two cars a year are produced with identical specification and optional extras. Porsche is the smallest independent manufacturer in the industry, with a workforce of around 4,600 in Stuttgart, which permits the increased flexibility needed to accommodate the different demands of their customers, many of whom choose to collect their cars personally from the factory. It takes three days to produce each 911 Carrera from the individual body panel stage to a fully functional vehicle, and this includes a thorough quality control. Once each car reaches

the QC stage, a qualified engineer with many years of experience in the Porsche engineering department, takes every vehicle out on to the streets of Stuttgart on a set 30km route to check for any faults with the car, before being parked in the yard ready for dispatch. This is obviously a process that works well, as fully 60 per cent of all Porsches are still running. There is understandably, a long list of applicants for the jobs as test drivers with Porsche, but management sticks to its tried and tested method – no vacancies there, unfortunately.

'Carrera' marketing

It has been a long and winding road since the early days of the limited Porsche 356 line-up, in which new model introductions were few and far between. It seems, by comparison, that in recent times and with each passing year a new model or variant of the 911 is introduced, but the market profile of the sports car buyer today is so different

BELOW This silver 996-series 911 Carrera Cabriolet was photographed at a yacht club in Detroit, Michigan. (Author)

compared with that of the 1950s that these market peculiarities have now become a requirement in the current market. New model descriptions abounded with each new introduction, for example, the Lightweight (Leichtbau), with increased performance (Leistungssteigerung), Turbolook, 30 Jahre 911, Millennium, 40 Jahre 911, and many more.

During the tenure of Peter Schutz's chairmanship of the company, sales of Porsche cars in the USA were struggling, and a shot in the arm was needed. It is fair to say that the weakening dollar exchange rate also hurt the company's bank balance, as selling prices had to be increased in America just in order to break even, much to the displeasure of would-be buyers over there. The car, the Americans argued, had not changed that much and yet the prices had rocketed up.

Following the demise of the SC, from 1983 onwards all 911 variants, with the exception of the Turbo, were given the Carrera name. To some this was a logical step, to others it was confusing, and to still others it was an improper use of a highly respected name. As Klaus Bischof, manager of the Porsche Museum explained: 'That was decided by the marketing and sales departments who said very clearly – the 911 is now the top model.'

Bischof again: 'With the Carrera name, the logic [of the model name] for us used to be in the technical specification, now you can see it is purely marketing, and defies any logic.' Other factory staff agree, that the Carrera name was synonymous with sporty and performance orientated cars, but it has now also come to mean 'top class', in a luxury context. Controversial, perhaps, but a potentially damaging sales outlook in the 1980s called for drastic measures and so the Carrera badge played its part in the upturn in the company's sales slide, which you would argue, if you were an accountant, was successful.

However, this has also led to the strange and unforeseen situation arising where the entire range of sports cars, including the new (2003) Carrera GT, bear the name of Carrera (with the exception, of course, of the Turbo). It is easy to sit back after the decision was made and to say: 'Now look what you've done', but it would be suicidal to withdraw the Carrera name from the whole range now.

There would be no question in the mind of any Porschephile, and any sports car enthusiast for that matter, that the new Carrera GT carries its name with pride and justification as the top supercar in the company.

The question of whether the naming of the whole 911 range by the name Carrera was the right decision in the long term remains one of divided opinion, even within the company. There are those who see no problem with this, pointing out the fact that it certainly played a role in helping Porsche out of the doldrums in the 1980s, and the company turned to the one name that could lift them out of that situation. With the value of the name Carrera that had been built up over the years, it was this heritage which was then attached to all Porsche cars to leave the factory and this had the desired result of lifting the company's fortunes. Equally though, there are those who do not support this move, saying that the name of Carrera should be reserved for the top performer of the range only, or some special limited edition with noteworthy positions within the Porsche range.

Porsche's heritage has been built around its motorsport achievements, and with the company no longer competing against the other major

ABOVE The badge on the engine lid of this 911 Carrera Targa says it all – a royal heritage. This vehicle is a Carrera Targa 3.2 (1984–89 Model Years). (Author)

manufacturers as they did in international racing
events from the 1950–1990s, it is harder for the
company to use their racing achievements to
promote their cars. As Rolf Sprenger points out:
'We do not any longer compete in any major
competitions, except the Porsche Cup, because in
competition we could show how good and how
strong we were.'

Porsche Museum manager, Klaus Bischof says,
'As far as I am concerned, if I had any say in it
because I have been involved very much with the
historic vehicles and the tradition, I would have
used the word Carrera as they have used the word
Turbo, as this refers to the technical specifications. I
had always used the word Carrera for a special 911.'

For the very reason that the name Carrera was
reserved for the top-performing road car at any
time in the company's history, it is logical that the
new 2003 Carrera GT (see next chapter) received
this name. The unfortunate situation has now
arisen, though, whereby the whole 911-range is
called Carrera as well as the top-performing road
car, the superb Carrera GT. With reference to the

decision taken back in 1983, Jürgen Barth feels: 'I
don't think at the time anyone thought about it.'

The future of the 911 Carrera will not be
dependent on the title Carrera alone, reasoned
Jürgen Barth, 'No, I think it is not only Carrera,
but it is the continuation of the "C" theme with
the Cayenne and the new Cayman, but I think the
name Carrera will always be connected to a
powerful street-going car.'

However, Herbert Linge, a long-time employee
of the company and noted Porsche racing driver,
feels that the name of Carrera, which meant
something really special back in the Fifties, is a
name that has been given to the whole Porsche
range in order not to have the model name change
every year. The name of 911 Carrera brings some
consistency to the range instead of always
identifying each new model with a different
product code such as 964, 993, 996 and so on.

Whichever way it is argued, in naming the latest
911 Carrera the 997, this three-digit numerical
sequence no longer offers the company much
scope in terms of future model identification. For

this reason alone, the follow-on to the 997-series would had to have been called by a new name, if not 911 Carrera.

Rolf Sprenger sums up the situation as follows: 'Carrera is a synonym for 911 and no longer for the top engined 911. A lot of people including myself do not say any longer, "I have a 911 Carrera", we just say "I have a Carrera Cabriolet".'

Porsche Carrera Cup origins

For those customers who wanted to go racing, in 1988 Porsche introduced a series of factory-built competition cars to run in what became known as the 944 Turbo Cup. That series proved so successful that Porsche lured Herbert Linge out of retirement to manage a new single-make racing series to follow on after the 944 Turbo Cup.

Initially, the company wanted to emulate the success of the front-engined 944 series by launching another series, but this time comprising the 928 model. 'The idea was, that after the 944 Turbo Cup, to do it with the 928 and I told them immediately if you want to do it with the 928, I am not going to do it', Linge explains. The 928 was never intended to be a race car, it was too heavy, too big and would cost too much to make it competitive. 'I told them if I am going to do it, I will do it with the 911', he remembers clearly.

Having convinced the powers-that-be in Stuttgart, the 964-series 911 Carrera 2 model was selected and Linge set to work to get the series off the ground. With production of the new 964 Cup cars having begun in late 1989, the front-engined 944-series would be replaced for the 1990 season.

BELOW
Carrera 3.4 Cabriolet
(1999 Model Year).

ABOVE A 964-series 911 Carrera in the Eifelrennen Carrera Cup at the Nürburgring in April 1991.

OPPOSITE TOP The 993-series 911 Carrera was introduced in 1995. Here, Gerhard Müller is seen in action during the 1996 season.

OPPOSITE BOTTOM Porsche's 996-series 911 Carrera ready at the start of the 2004 Carrera Cup Great Britain. The livery depicts all the global regions in which the Carrera Cup is held – Great Britain, France, Germany, Australia, Japan and Asia. (Porsche UK)

The car was called Carrera 2 Cup and it was raced in the Porsche Carrera Cup in Germany from 1990 to 1994. The name Carrera was used to good effect in this race series as this powerful name conjured up images and memories of Carrera's rich motorsport heritage.

Starting with a standard Carrera 2 Coupé, each Cup car, technically identical, was equipped with shorter and stiffer coil springs, Bilstein gas pressure dampers and adjustable anti-roll bars. Ride height was dropped by 55mm and the 911 Turbo's cross-drilled and ventilated disc brakes with four piston aluminium callipers were installed. The ABS was retuned for racing and the steering stripped of its power assistance, a quicker ratio steering rack and three-piece Cup-design wheels also being fitted. Output was up by 15bhp over the standard Carrera 2, 265bhp now being developed at 6,100rpm thanks mainly to a free-flow exhaust system. The five-speed manual transmission had shorter ratios on third, fourth and fifth gears.

Few alterations were made to the bodywork, an aluminium front lid saving a few pounds while smaller exterior mirrors offered marginally less wind resistance. The most radical changes were reserved for the cabin where practically every luxury fixture from the regular Carrera 2 was thrown out. Porsche fitted a Recaro racing seat with competition harness, an FIA Matter roll cage and thinner side and rear glass. The soundproofing and underseal were also stripped away, all of which resulted in the 964 Cup weighing in at just 1,120kg (2,470lb), an amazing 235kg (518lb) lighter than the donor car. All cars were supplied directly from Porsche AG, Stuttgart, and apart from those improvements mentioned, no further modifications were permitted. Indeed, 90 per cent of the Carrera Cup car's components were shared with the road-going model, which highlighted the strength of the standard road car.

No major developments were made to the cars until 1992, at which point all Cup cars were based on the Carrera RS instead of the Carrera 2. The use of Super Unleaded fuel led to an extra 10bhp being developed, output now registered as 275bhp at 6,500rpm. Weight was further trimmed thanks to the use of even thinner glass in the side and rear windows while the front hubs and new three-piece 18-inch wheels were now fabricated from magnesium. The 964 soldiered on until the end of the 1994 season, at which point the new 993 Cup 3.8 replaced it for the 1995 season onwards.

Over the years the idea of a one-make cup with the 911 proved very popular and ever since 1993 the Porsche Pirelli Supercup has been run as a support series to Formula 1. In 2005, seven Carrera Cups (Germany, Asia, Great Britain, Japan, France, Scandinavia and Australia) were run in 15 countries. The numbers of cars to be delivered to racing customers rose respectively and in the winter of 2005–06, approximately 170 of the latest Cup 911 cars were built.

TIMELINE:

Late-1990s	2000	2003	2004	2005
LMP 2000.	Carrera GT Paris Show car.	Carrera GT introduced.	911 Carrera 997-series.	50th anniversary of Carrera.

CHAPTER TEN

Starting it all again

'It had to be the Porsche among the supercars.'

Michael Hölscher, Project Manager, Carrera GT.

Surely the Carrera GT more accurately portrays the true art of GT driving and the significance of the Carrera name, more than any other road-going Porsche.

Following the historic double victory by the Porsche GT1 in the 1998 Le Mans 24-Hour, Dr Wendelin Wiedeking and the board of directors gave the task to a small group of engineers to develop a car for the road using the technology of the GT1. A limited number of 23 GT1s were adapted for the road and sold to private customers, but the Board wanted a distinctive road car which used the GT1 race technology that would sell in slightly larger numbers. 'You cannot take a race car and only put licence plates on it – you can, but you cannot sell many cars', said Michael Hölscher.

The group of engineers assigned the task of developing this awesome machine presented their car, designed by American Grant Larson, at the Paris Motor Show in 2000 and the public's response was overwhelming. At the same time as the Paris show car was being prepared, the engineers also began work on the concept of a real car so that they would also have a good idea of how this car might be made in a production environment should the idea gain approval.

Michael Hölscher later received a phone call from Horst Marchart, former director of engineering, asking if he would like to take over the project management for a super sports car. 'Well it took some time to take it all in, about five seconds, and of course that was a chance where you do not normally think twice', Hölscher commented with a broad smile.

Hölscher and his team were given more freedom than is afforded most new car projects. The normal procedure would be to carry over either an engine, gearbox and drive train, or perhaps the bodywork, or at least parts of the body. Unlike the 959 project, where the flat-six engine had to be used and part of the 911 body, the Carrera GT was intended to shock, and would therefore need to be different from anything else they had done before.

Despite the fact that the 1953 Porsche Typ 550 was a race car, there is some argument in highlighting the similarities between it and the Carrera GT. The low style, the two-seat configuration, mid-engined layout, all contribute to a family likeness. Under the skin, there is the attention to detail in weight-saving measures and both cars have a four-overhead cam engine, although that is where the technical comparisons do end.

The important comparison to be made, though, is where both cars emphasised the company's strong engineering foundations and technical innovations. Both vehicles were what the author refers to as a 'landmark vehicle' – where the result of painstaking effort, design, research and engineering prowess has produced a vehicle of such significance that those cars that follow it will be measured against this model. The 550 set the platform for the RS and RSK series that followed which lifted it above the competition. In the same way, the Carrera GT is just such a vehicle in that it is so advanced, so innovative and so dramatic, that it stands out from its competition.

In many ways, creating a car like the Carrera GT was a departure for Porsche in that it was only ever going to be a one-car model, and that model would represent the flagship of the whole Porsche range – Boxster, 911 and Cayenne. When the 911

OPPOSITE Pictured here with the immortal 917, the Carrera GT returns to the home of many of Porsche's most significant race wins, Le Mans.

Carrera RS 2.7 was launched in 1973, it was unquestionably a dynamic performer for your money and it sat somewhere in the middle to higher echelons of the sports car world dominated by the likes of Ferrari, Maserati and Lamborghini. The 2003 Carrera GT was different though, and was never intended to be anything but the best on the market, competing unambiguously with the top performers of the day for the crown as the best 'super sports car'. Porsche had not been a regular visitor to the realms of super sports car manufacture, and although the 959 and GT1 road cars were in that league, the company opted instead for a market in which there was slightly more volume.

However, more than any model since the original 550 Spyder, the Carrera GT epitomises the very essence of Porsche, illustrating what

Porsche has always stood for – high performance, excellence of ride, technological innovation. Overall design responsibility for both the Paris Show car and the production model fell to Porsche design supremo Harm Lagaay, while Tony Hatter was accountable for the design detail on the production model. Contrary to most prototypes conceived only for racing, clever re-interpretation of existing design features combined with new styling statements, provide more than a passing resemblance to current production vehicles and Porsche's legendary racing cars. Although it was not intended to be the fastest car on the road, as that description in itself conveys only a single message, rather, the Carrera GT is a vehicle that can surely hold its head up high in almost any company as a genuine all-round supercar.

When your products have for years been regarded, by both customer and competitor alike, as the pinnacle of motoring innovation, then as a company you have a responsibility to live up to that reputation. It is not a reputation that is short-lived or belongs to just one model in the range, rather, there is an expectation by the market that you will continue to carry that mantle with pride and determination. Not since the 911 Carrera RS 2.7 of 1973 had there been a truly special Carrera model that took away the collective breath of the motoring fraternity, and perhaps Porsche has been too conservative in its development of sports cars. Not to take anything away from the superb 911 Carrera range, or the practical Boxster, but the Stuttgart manufacturer had not given the Italians much to worry about for decades.

The Carrera GT has pulled Porsche back to its roots more than any other car in recent times. This is a dramatic car in every sense of the word. It is as dramatic as the Porsche 356 No.1 was in 1948, and with the Carrera GT Porsche has successfully recaptured the magic of that name in this vehicle. It is also an inspirational car, it grabs your attention. It is all-absorbing and evocative, almost sensual, and it recaptures what Porsche set out to do in 1950.

Stepping back in time to the 1950s, the reputation of the 550 on the track and later the RS-series racers, earned them the nickname of 'giant killers' at that time. The 356, too, in its

ABOVE Only a handful of the GT1 road cars were produced (1998).

various Carrera guises took the market by storm and when the 911 was introduced it too performed miracles on both the track and in road-going form. But by the late 1990s, the 911 had been on the market for 35 years and, although it was still capable of thrashing the competition in either road or track dress, it had all looked very much the same, for a bit too long. Porsche's reputation for technical innovation was being stretched a little and there were some questions being asked along the lines of 'when are we going to see some of that old magic again?' – it was
when this question was asked by Dr Wendelin Wiedeking, that things started to happen.

Carrera GT (2003)

The starting point on the proverbial blank sheet of paper for Michael Hölscher and his team, was that the new car was to utilise the technology embodied in the GT1 race car. Interpreting that requirement did not mean that they had to use the engine, which was the turbocharged flat-six boxer engine, nor did they have to borrow the chassis or bodywork of any previous model – the development engineers literally had a blank canvas.

However, they did have a useful piece of equipment left over from the stillborn LMP 2000 project, which to this day, remains under wraps,

OPPOSITE TOP The original prototype show car, here displayed at the Geneva Motor Show, 2001.

OPPOSITE BOTTOM A Carrera GT at the British Motor Show, Birmingham, England, 2004. (Author)

deep in the vaults of Weissach. The Porsche engineers had produced a magnificent V10 engine of 5.5-litre capacity that had been intended for capturing the laurels in the endurance sports car racing world yet again. Although the LMP 2000 project is shrouded in secrecy, the engine and layout configuration does in some ways hint at the possible style of the car itself. Having said that, Hölscher emphasised that none of the other elements of that car could be absorbed into the new Carrera GT. For starters, the LMP 2000 had no doors or roof, and with the engine being bolted directly to the chassis, an alternative mounting procedure would have to be devised for the new road car.

The carbon-fibre monocoque was the only other shared component between the GT1 and the LMP 2000 that would be common also in the new Carrera GT, but this was shared only in concept, as the new monocoque for the road car would have to satisfy a whole raft of different safety criteria for road use. This gave the development engineers two generations of race car technology in the field of carbon-fibre body construction from which to draw when creating the shell for the new GT.

When designing and building a car in carbon-fibre, one cannot first complete the task in sheet metal and then simply substitute the new material as a last step in the process. The engineers had to learn to 'think' in carbon-fibre due to the distinctive material properties and strength characteristics, which are quite different from sheet metal. Building the monocoque alone would take a week, comprising up to a thousand individual operations.

Design of the Carrera GT was the responsibility of Weissach and, although this car is like no other in the Porsche range, there are some elements of previous models evident in it. 'You can see some elements from the 356, from the very first Porsches, for example the front hood, then of course there is some heritage of the 550', explains Hölscher. The evocative tail incorporates a rear wing which rises automatically at 75mph (120km/h) to a height of 160mm, retracting again at 50mph (80km/h).

During the design phase, the company relied almost entirely on internal input in terms of styling and the proposed market size. Porsche conducted discreet research amongst its worldwide dealer network, where certain potential customers were questioned on the marketability of such a model, but at no stage was the feedback of any customer car clinics sought. Wanting to set the trend with this vehicle rather than follow the style of any competitors, Porsche relied very much on the vast experience of its own race department. So critical was the success of this vehicle to the company, that Chairman Dr Wendelin Wiedeking insisted that the Carrera GT would not be released to the public without a stamp of approval by world-renowned Porsche racing driver, Walter Röhrl. Röhrl spent many hours testing and improving the GT on the test circuit at Weissach.

Hölscher went on to say, 'Walter Röhrl was involved as soon as we had hardware. He had already made an assessment of our seating buck in order to evaluate the ergonomics with the view of a professional race driver. His main job began when the first drivable prototypes were available.'

The basic suspension set-up was tuned by Roland Kussmaul at the Weissach test track after which the chassis engineers went to several race tracks with Röhrl and Kussmaul. The main focus at the Nürburgring was to tune the driving dynamics to the optimum, including such aspects as suspension kinematics, spring and damper ratios, tyre behaviour and aerodynamics.

The decision to build the engine support structure in carbon-fibre was one which produced much head-scratching because, according to Michael Hölscher, nobody had built such an engine frame in the 'hot area' before. Due to the critical temperature properties of carbon-fibre, it suddenly loses its strength without warning as it approaches this breaking point. However, in overcoming this challenge, it gave the engineers the opportunity to style the engine frame, a feature that few would even notice, but which shows that such synthesis between performance and aesthetics even in the engine compartment is possible.

The decision to go with the V10 engine was not a given factor from the beginning. Although this was a state-of-the-art piece of technology, the

BELOW A cutaway view showing the position of the engine in the Carrera GT. This illustrates perfectly how low the engine unit sits in the frame.

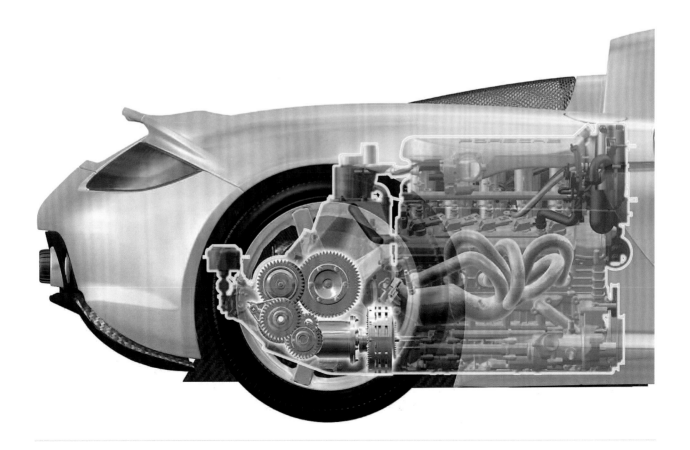

tried-and-tested power of the GT1 power plant was a known factor and would have been the safer option. However, contrary to what one might think, the V10 actually provided a lower centre of gravity than that of the flat-six boxer unit. In the words of Michael Hölscher, 'You should not look at the component, you have to look at the [whole] car.'

The boxer engine, with its exhaust system which first bends upwards and then curves down and under the engine, would result in an air gap under the motor to accommodate this pipework, and, as a result, the motor would sit unnecessarily high. In placing the motor as low as possible, the clutch required a comprehensive rethink, as Hölscher explains: 'If you have such a "pizza" plate behind the engine, you have to raise the engine only

because of the clutch.' Looking at Formula 1 technology, this is the reason they have a 125mm carbon-fibre clutch, and so that seemed the obvious route to go. But in this case, carbon-fibre was not the answer as these units only have a life of 10,000km (6,000 miles) which would mean the Carrera GT owner would be changing his clutch more often than the engine oil. This brought about a world first for Porsche when they developed the Porsche ceramic composite clutch (PCCC), with a diameter of 169mm.

These units combined to allow the engineers to proceed with the V10 power plant, although not in exactly the same form as in the LMP 2000. For reasons of emissions, durability and servicing, the engine capacity was increased from 5.5 litres to 5.7 litres (5,733cc) giving a maximum output of

BELOW The interior of the Carrera GT is a comfortable blend of comfort and functionality. After all, this car is all about power and performance. Note the laminated Birchwood gear knob.

CARRERA GT PERFORMANCE FIGURES	
0–100km/h (62mph)	3.9 seconds
0–160km/h (99mph)	6.9 seconds
0–200km/h (124mph)	9.9 seconds
Top speed	330km/h (205mph)
Source: *Porsche AG*	

612bhp at 8,000rpm. The four overhead cam motor had a bore of 98mm and stroke of 76mm, with a compression ration of 12.0:1, and produced staggering performance and acceleration statistics. Despite such impressive figures, the Carrera GT could still return an extra-urban fuel consumption of 24mpg (11.7 litres/100km).

By placing the 2000 Paris Show car and the final production model side by side, one would be hard pressed to see any differences, as Michael Hölscher explains: 'Of course, we took the styling data from our Paris model, but we had to revise every square millimetre because of legal requirements and internal requirements like wheel travel, but the challenge was that it should look like the show car.'

Making it look like the show car was harder than it might seem, as the Paris model had no roof and no side windows. This concept model also had no engine supports as the V10 was bolted directly to the chassis, but it did boast a video camera which would enable the driver to view his laps of the Nürburgring in the comfort of his home later. However, after several comments from prospective customers that they might be regarded as 'schoolboys' by their neighbours and friends were their supercar to possess such gadgets, it was decided to drop this from the production model.

The roof created its own problems as most cars in this market at the time all featured electric folding roof sections, but this would have added too much extra weight at a high level, upsetting the purposely low centre of gravity the engineers had worked so hard to achieve. One of the design briefs was that the magnificent V10 engine should be visible through a transparent engine cover, and so no folding roof should be allowed to obscure this. In the end, the designers opted for a light, two-part, manually removable roof which could be neatly stowed in the front luggage compartment.

So as to be under no illusions as to the intended market for this super sports car, the seats were constructed from a composite carbon-fibre and Kevlar, and upholstered in leather. The interior features a Porsche Online Pro navigation radio including a Bose sound system which offers not only audio entertainment but also houses the navigation system, telephone with hands-free operation as well as email and Internet functions. Each Porsche Online Pro system comes with its own email address, while the CD player can also play compressed digital music data files on MP3 CDs. Further enhancing the exclusivity of this vehicle, the GT comes at no extra cost with a full leather five-piece luggage set for those essential weekend getaways.

Although air conditioning is an optional extra (for reasons of weight saving), there is another innovative weight-saving feature which is a throwback to the 1970s, and the days of the 917. When the designers of the immortal 917 were challenged to cut the weight of certain components by 30 per cent, one technician responded by fitting a gear knob made of balsa wood, which was that much lighter than aluminium. This principle was followed in all subsequent Porsche racing cars and has now become a feature of the Carrera GT, although the gear knob on the new car is made of laminated Birchwood.

The company has guaranteed that only 1,500 cars will be made, and each one receives a plaque with the vehicle number in the series, mounted on the centre console. In order to ensure exclusivity, Hölscher is emphatic that this is a limited model only: 'We made the decision that the project will not have a successor right now.' The first car off the production line now sits in the Porsche Museum in Stuttgart. 'That is number one. You know normally, after twenty or thirty years the company tries hard to buy back the number one car, and that we want to prevent by taking the number one.' That means that, apart from the three test cars, which no longer look very beautiful after a gruelling test life, there will only ever be 1,499 Carrera GTs in private hands when manufacture ceases in 2006.

The sleek lines and low stance give this supercar an awesome sense of presence on the road.

Due to the demand for highly skilled technicians as well as advanced manufacturing equipment, it was not possible to manufacture the Carrera GT in one location. The plant in Leipzig had spare manufacturing capacity, but not the facilities to assemble and test the complex V10 engine on site. The main assembly plant in Stuttgart-Zuffenhausen could not accommodate the assembly of another model line, but they did have the space to produce the engine, although not to run the full test programme. This meant that the engines built at Zuffenhausen are tested in Weissach and then sent to the Leipzig plant for installation in the car. Leipzig was also chosen as the most suitable assembly plant as this is one of the favoured locations for customer collections. It offers a comprehensive test track for customers to drive the Carrera GT and to receive driving instruction prior to having the keys handed over.

The designing and developing of a supercar of such complexity with cutting-edge technology, one might imagine, would require a team of at least several hundred staff across all disciplines. After the initial start-up team of just ten engineers had set the ground rules and design parameters, Michael Hölscher assembled a core team of 50 skilled engineers to continue with the project. Peaking at 150, the team was drawn from the different departments from across the company as and when the skills were required, with all technicians returning to their roles from which they had been taken. In that way, the added skill and experience gained on the project was retained within the company.

Carrera GT engine assembly plant

When Porsche moved its operations back to Stuttgart-Zuffenhausen in 1950, it occupied part of the Reutter's factory where the bodies of the infant 356 had been constructed. As sales increased, the company built its own facility on the surrounding ground and eventually took over the Reutter company in March 1964. The old Reutter's body shop was converted into a seat-making facility for Porsche (Recaro), but when the building was classified as protected in 1993, Porsche was faced with having to expand around this building rather than demolishing it to erect a more modern facility.

In many ways this is perhaps a more pertinent outcome for the building, as Porsche decided to assemble the impressive Carrera GT power plant in the old Reutter's building. Converting the internal space of the old building proved no problem. Looking at this development philosophically, this is where the early Carrera bodies would have been made, but today it is where the modern Carrera GT engine is assembled – a rather fitting tribute to the illustrious heritage of the old factory.

Being given access to this hallowed chamber, is not a privilege meted out to many, and the author counts himself among the fortunate few to have been given a guided tour of this facility. Being greeted at the entrance by Master Engineer Thomas Hartmann (Meister in GT Motorenbau), we were led into the engine assembly area where a handful of carefully selected technicians were busy with various assembly functions in what can only be described as laboratory-like conditions.

Only three engines are assembled per day by a team of two technicians each. A further team of two – and these highly trained technicians are carefully paired together for reasons of compatibility – are charged with pulling from stock the meticulously matched and blueprinted components for the assembly of the next day's batch of three engines. These are placed on specially designed consignment trolleys and wheeled to each work station ready for assembly. The technicians selected for work on the Carrera GT engine assembly line are all taken from the main factory, where they would have gained valuable experience on the Turbo or the Carrera Cup engine assembly line. A good understanding of the workings of a high-performance engine is essential in this particular job and, understandably, the queue for a position on the GT engine assembly line is a long one.

Every morning, the engines assembled the previous day are sent off to the test facility at Weissach where they undergo a full two-hour test programme on the engine test bed. As those engines are being dispatched for testing, so the engines from the day before are returned to the Zuffenhausen assembly line from Weissach where they are prepared to receive the special gearbox, designed only for the Carrera GT. Made by Hör, the six-speed 'box is then mated to the already-tested engine and then run again on a smaller test rig in Zuffenhausen (old Reutter's building) to check for any leaks in the hydraulics and the fluid connections as a result of this final assembly stage. A quick demonstration by Meister Hartmann on the small Zuffenhausen test rig reveals the awesome power and noise created by the engine as he runs it up through the rev range.

As an additional quality check, once a month, one of the Weissach-tested engines is then stripped down completely to the last component and checked for assembly and wear faults. This strip down is fully documented and recorded for later reference should any changes to the assembly process be required.

BELOW Here, a technician carefully mates the gearbox with the already tested engine from Weissach prior to a final test on the smaller Zuffenhausen test rig. The gearbox also contains the oil tank for the engine.

A POWERFUL STATEMENT

In the media conference room of Werk 1, Zuffenhausen, hangs a poster of the Carrera GT at speed on the open road. The caption below in three different languages (English, Russian and French) reads: 'You are now leaving the American zone.' The message is simple, but very powerful. There are few cars in the world capable of equalling, yet alone challenging, the Carrera GT in terms of performance, technology and roadability, fewer still that come even close in terms of looks. The owner of this Porsche is left with no doubt that he is leaving behind the confines of the ordinary world – welcome to the special world of the Carrera GT.

Once the final engine and gearbox assembly and testing has been satisfactorily completed, the units are then sent to Leipzig where the Carrera GT sports car is assembled. It may seem a rather round-the-houses way of doing things, but it works well and assembly procedures and quality are checked and monitored every step of the way and, on a €450,000 super sports car, it is well justified.

Were it not for the LMP 2000 project, perhaps the Carrera GT would not have been powered by anything quite as exotic as the superb V10, which, for a company having grown up on flat boxer engines, in itself represents quite a departure for the Stuttgart firm. Porsche had always prided itself in leading the way in terms of technological innovation and in staying a step ahead of the competition, but more recently the 'WOW' factor was somehow missing from the model range. The company needed to inject some of that old spirit, that special Porsche DNA that existed when the 550s and the 356 Carreras ruled the roads. It was time to claim that lead back again – the Carrera GT has certainly done that.

The 997-series (August 2004)

In many ways the 911 of today is a far cry from the original, slim 911 of 1963, satisfying the vision that Ferry Porsche had back then of a light-weight, nimble sports car. He was heard to say that if he had known back in 1963 that the boxer motor would ultimately grow to this size, he would have put a cap on it much earlier. But then, for the 911

BELOW
This factory publicity shot shows the 997-series 911 Carrera (left) and the 911 Carrera S.

to have survived in its various guises for over 40 years, which must surely rank as one of the longest production runs in auto history, it was inevitable that the car would change in many ways during that time. Today, the 911 Carrera, or 997 to give it its factory reference, is filled to the brim with technology which has enabled this classic to keep pace with its competitors over the decades, while still retaining the same basic silhouette. Other manufacturers in the market have introduced countless new models to replace earlier ones, but the basic 911 shape has remained true to its origins.

So successful and simple was that original shape that thousands of customers have returned to buy the next model upgrade, resulting in 60 per cent of all Porsches, which means that a high proportion of all 911s, are still on the road today. This has resulted in Porsche actively working to retain the original 911 silhouette rather than seeking to change it, which is an interesting principle in itself, and a concept strongly avoided by most other manufacturers, but not Porsche, where things don't change easily, and certainly not without good reason.

The 911 Carrera (2005 Model Year)

With the return of the oval front headlamps, the visual similarities between the 1963 Porsche 911 and the new 997 were emphasised. But there is, however, another similarity which both the 996 and 997 Carreras share with an even earlier model, the 356 A Carrera of 1955, and that is they all run with twin overhead camshaft engines – but that is where the mechanical similarities most definitely end. For the first time since 1977, the new 911 Carrera is offered with two different engine sizes – the Carrera comes with a 3.6-litre unit while the Carrera S is fitted with the new 3.8-litre motor.

A significant design cue taken from the earlier 356 can be seen in the 997, with its tensed rear haunches, but even here, the 997 is vastly different from its immediate predecessor, the 996 Carrera. Slightly shorter but significantly wider than the 996, the new model offers all-round improvements in body stiffness and for the first time, Porsche active suspension management (PASM) is available as standard on the Carrera S.

RIGHT The 997-series marked a return to the familiar oval front headlamps. (Author)

BELOW Firm lines and tight haunches characterise the rear end of the 997-series 911 Carrera (2004). (Author)

With the 997, gone are the slim and sleek lines of the original 911, which are replaced with muscular power bulges. However, these increased dimensions have been cleverly constrained and the original silhouette is still clearly evident.

Although offered only in rear-wheel-drive configuration at launch, the 997 Carrera is bristling with new technology. While standard on the Carrera S, Porsche's new active suspension, PASM, is also available as an option on the regular Carrera. At the touch of a button, PASM allows the driver to select one of two suspension settings – 'PASM Normal' for everyday travel or 'PASM Sport' for a more competitive vehicle set-up. In the 'Sport' setting, the system lowers the whole car by 10mm, activating harder damper control and thus providing a driving attitude and qualities comparable with those of an all-out sports suspension.

The 997 benefits from a new generation of Porsche stability management (PSM) which enhances the ride and safety of the Carrera still further. In addition, both the Carrera and Carrera S are available with the optional Porsche ceramic composite brakes (PCCB) weighing up to 50 per cent less than the cross-drilled steel discs, but these come at a hefty premium of over £5,000.

For those wishing to live life to the full, the sporting experience can be sharpened with the Sports Chrono Package Plus option which includes an analogue/digital stopwatch mounted

ABOVE This factory press car shows the front end treatment for the 997-series – the headlamps have been moved further back and more to the outside while the indicators and additional lights have been removed from the main headlight unit. This development gives the front end a wider and lower appearance. (Author)

Although the sixth-generation 911 Carrera 997-series obviously owes much of its shape and heritage to the original 1963 car, the latest offering has undoubtedly put on a substantial amount of weight, which is also evident in its increased width and heavier front and rear proportions. Much of this extra weight is down to the complexity of the machine, additional features, and a much bigger engine – almost double the capacity of the first 2.0-litre unit in 1963.

COMPARATIVE DIMENSIONAL DATA COVERING THE LAST FOUR GENERATIONS OF 911				
Details	**1989** 964 Carrera 2	**1994** 911 Carrera 993	**1998** 911 Carrera 996	**2004** 911 Carrera 997
Weight (unladen, manual car)	1,350kg (1,450kg – C4)	1,370kg (1,420kg – C4)	1,320kg (1,375kg – C4)	1,395kg (1,420kg Carrera S)
Length	4,250mm	4,245mm	4,430mm	4,427mm
Width	1,652mm	1,735mm	1,765mm	1,808mm
Height	1,310mm	1,300mm	1,305mm	1,310mm (1,300mm – Carrera S)
Wheelbase	2,272mm	2,272mm	2,350mm	2,350mm
Source: *Porsche AG factory press kits*				

amidships on top of the dashboard for monitoring track times, acceleration and additional performance data. By pressing the 'Sports' button on the centre console, this package opens up a whole range of performance management enhancements, tightening up response times to acceleration input and throttle lift-off, while the PSM changes, allowing greater agility and driving dynamics. The Sports Chrono pack allows the driver to monitor the car's performance by flicking an additional stalk control on the steering column which shows performance data on the monitor of the Porsche Communications Centre in the centre of the dash.

The engine powering the 997 Carrera has been increased in size to 3,596cc (996-series: 3,387cc) and now generates a maximum output of 325bhp. This new Carrera power plant is good for 177mph (285km/h). The Carrera S on the other hand has also received a new engine, this time the largest capacity boxer engine ever made, giving 3,824cc, which generates 355bhp and can propel the S to a top speed of 182mph (293km/h). A new six-speed manual gearbox was developed to cope with the extra power and torque produced by these new engines, and both models can be purchased with the five-speed Tiptronic option.

External improvements included the return to traditional 911 oval headlamps being separated from the indicator clusters, and have been specially designed to give a distinctive front-end signature with the light units moved further back and towards the outside of the fenders. Even the exterior wing mirrors have come in for some special treatment. With the design concept taken from the Carrera GT, the mirror housing with twin arms actually increases downforce on the front axle as well as aiding the flow of air to the back of the car where the extendable rear spoiler provides extra downforce.

BELOW New suspension and stability management ensure a safer ride and firm attitude in cornering.

For the 2005 Model Year, the 996-series Carrera 4S Coupé and Carrera 4S Cabriolet versions continued in production pending the introduction of the 997 models of those variants. When the 997-series Carrera 4 Coupé and Carrera 4S Coupé models were introduced, they came with widened fenders (an extra 22mm on each side) to accommodate the extra-fat rear wheels measuring 295/35 ZR 18 on the Carrera 4 with even bigger 305/30 ZR 19 rubber on the Carrera 4S. The 'S' version in both Carrera and Carrera 4 models are 10mm lower than the non-S cars, reducing the drag coefficient still further, to an incredible 0.29.

Launched in October 2005, the Carrera 4 Cabriolet and Carrera 4S Cabriolet completed the 997-series line-up. These two models are powered by the same 3.6-litre and 3.8-litre flat-six engines as in the equivalent coupé versions, with the open-air 4 Cabriolet posting a top speed of 174mph (280km/h) while its 4S stablemate tops out at 179mph (288km/h). The 4S Cabriolet can reach 100km/h (62mph) in an impressive 4.9 seconds.

Additional specific reinforcements to both the four-wheel drive and the Cabriolet body give the bodyshell of this car a very high standard of stiffness. The car's soft top and hydraulic mechanisms weigh only 42kg (93lb), which is only half as much as a comparable retractable steel roof, having an advantageous effect on the car's low centre of gravity. The entire roof mechanism can be operated at a speed of up to 31mph (50km/h), the roof opening or closing together with the windows in a mere 20 seconds. As a result, the Carrera 4 Cabriolets pass the wind tunnel test with a drag coefficient of 0.30 (C4) and 0.29 (C4S); extremely impressive for a cabriolet body style. Available as an optional extra, the sturdy detachable aluminium hardtop weighs only 33kg (73lb) enabling the owner to enjoy their cabriolet throughout the winter.

In keeping with the concept of a 'business-style' executive sports car, the Porsche communication management (PCM) is fitted, offering the now expected range of entertainment and performance data options for today's sophisticated buyer. However, included as a new feature is the innovative electronic trip recorder interacting with the navigation system to record up to 1,500 trips, depending on the driver's requirements. All the driver has to do is confirm, either prior to setting out or during a journey, whether he is travelling on business or privately. The data recorded may then be conveyed via the PCM infrared interface to an appropriately equipped laptop or PDA, subsequently being processed by means of the software provided together with the system. This new option meets all the requirements made, for example, by the authorities in Germany and elsewhere around the world, of an automatic trip recorder with a logbook function. This is just one more example of how the 911 Carrera has changed from an out-and-out sports car – as seen up to the mid-'70s with the Carrera RS 2.7 – to the current day 'business-mobile' for the high-flying executive.

RIGHT The 911 Carrera S Cabriolet offers serious performance with top-down motoring.

BELOW The 911 Carrera Cabriolet is all about luxury, open-top cruising – a far cry from the days of noisy engines and spartan interiors.

TIMELINE:

1948	**1955**	**1963**	**1973**	**1998**	**2003**	**2005**
First Porsche 356 launched.	356 A Carrera launched at IAA.	Porsche 911 launched.	911 Carrera RS 2.7 introduced.	Ferry Porsche dies.	Carrera GT supercar introduced.	50th anniversary of Carrera name.

CHAPTER ELEVEN

Carrera into the future

Whether 50bhp or 650bhp, the Porsche sports car has always possessed that unique ability to attract, to entertain and engross the driver, at almost any speed – even standing still.

Author

You cannot mention the name 'Carrera' without thinking 'Porsche', the type of fact which would spell success for any manufacturer. Success not only in the strong heritage of the name, but also the image which has become synonymous with performance, reliability and everyday practicality. At no stage in those early, formative years, was there any talk of a marketing plan for the Carrera name, not when the name was first applied to the Fuhrmann engine in Mexico by the mechanics, and neither when the 356 A Carrera was launched in Frankfurt in 1955. Nothing was set in stone in those years, it was all done by trial and error in the immediate post-war years.

Legends are created over time, they do not happen overnight. The basic 911 shape, launched in 1963, six years before man first walked on the moon, continues to inspire today with the same level of fascination. Having survived several world energy crises, countless new design fads and styles, it was even threatened with the 'chop' in the 1980s, but the 911 model still stands as a testament to the ingenuity of its creators. Increased in dimensions here and there, improved and packed with technological innovations, the 911 platform has kept pace with the market and in the process silenced most, if not all, of its critics over its forty plus-year lifespan.

To have such a track record, there must be certain essential elements present, such as a good starting point, steady and positive progress with model development, the aim to always improve, and the all-important respect of the market and opposition.

The strength of the brand as perceived by the customer, is embodied in the expected delivery and satisfaction created by the product. Looking at the extended wheelarches and the lines of the 996 and 997-series today, these mimic the powerful and muscular styling of the 911 RSR Martini Porsche of 1974, creating a 'must have' desire for any prospective buyer.

When asked for his opinion on Porsche's position in the world of sports cars today, Jürgen Barth replied: 'I think we are quite unique in the industry in that we are building 60–80,000 cars a year compared to Ferrari who build only 4,500 cars. We are located in between the big manufacturers and the small manufacturers and so we are in a quite unique position building only sports cars, in a quite big number.' Towards the end of the 1980s, Porsche delivered cars to around 35 markets (countries), today this number is closer to 100, so there has been tremendous development of new markets in recent years.

OPPOSITE A 2004 Porsche 997 Carrera, pictured in a regal English setting. (Author)

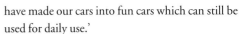

ABOVE That magical lettering on the engine cover of a 356 B 1600 GS Carrera (1960).

BELOW The 911 Carrera RS 2.7 Coupé in everyday use (November 1972).

There are many manufacturers who produce a sports car model based on a platform shared with other models in the range. These cars are built up sports cars and are therefore not exclusive in the same way that the 911 Carrera is a dedicated sports car model. Barth continues, 'So I think we are unique and I think that it is quite good to be unique in a certain way because our engineers have made our cars into fun cars which can still be used for daily use.'

There has been a great flood of supercars onto the market in the past ten to 15 years, from the Ferrari F40, to the Zonda, from the Jaguar XJ220 to the Lamborghini Diablo, or the McLaren F1, and many others besides. All of these are exclusive due to their low production numbers, all are expensive and all are very capable and staggeringly quick machines. With a few exceptions, most of these cars are made for the road and will never be driven anywhere near their true performance potential by their owners. But few of these exclusive machines offer the same level of everyday practicality and affordability as the 911 Carrera offers – granted, the standard Carrera does not offer the 200mph (320km/h) plus speed of some Ferraris, but very few owners will ever explore these boundaries anyway.

Taking a step back in time to 1973 when the original Carrera RS 2.7 was introduced, the car was basically intended for competition use, although Porsche knew full well that many would not see track action. The '73 Carrera was built for sport first and comfort next while image didn't really feature anywhere in the equation. Today's supercars are almost entirely about image, with hardly a thought for real competition use. When you try to build image into a car, it becomes a fashion or social statement, because that is the appeal that the manufacturer is trying to create and, as such, the appeal will usually be of shorter duration. Unfortunately, too many supercar manufacturers today are trying to build a 'classic' first, with less and less thought given to continuity and heritage.

Classical lines never date or go out of fashion and it is a testament to the different designers at Porsche over the past forty years that this styling has remained largely untouched. Much of this success is down to simplicity of lines, uncomplicated style and a lack of adornments. In this, the Porsche designers have stuck to the original 911 design brief of 1963 – all things have a starting point, if that starting point is good, then the potential for that product to become a classic in the future is much stronger. In Porsche's own terms, the three design elements that have always been adhered to are: timelessness, a sporty attitude and independence. Each of these three elements, if studied individually, will confirm in every way that the Porsche designers have successfully achieved their goal over the years.

The attitude of the engineers at Porsche is like a thread that runs throughout the company, be it in design, assembly, racing or any other discipline in the manufacturing process. Jürgen Barth again: 'I think the spirit of our engineers and the spirit of Porsche is a bit different.' This simultaneous approach to quality and simplicity can be seen in the all-conquering 917, as Barth explains, 'but it's the same thing which, again, our engineers and the racing guys could manage with any racing car. You know, with the 917, you turn the key and you go. In the paddock after the race you stop, next race you start it again, you could go on like this – it's like a Volkswagen engine. With the 917 it was so funny, everyone else would run off one cooling lap and we just cut the engine off and that was that.'

At the Porsche works in Stuttgart-Zuffenhausen, this sense of professionalism and pride is tangible. When the production goal is the same for everyone, then this shows in the products.

Will the Carrera name endure?

We are constantly being told that communication is a two-way street. In the context of the Porsche Carrera, it is also a two-fold statement. There is first the communication between the car and the driver, ensuring the most pleasurable and efficient drive, while the second communication is between the car and its audience. In this latter element, the owner is telling his admirers through the vehicle that this car has been selected with careful thought, not just purchased out of a catalogue. Consideration goes into choosing the right Porsche Carrera and it says that this owner has taken his or her time in this selection.

Will the name of Carrera endure? Klaus Bischof thinks so: 'Well, I am now totally convinced that the 911 is here to stay and that the word Carrera will stay. I am convinced that just as long as the 911 exists, it will have the name Carrera on it. I am totally convinced of that.'

BELOW The name says it all – the 'Carrera' badge has come a long way since the early days. There is now 50 years of experience between the first 356 A Carrera of September 1955 and the current model. (Author)

BELOW In this press photograph, the heritage of the 996-series Carrera Cabriolet can be clearly seen when compared to Porsche's first Roadster, the 356 No. 1 of 1948.

OPPOSITE TOP It was the 356 that gave the Carrera name a meaning, but this heritage is carried with pride in the new 997-series 911 Carrera 4S. (Author)

OPPOSITE BOTTOM The business end of the Carrera GT. There can be few other shapes on the road today that are as evocative and stylish as the Carrera GT. (Author)

Jürgen Barth agrees. 'I think the 911 will be there for ever, you know, so there is no question about it and there is so much potential also still to go. I think even from the 996 to the 997 you can see the potential, where the engineers improved it and I'm sure they have some more ideas in the future.'

It is amazing how valuable that concept of slow, deliberate and measured progress has been for the brand, from that first car in 1948, right through to the current 997 today. Klaus Bischof again: 'You can see it in each car body which started with 356 No. 1. If I line up this first Roadster next to the mass-produced cars everyone can recognise the kinship and the line, of course with a bit of fantasy, and that is what Ferry Porsche wanted to achieve.'

There is no question in the minds of any of the Porsche personnel interviewed for this book, that the value of the Carrera name to the company has been immeasurable. A nameplate that has been a synonym for performance, and a major part of the fabric of Porsche since not long after the company's inception, will always be greatly treasured by those

who have been closest to it. From a publicity angle, the value of the word Carrera was first shown in Porsche's ability to make strong endurance race cars, as they demonstrated in the Carrera Panamericana. For Rolf Sprenger, 'The value comes from racing, [it] comes from the top of the line engined car and stayed with the famous and classical 911.'

Porsche – the story of survival

The senses cannot work in isolation when examining and describing the performance and quality of a Porsche. The eye can see, but only the fingers can feel the curves, and only the ear can appreciate the distinctive wail of the flat-six boxer engine. Individually, the senses can identify different qualities and attributes, but together with all the senses in harmony, you can appreciate the whole package. In the same way, the Porsche is not just made up of a good engine or a timeless design, but its strength is the sum of the parts, the character and blending together of the

combination of these parts that make the whole package so desirable.

Porsche as a company, grew up in an era when model developments were done because they improved the quality or performance of the car. These changes were carried out with the minimum of fuss and formality, and with respect for the person recommending the change or improvement, as it was accepted that that person was an expert in his or her particular field. Unfortunately, in today's over-regulated corporate environment, much of this type of autonomy has been quashed by a variety of factors, namely regulations (safety, etc.), finances or fixed product life cycles. In the early days, it was easier to create more evocative shapes such as the 356, 904, 906 and 911, and the creative genius of the pen master can be clearly seen in these vehicles. Fortunately, this same kind of skill and talent has come through in the Carrera GT of 2003, as CEO Wiedeking gave the project engineers a blank sheet of paper with very few, if any, rules and the express instruction to produce a vehicle that would once again show the world what Porsche stood for.

Very few cars that leave the production line today are ever 'instant classics'. That title is something that the car earns over time either through competition, quality or pure exclusivity. However, the original Carrera RS 2.7 was one such car, as were its successors in the Seventies. In our image-conscious society today, unless the manufacturer's focus swings back towards the real reason for building sports cars, that is for sport or competition, we will continue to see shapes and styles made to appeal to the image set and not the competitive driver. Understanding the raison d'être for a sports car in the first place is part of the success behind that timeless classic, the 911 Carrera RS 2.7.

For Porsche, swimming upstream against the flow of water has produced results that would have drowned the resolve of many others. From the start, with the early 356 and its reverse engine layout, the company has learned and refined its products. Through these struggles, Porsche has not had the luxury of large advertising budgets to flaunt its achievements through expensive promotional campaigns, but it has had to gain

market share and acceptance through racing achievements, which is the tough way, but it has produced a purer breed.

The 2003 Carrera GT was not built as a competition car, and very few will ever see track action, but the important issue for the company was that through this car the company was able to assert its position as a technology leader in the world of super sports cars. For those people who are lucky enough to acquire a Carrera GT, they will do so because of what the car is, not for the impact it would make in society.

Through the Carrera GT, Porsche has once again captured the magic of the original gravitas of that coveted Carrera badge, earned by those early sports cars in the harshest of conditions and carried with pride since the Fifties. While it may have made good marketing sense to use the Carrera name for the whole 911 range back in the 1980s, it unfortunately conveys a mixed message to the market by being applied to two completely different models in the Porsche family – the 911 range as well as the flagship Carrera GT. That marketing initiative may still dilute the name of Carrera for some time into the future.

Staying the same

Producing a good car is only one part of the challenge, the other is attracting the attention of potential buyers to try the products. For normal road-going cars, this equates to good sales and customer loyalty. For racing cars, this means the driver must win races. Ferry Porsche had an uncanny knack of understanding the needs of a racing driver, interpreting those needs and then producing a car in which that driver could perform brilliantly. This is an oft overlooked quality in early motoring pioneers, and is unfortunately increasingly absent from most boardrooms today.

Understanding what the drivers wanted and understanding the challenges and dynamics of a racing car is something which comes from working with the engineers constantly. Jürgen Barth expands on this: 'Yes, sure, because they were close and they understood racing much better. You have the best example, where you get Mr Bott and Professor Fuhrmann dismantling the engine themselves. Dismantling it, just to see what is happening and they were the chief of development and the chairman. I would hardly see Dr Wiedeking dismantling an engine today.'

A close association with his engineers was always something that Ferry Porsche nurtured, but it wasn't just for the sake of having a chat, it was also to understand the engineering issues confronting his staff in the workshops. Today, it's called 'keeping your finger on the pulse of the company', the difference being for Ferry Porsche was that his staff were the company. Jürgen Barth remembers those days well, 'But also the important thing was in the 1950/60s, Ferry Porsche came down nearly every day to the production line, talking to the guys there, and even to us apprentices, he came and said, "How are you", and things like that. Well, it was like a big family firm.'

Quite frankly, if Porsche was another company, it would have ceased to exist long ago. It is not only the strong heritage that prevails, but the indestructible attitude of its personnel, the pride and commitment with which they carry out their work and the belief that they have in the products they make. This belief is a tangible feature when walking around the factory and pride is something that is in evidence in almost all areas of the plant, even in the company canteen, or 'Casino' as it is called. Just for the fact of surviving 50 years in the market place alone, you can only have the highest regard for the Carrera name, and the greatest admiration for the engineers who have ensured its continued improvement and technological developments.

How has Porsche been able to successfully retain such a strong and faithful following with a design that is basically unchanged since its introduction in 1963? The Stuttgart engineers have worked hard at retaining the old magic in a car that is now more than 40 years old. That is the irony in this whole story – what other manufacturer would put so much effort into trying to stay the same? By virtue of progress and the natural course of events, designs move on and technology requires that today's cars are

OPPOSITE TOP Jürgen Barth and Klaus Parr in the Porsche Historisches Archiv, Stuttgart-Zuffenhausen in 2005. (Author)

OPPOSITE BOTTOM In the workshop – Ferry Porsche with factory foreman Bruno Trostmann, discussing a Typ 547 engine in 1954.

BELOW The 911 Carrera RS 2.7 did so much to carry the Porsche name through the difficult 1970s period; what with the energy crisis and falling demand for sports cars. (Author)

OPPOSITE TOP The 1,000km Nürburgring race, 1961 – Herbert Linge and Sepp Greger in a 356 B Carrera GT (692/3A engine) chasing Stirling Moss and Graham Hill until the Spyder blew its engine. Moss then finished the race in a 356 with Linge completing 43 laps, only one lap less than the winning Maserati 'Birdcage'. (E. Beck/Archive Marinello)

BELOW The 997-series 911 Carrera still retains the same distinctive profile as the first 911 shown in 1963, and indeed, the 356 before that. (Author)

built differently and therefore need to look different. This is where the quality of design and engineering is so strong in Zuffenhausen, because, with these pressures brought to bear by new technology on what is an essentially old design and layout, through this the Porsche engineers have been able to retain the same basic shape of the car. The fact that the company works so hard at trying to keep the 911 model looking familiar, sets Porsche apart from all other manufacturers today.

Looking at competitors in the market, other sports and supercar manufacturers, the likes of Ferrari and Maserati, Lamborghini, Aston Martin and many others – these makers try to retain a vestige of their heritage in the current designs. But none of them try actively to retain the same basic silhouette as their models of four decades ago. Porsche has not only succeeded in achieving this seemingly illogical goal, but it has done so by incorporating all the latest technology and safety features found in any other supercar.

Some memories from a bygone era

In the 1950s and '60s, when the world was a far simpler place, motor racing was a profession that was still carried out by gentlemen with pride, loyalty and a big dose of adventure. Herbert Linge recalls how Moss, Hill, Bonnier and others drove Porsche cars: 'If they didn't have a Formula 1 race, they came to us, and one time Moss and I drove an experimental car in a 1,000km race at Nürburgring. We had the Porsche disc brakes, the first synchromesh transmission and some other bits, so they put this car into the sports car class. Stirling Moss said "OK, let's drive, we want to see how [it performs]" – we won the sports car class with a 356 Coupé experimental car!'

It is difficult to put into words sometimes the triumphs and the disappointments, the endless hours spent working against impossible odds, to achieve something that may go unnoticed by most. To try to adequately capture the close personal and working relationships of people who have started at the bottom and through dedication and

commitment, achieved monumental success, is nigh on impossible, because we are referring to an era long gone. Today, trade unions and human rights all come into the picture, and one can no longer 'expect' things to get done no matter what it takes. Hard work and a strong desire to see the object of your labour succeed, created a strong bond between not only co-workers but also, in the case of Porsche, between workers and the head of the company. To a large extent, much of the success of the company in those early years can be put down to worker loyalty and pride.

In an attempt to recreate in mere words the atmosphere of the struggles, the failures and the repeated efforts to succeed, one would lose much of the true emotion of how dedicated those early engineers were. Not to try would be to leave a chapter of history untold, so in striving to capture a meaningful element of the emotional and personal contribution made by the staff in the 1950s and '60s, it is best to share some of these memories with those lucky enough to have been there.

Herbert Linge recalls: 'And in the beginning, when we were building the aluminium coupé for racing, he [Ferry Porsche] came down every day to the shop when I was a small mechanic, you know, just that high', he indicates laughing, '… he came down, took my hand, took me into a corner and said: "Now I want to know your mind, but your mind, not mine, yours", and he listened to you whatever you told him.'

At this point in the interview, Herbert Linge looked quite absorbed, almost distant, as one could see him recalling those very personal memories which he no doubt cherished. These were golden moments for him. He continued, 'He [Ferry Porsche] never answered anything, he walked away, maybe two days later or so he came back and would say: "I got an idea, ja it's working".'

Again, Herbert Linge recounts another time when his opinion was needed by Ferry Porsche, 'When I came back from the States, every weekend I was at the race track. He didn't want my report that I had written to my boss in the department. He said: "I want him up here in my office and I want to talk with him with four eyes", and I could tell him everything I have seen there.' Once again

the great man would walk away and the next day there would be a sign in the experimental department announcing some new measures or procedures. Linge continues, 'He never said it is coming from there or there, my name was never mentioned, but he was putting my suggestions into action. Very quiet and nobody realised what was going on. It was unbelievable.'

BELOW Herbert Linge stands alongside a collection of racing memorabilia depicting his illustrious motorsport career with Porsche – at the Stuttgart Retro Classic 2005. (Author)

There was no favouritism, no big song and dance, just the quiet, strong manner of a man who listened to those unsung heroes on the workshop floor. Herbert Linge again: 'Sometimes he came when we started with something new, we worked round the clock, in the middle of the night, he came to the shop and brought us something to eat and drink, asking if everything was going all right.' Again, the emotional recollections were deep and respectful, there was a tear in his eye as one could see him reliving those cherished and personal moments in his mind, in the company of the one man he admired so much.

He continued, 'It was in 1963 or '64, he [Ferry Porsche] invited all the mechanics who had been at Le Mans to his private house, and we had a meal in the night and talked together in his house. Not in a restaurant or somewhere, in his house. His wife was cooking and talked to each one. He knew everyone personally.'

The author tries, inadequately, to contribute to this emotional and deeply sensitive conversation, while in the company of someone who has himself achieved more than most modern racing drivers and engineers could hope to in two lifetimes. Herbert Linge has raced in the Carrera Panamericana, Le Mans, Targa Florio, Monte Carlo Rally, Sebring, Daytona, Nürburgring – in fact, the list is endless. Besides racing, he has contributed to the production of most Carrera sports cars and race cars, as well as managed race teams. He oversaw the construction and installation of the test facility at Weissach.

He picks up the story, 'When we were building the experimental department in Weissach, I was in charge of all the workshops and everything, so I was out there maybe 11 or 12 o'clock at night. Sometimes at 9 or 10 o'clock, Mr Porsche, all by himself, walked to the place. He didn't want formal reports from the bosses out there, he wanted to talk to me or to another workshop man about what he thinks and if everything is going all right.' Despite being the head of an organisation and having one of the most dedicated workforces in the industry, Ferry Porsche was himself, one of the hardest working members of staff in the company.

In many ways, Ferry Porsche was a remarkable man. He had the respect of all who worked with him and especially those who drove his cars. The Carrera was a car, a legend, that grew up in a different time, when engineers, mechanics and racing drivers mixed socially with the company's management and it was all just accepted back then as the way things were done. This type of camaraderie was commonplace and it ensured a greater understanding of engineering issues both up and down the chain of command. Ferry had seen the birth of the Carrera legend in 1955, but with the launch of the 356 A Carrera model at the IAA in Frankfurt, he could never have imagined at the time that the name would still be emblazoned on his cars 50 years later. The Carrera name has played a vital roll in the fortunes of the Porsche marque, having survived model changes, applications for road as well as race cars, and even been dropped altogether for a time.

For the Carrera, it has truly been a long and winding road, but one that brought as much enjoyment to the drivers of these great cars as to those who made them. Like all true nobility, it is the royal bloodline which allows succession to the

OPPOSITE Ferry Porsche at the wheel of a Boxster. This is one of the last photographs taken of Ferry at his home in 1997.

BELOW An aerial view of the Weissach testing ground, known as Werk 8, just outside Stuttgart.

throne for the next in line, and, in this way, the Carrera bloodline can be traced right back to those dusty, twisting and dangerous roads in a barren wilderness – the Carrera Panamericana, Mexico, November 1954.

The Porsche Carrera is all about driving, not being still – it always has been, it always will be.

In conclusion

The mystique of Porsche is not something that was intentionally created by the company. On the contrary, the mystique of the Carrera badge is something that has been created by the customers and enthusiasts alike, over more than half a century.

This abstract phenomenon of some mystical value, is something that is earned, not built into each car on the production line. It says something about the cars that no corporate document, public relations or advertising agency could ever hope to equal in the most creative or complimentary of ways. No amount of money or effort on the part of the company could come close to emulating the aura in which the Carrera badge is held – in fact, if they tried, they might just possibly destroy what so many hold dear. No, the mystique of the Carrera is something that has been created by the market, a laurel that has been earned by the company as a result of the respect of its customers.

Born in Vienna, Austria in 1909, Ferry Porsche died on 27 March 1998, not far from Gmünd and had thus come full circle as this was not far from where it all started with the building of the first Porsche cars by his father Dr Ferdinand Porsche. The cars that bore the family name, and which Ferry had had such a pivotal role in creating, have also come full circle with the name Carrera once again adorning the bodywork of the company's flagship, the Carrera GT.

'Life itself is a race, marked by a start, and a finish. It is what we learn during the race, and how we apply it, that determines whether our participation has had particular value. If we learn from each success, and each failure, and improve ourselves through this process, then, at the end, we will have fulfilled our potential and performed well.'

Porsche Cars North America Inc.

Biblography

Books

Wood, Jonathan, *The Ultimate History of Fast Cars* (Paragon Books, 2002)

Howlett, John, *James Dean, A Biography* (Plexus Publishing Limited, London, 1983)

Heinrichs, Steve, Marinello Marco, Perrin Jim, Raskin Lee, Stoddard Charles A., Zingg Donald, *Porsche Carrera Speedster Typ 540, The Quintessential Sports Car* (Big Lake Media, Inc., Incline Village, Nevada)

Seiff, Ingo, *Porsche – Portrait of a Legend* (Macdonald Orbis)

Morgan, Peter, *Original Porsche 924/944/968* (Bay View Books)

Morgan, Peter, *Original Porsche 911* (Bay View Books)

Long, Brian, *Porsche 356* (Veloce Publishing)

Long, Brian, *Porsche 911: The Definitive History 1971-1977* (Veloce Publishing, 2004)

Long, Brian, *Porsche 944* (Veloce Publishing)

Bongers, Marc, *Porsche: Serienfahrzeuge und Sportwagen seit 1948* (Motorbuch Verlag 2004)

Frère, Paul, *Porsche 911 Story, 7th ed.* (Haynes Publishing, 2003)

Ludvigsen, Karl, *Excellence Was Expected* (Bentley Publishing)

Harvey, Chris, *Porsche 911 Carrera, Super Profile* (Haynes Publishing, 1982)

Bischof, Klaus, *The Museum* (Dr Ing. h. c. F. Porsche AG)

Adler, Dennis, *Porsche 911: Road Cars* (MBI Publishing)

Vivian, David, *Porsche 924/928/944/968* (Crowood)

Seiffert, Reinhard, *Carrera 4: Porsche Allrad 1900-1990* (Christophorus)

Meredith, Laurence, *Porsche 911* (Sutton Publishing)

Starkey, John, *Porsche 911 R-RS-RSR* (Veloce Publishing)

Leffingwell, Randy, *Porsche Legends: Inside History of the Epic Cars* (MBI Publishing)

Sloniger, Jerry, *Porsche: The 4-Cylinder, 4-Cam Sports & Racing Cars* (MBI Publishing)

Maltby, Gordon, *Porsche 356 & RS Spyders* (MBI Publishing)

Deiss, Jutta, Brümmer Elmar, Schloz Reiner, *Porsche 911: Enduring Values* (Delius Klasing Verlag, 2004)

Brümmer, Elmar, Deiss Jutta, Schloz Reiner, *Porsche Carrera GT* (Delius Klasing Verlag, 2003)

Magazines and journals

Porsche Panorama

Road & Track

Sports Car World

Christophorus

356 Registry

911 & Porsche World

Automobile Quarterly – Vol. X No. 2 – 'The Baron of Park Avenue' (Ludvigsen)

Classic & Sportscar

Rand Daily Mail – newspaper, South Africa

Excellence

MotorSport

GT Purely Porsche

Index